The 5 Laws
of Innovation Success

Generating Critical Momentum for Products,
Services and Ideas

G. Douglas Olsen

Novetics Press

The 5 Laws of Innovation Success
Generating Critical Momentum for Products, Services and Ideas
By Douglas Olsen

Published by Novetics Press, Phoenix, Arizona

ISBN: 061546565X
ISBN-13: 9780615465654
Library of Congress Control Number: 2011925810

To Lana, Mark, Nathanael and Timothy.

ACKNOWLEDGMENTS

As with many projects, the completed work is the sum product of many different individuals and institutions. I would like to thank James Lam, Allison Minkus, Jaelan Petrie and Adam Zukowski for their research assistance, as well as incredible conversations with Chris Lynch and Cameron Linke regarding this work. I am also indebted to the constructive feedback of a number of friends and colleagues who were kind enough to review earlier versions of the manuscript, as well as the advice from Diane Davis on many of the figures contained in this book.

Gratitude must be expressed to my academic families at the University of Alberta and at Arizona State University for their support while writing this book. In particular, I would like to thank Michael Percy, Richard Johnson, Michael Mokwa and Michael Crow for their leadership during this time.

A major impetus for this book came from observations made in the field regarding biases in decision-making and the realization that in many change situations a complete model regarding how to approach the situation was not present. For this reason I am especially grateful to my colleagues on the applied side, especially discussions with my collaborator and friend Ian Montgomerie. Interactions with faculty, staff and members at the Center for Services Leadership at the W.P. Carey School of Business at ASU have also been invaluable, with a special thanks to Mary Jo Bitner, Steve Brown, Kevin Burkhard and Alicia Holder.

Friends on a personal level have also played a pivotal role in providing a network within which to live and create. Eckhard Strelau, Martin Friedrich, Dan Heiling, John Roumas, Steve Ramsthel, Bill Religo and Gabe Gonzales have all acted as strong change agents in my life and I am thankful for their wisdom and encouragement. Finally, I would like to express unbounded thankfulness to my wife Lana who has been a pillar of support both during this project and throughout my career.

TABLE OF CONTENTS

Chapter Five – Bias in Search and Choice Must Be Overcome

PART I

THE FIVE LAWS OF INNOVATION SUCCESS

In order for any product, service, policy, or idea to be successful, it must possess gravity—that critical level of "I want that" attraction required to wrestle the individual away from his or her current state of being. The overview chapter of this book lays out the five laws of innovation success and provides a review of product-, service-, and policy-related innovation contexts where change was less than successful because one or more of these laws were violated. The next five chapters then present a detailed understanding of factors impacting each of the five primary laws of innovation success. Part II grounds the model further, applying it to a broad range of personal and professional contexts.

OVERVIEW

ON DRIVING INNOVATION

WE LIVE TO INNOVATE AND MAKE CHANGE

We live to innovate and make change in the world around us—both personally and professionally. Stated differently, we are frequently in the process of moving from point A (the current state) to point B (the new and desired outcome). However, innovation will falter when the new concept does not generate enough attraction—that critical level of support and buy-in needed to gain momentum and be successful. One might think of this "I want it!" attraction as a gravitational pull, with various factors either increasing or decreasing the level of pull that a given alternative exerts. There are five major contributors to the level of attraction possessed by a given offering, and while these work together and interact, the failure of any one of these dimensions is capable of rendering an option impotent. Dead and useless. To successfully foster innovation, it is imperative to have a firm grasp of all five.

THE FIVE LAWS OF INNOVATION SUCCESS

Law 1. There must be superior value.

Law 2. The stability of the existing alternative must be reduced.

Law 3. Uncertainty/fear of the new alternative must be reduced.

Law 4. Outside independent influences exert an impact.

Law 5. Bias in search and choice must be overcome.

The goal of this book is to present a straightforward framework that applies to any innovation setting where there is a desire to move people from one "system" to another, where a "system" may be any product, service, behavior, or belief. As a result, while the ideas might be pertinent to migrating a person from one financial services provider to another or choosing a new laundry detergent, the concepts have equal relevance when adopting "not smoking" over "smoking," or selecting alternatives that reduce water consumption. *Innovation incorporates any situation where one would like to see change occur—not simply high-technology contexts.* Of course it is relevant in these areas as well.

The motivation for this book stems from a number of years of consulting and watching business success and failure. My view of what is considered "business" is rather broad. Robert Louis Stevenson sagely noted, "Everyone lives by selling something."[1] Whether you are administering a health care program to increase child inoculation rates, implementing a new software system to improve project management, or lobbying to reduce the incidences of pollution and carbon emissions, it is essential to understand the factors that contribute to adoption of an alternative, as well as those that inhibit it.

Ralph Waldo Emerson suggested, "Build a better mousetrap and the world will beat a path to your door."[2] Imagine for a moment you actually built the world's best mousetrap and every living mousetrap technician was willing to sign an affidavit confirming the pre-eminence of your contraption. Should we assume, then, that it will sell like crazy? Maybe. However, there are many reasons why an absolutely superior mousetrap may not generate a level of attraction sufficient to succeed. A brief list might include: (1) there is currently no problem with mice, (2) people have already invested heavily in existing, albeit inferior, technology, (3) the trap seems complicated and there is still some confusion as to how it works, (4) media and special interests groups have recently begun to decry the killing of mice, or (5) the government requires a nine-year approval process before allowing the device to be placed on the market. The list of possible mitigating factors could be expanded, but even this brief list serves to underscore a fundamental truth—better mousetraps do not always win.

CASES FOR CONSIDERATION

In an effort to underscore how well-meaning and solid organizations can fail to generate sufficient attraction to their innovative offering, a number of examples are presented. In each of these cases, the product or service has some appeal if examined in the right light (granted, you may have to squint). Nonetheless, it is painfully apparent post hoc that there were obvious reasons why sufficient attraction to the concept was not present—and, consequently, why the innovation failed. In each case, one or more of the five laws were violated.

The Three-Piece Suit—Levi's (c. 1980)

Levi's has an excellent reputation and a solid history.[3] Perhaps this is why the company thought that the marketplace would be receptive to a new line of garments in 1980. With great determination, Levi's sought to develop three-piece suits. A top flight fashion designer was employed. Quality fabric was purchased. Advertising was lined up. Experienced managers and sales personnel were in place. It seemed that all of the key elements were there.

At the time, Levi's conducted extensive survey and focus group research. It was clear that the primary segment for a three-piece suit was an individual who shopped in boutique outlets and did not mind paying extra for expert tailoring. The mismatch between the desires of the segment and the intended execution (a pretailored, off-the-rack version, distributed through department stores) should have set off the fire alarm. In fact, the entire sprinkler system should have kicked in. Additional problems might have been recognized when research indicated that although the target group thought that Levi's could produce good jeans, they were not supportive of Levi's making a suit. About one year from the time of commencement, the penchant to pursue suits dematerialized.[4] The primary problem here centered on not having the right type of product/image for their target market (part of Law 1) and substantial uncertainty associated with it (Law 3).

Home Banking—The Pronto System by Chemical Bank (1982)

Today the concept of using your computer to access bank account information via the Web is so commonplace that for many it would be hard to imagine life without this convenience. This said, how long have you banked over the Web? Most people are surprised to learn Chemical Bank in New York spent about $100 million to develop a home banking system over a quarter century ago.[5] The system delivered many of the services offered by present-day home banking providers, including the ability to access balance information, transfer funds, and pay bills. As well, the system permitted home budgeting and the ability to send e-mails to the bank and other Pronto customers.[6]

Field trials excitedly commenced in February 1982, with the full-blown launch taking place in New York City one year later. Fliers, in-store promotions, and the introduction of both print and television advertising heralded the arrival of Pronto. One magazine advertisement portrayed a man in his pajamas in front of his television screen, with the heading, "Chemical would like to open a branch in your living-room." Despite some early success, the Pronto home banking system was shut down in 1989.

What were the key factors contributing to the demise of the Pronto system? The fixed cost of the computer and the monthly system access fees may have been an impediment for many individuals. Another hurdle might have been the lack of a platform common to all computer users—the initial system required an Atari computer.[7]

Beyond these obstacles, there is no question it can take time to shift to a new paradigm and get to the point where we see using the new system as "the way we do things." In Pronto's case, people were still used to going to the bank and dealing with a teller. For many, making people bank in two different ways probably seemed like a redundancy, or perhaps an aberration to their way of being. Issues of trust and security, as well as a limited understanding or anxiety regarding the use of emerging technologies, would also have been barriers. In this case, Pronto was not compatible with either how people did banking or with existing technology (part of Law 3), and was likely perceived as just a little "too new" to be considered (part of Law 5).

New Coke (1985)

Given the notoriety of the New Coke debacle, it is tempting to omit it completely. Nonetheless, it does exemplify how a company can get so focused on achieving one goal that it misses out on the problems that might arise in other areas. For years Coke had been plagued with the Pepsi Challenge. Blindfolded participants would be given a sample of the two colas and asked to decide which one they liked better. Coke lost in the majority of cases. Pepsi tasted a bit sweeter, and in cases where people had just a small sample, Pepsi came out ahead.

Coke went on a mission to reformulate its taste. The company's research revealed this new flavor was preferred not only to the previous version of Coke, but to Pepsi as well. If Pepsi continued to be so bold as to run their Pepsi Challenge using New Coke, they would do so at their own peril and a new taste champion would bubble to the surface.

It turned out Coke drinkers were not appreciative of the efforts to improve the flavor. In fact, they were downright indignant. What had happened? Coke had focused so much on the taste that it forgot a major component of the consumers' purchase decision was the emotional relationship with the brand. By changing the flavor, Coke had killed the relationship with a lifelong friend. As one commentator put it, it was like they had trampled the American flag. Within four months of the launch, New Coke was nixed.

Some posit this was all part of a general plan by Coke to reinvigorate the passion for the brand name and/or generate sales through the controversy. There are a number of conspiracy theories, many involving aliens, that have a far greater likelihood of being true. This was a classic case of a company completely misreading what the reaction of customers would be, even if Coke's goal was noble. If the road to hell is paved with good intentions, Coke unquestionably provided enough material to create a freeway. Given the stability with the existing product, a violation of Law 2 was Coke's major downfall.

Parfum Bic (1988)

Bic's underlying business model is to produce items of value, with value defined as quality divided by price. Few would try to argue that a Bic pen is of better quality than a Mont Blanc. However, the low price of the Bic pen, combined with its ability to work well for a long time, results in a product of high value. Similarly, Bic lighters and Bic razors are not typically considered "top of the line" in their respective arenas, but what you get for a small sum reinforces the value associated with the Bic name.

In 1988, Bic sought to build on their empire. They probably considered a number of options that would fall in line with their value model and the extent to which such options would link with their distribution channels, like stores that sold stationary. Perhaps a new line of pens? A foray into the stapler market? While such ideas might have had merit, another apparently appealed more.

Maybe it was the location of Bic's head office in Paris that resulted in the eventual concept put forward for development—perfume. Contained in a small bottle not too dissimilar from a see-through Bic lighter, this scented concoction would retail for a mere $5. Four different fragrances were produced: two for men and two for women. Bic described these perfumes as products "that combined high quality with affordable pricing and stylish, portable design."[8] Sure, it might not be the best-smelling fragrance on the market, but for such a low price, value was assured. Bic was confident they had done it again and invested $20 million in advertising to launch the product.[9]

What happened? In 1991, Bic decided to discontinue the Parfum Bic line at a loss of approximately $25 million.[10] Looking back, it would seem like Bic perfume was doomed from the beginning—certainly from an outsider's perspective. The notion of spraying yourself with a container that looked like a butane-filled lighter was no doubt a little less than alluring to many. Further, while Bic had been associated with lower-end utility goods, they had not been associated with luxury products. Hence, when considering perfume, a product that is so closely associated with personal image, it is not surprising the connection with the consumer was not a positive one.

How could Bic make this mistake? They got locked into aspects of "why will they buy?" such as value and distribution, and forgot to pay heed to issues associated with "why wouldn't they buy?" such as image and perceived quality. To be fair to Bic, I was intrepid enough in 1990 to actually purchase a bottle for myself and was actually surprised at how pleasant the scent was. Despite very reasonable product quality, the downfall of Bic perfume was assured by violations of Law 3 (fear and uncertainty) and Law 4 (in this case, issues regarding changes in fashion and concerns regarding what other people would think).

OS/2 Warp (1994)

OS/2 Warp began in 1985 as a joint initiative between IBM and Microsoft.[11] This alliance continued until 1990, when the two decided to go their separate ways. Microsoft would continue with the Windows operating system, a system that was technically inferior but remarkably successful from a commercial perspective. This paved the way for IBM to create a bigger and better operating system on its own. If anyone could compete with Microsoft, it would be IBM. Warp had a number of very strong points relative to Windows: it was compatible with Windows and Windows applications; it was able to run multiple programs at the same time; it had an arguably better interface; and it had a high level of system stability given that each application ran independently. Thus, an error in one program did not mean the entire system would freeze as it typically did with Microsoft Windows at the time. Many believed IBM had built the better mousetrap.

So what went wrong? There were some issues regarding hardware compatibility, but this was not the biggest stumbling block. Instead, it was Microsoft's prevailing ability to get computer manufacturers to preinstall Windows instead of Warp as their base operating system. To add insult to injury, IBM even started preinstalling Microsoft Windows on the computers they manufactured, instead of their own (supposedly beloved) OS/2 Warp. IBM eventually conceded the consumer market to Microsoft, but continued the push toward the business market. The stability of the system made it ideal for mission-critical applications, and IBM took pride in the banks and nuclear facilities that chose Warp for their platform. However, high levels of adoption were never achieved, and it was difficult for IBM to justify the ongoing maintenance of the Warp system. While the system was somewhat on its last legs by the end of the century, it was kept on life support until the end of 2005, when IBM finally hit the delete key. Unfortunately Warp failed to produce something that was perceived to be significantly better (Law 1) and certainly was not strong enough to destabilize the existing system (Law 2). Issues of uncertainty and fear regarding how existing programs and files would be affected by installing Warp were also likely at a sizeable level (a violation of Law 3).

Canadian Gun Control Registry (Mid-1990s)

In the mid-1990s, an attempt by the Canadian government to reduce crime rates took the form of a database initiative that required every gun in the country to be registered.[12] It was first believed this registry would cost about $120 million and would be self-sustaining financially. However, the cost/benefit structure of the program was attacked when it became apparent the amount spent to develop the program was approximately ten times preliminary projections. Moreover, the registry was receiving a very poor reaction, especially from rifle owners in rural areas. They were being asked to pay $60 per gun to meet the new registration law. For some hunters and collectors who maintained multiple guns, this was a significant imposition. Worse, each registration would have to be renewed every five years, and failure to register could result in a criminal conviction. The perception of some was that good and honest law-abiding citizens would now be put in the rank and file of barbaric criminals if they forgot to register great grandpa's musket. Rumors also started that this was the first step in a government plan to confiscate all guns—first they would figure out who had them and then take them away.

Media reports did not help the growing state of uncertainty. In addition to stories regarding cost overruns, issues of database security were also being raised. The logic was that criminals could conceivably hack into the system, find out where firearms were located, and then steal them. Further, beyond mere claims of public safety, politicians and senior police administrators were questioning the true usefulness of the database.

In hindsight, the database was ill conceived from the outset. The general idea of fighting crime and controlling guns may have been noble, but the benefits of the program were not sufficiently articulated to the community. Additionally, high levels of uncertainty and some degree of fear were associated with many aspects of the program, including its intended purpose (hence concerns regarding possible gun confiscation). As a result, sentiment toward the program became progressively more negative, both among gun owners and the general population. The government had clearly misjudged how easy it would be to implement this program and the resistance it would face. They had also violated Law 1 (the provision of superior value) and Law 3 (uncertainty and fear of the new system).

The Honda Accord Hybrid (2005–2007)

The hybrid car market has been viewed with a great deal of attention and has experienced some mixed results. The Toyota Prius, complete with its distinctive design, confirmed there was a very real demand for such a vehicle. Honda recognized this. They knew people liked their Accords. And clearly, people seemed to like the concept of a gasoline-electric hybrid. Surely, then, people would absolutely fall head over heels in love if they combined the two. Honda went ahead and introduced the first Accord hybrid in 2005, with considerable critical acclaim. That year, *Consumer Reports* magazine dubbed it the number one family sedan.[13] Impressive, especially since it was compared to thirty-one other vehicles. Despite the accolades, the Accord hybrid never reached expected sales, and in 2007 Honda cancelled production.

What led to the demise of this well-intentioned vehicle? It may have been the extra $10,000 on the price tag relative to its gasoline-only counterpart. Another possibility is that, unlike its competitor, the environmentally friendly Prius, the Accord hybrid had no distinctive shape—for all intents and purposes, the hybrid looked like any other Accord on the market. Alright, there was one difference between the vehicles: the 2006 hybrid model had amber turn signals in the back, whereas the less ecofriendly gasoline version came with red signal lights.[14] For those environmentalists wishing to wear their car like a badge of honor, it was probably not enough to produce a car that would simply *do good*; it was important to produce a car that would help the environmentalist be *perceived as doing good*.

A difference in rear signal lights did not seem to achieve this objective, resulting in the automatic rejection of this alternative (part of Law 5 dealing with bias in search and choice).

Electricity Deregulation in North America (Mid-1990s to Present)

Deregulation of the electricity sector in the United States of America and Canada provides an example of a potentially sound idea gone wrong.[15] Prior to deregulation, customers seemed, for the most part, happy with electricity service—supply was sufficient and reliable, and, some grumblings aside, the price was reasonably affordable. It was an industry that worked well enough, with fairly stable market conditions. However, the prospect of consumers having choice and potential savings, which could be realized due to increased competition, loomed large. In addition, a free-market system might lend the kind of innovative spirit and efficiencies that would be far more advantageous than working within an outdated monopolistic system. Or would it?

Even with the prospect of potential advantages, the United States and Canada had seen other regions, such as the European Union, struggle with deregulation—certainly there were indicators that change might hold challenges and considerable risks.[16] This was evidenced by the 2003 blackout in the Midwest, Northwest, and Ontario, as well as the failure of utility companies whose bottom lines could not withstand soaring spot-market prices and price controls. In addition, increased competition did not seem to always fulfill the promise of lower prices for consumers—in some areas, such as in California and New York, it produced the exact opposite result.

The well-publicized rise and fall of Enron was also intertwined with electricity deregulation. Enron was one member in a cast of many characters that could not refuse the extraordinary profits that the newly deregulated environment could provide. Given the spillover of negative publicity from this debacle, some governments chose to either slow down or simply

withdraw from the process of deregulation. This pullback likely gave cre-
dence to those who had condemned deregulation in the first place.

Why was the process of electricity deregulation considered such a
disaster by some? Deregulation was supposed to promote growth in the
sector; develop more providers and more distributors who would effectively
spur competition; increase supply to meet growing demand; and ultimately
push companies to be leaner, more efficient, and provide energy at a lower
cost. Instead, mergers proliferated, and an aging grid was crippled by
rising energy demands.[17] At the time of this writing, more than half of
the American states still have regulated electricity markets. Until issues
are dealt with to demonstrate the real benefit of deregulation (Law 1) and
remove fear and uncertainty (Law 3), the required legislation to facilitate
deregulation (part of Law 5) is unlikely to make considerable headway.

THE FIVE LAWS OF INNOVATION SUCCESS

When one speaks of building attraction to an offering and thereby influencing change, one of two goals may be present. The first is to successfully
migrate people from one state or condition to another—to get them to do
something new and to be innovative. Conversely, another very real goal is
to figure out how to prevent change from occurring. Such might be the
case if one is trying to maintain and/or enhance customer loyalty to prevent
switching to a competitive product or service offering. This is also the goal
with many social issues, such as preventing young people from becoming
parents too early or reducing crime. In such cases the overarching objective
is to build enough attraction to the existing alternative that migration to
new options does not occur.

So far we have spoken about change as though it was always a case of
trying to convince people to exercise their own volitional will to adopt/
not adopt something new. However, on some occasions, innovation and the
associated changes are thrust upon individuals and they have no real say

about it. Examples might include when a company announces a general policy change regarding a benefit plan that applies to all employees, or when a government introduces mandatory legislation that alters vehicle registration fees. Under such conditions, when change is forced on individuals, the key outcome measure is not "willingness to change" but rather "acceptance of change."

Regardless of the specific change context, there are five key components that will influence how successful a given innovation will be. Subsequent chapters will serve to unpack each of the components and apply them to specific change contexts.

Law 1: There Must Be Superior Value

Core competency. Differential advantage. Unique selling proposition. A variety of terms are presented to describe the essence of what features and benefits the new option has that may help it compete with existing alternatives. Understanding the benefits of a given offering is an essential part of the planning and implementation process. In fact, one of the top cited reasons for new product failure is the absence of a truly superior value proposition. In fairness, this aspect of change success is frequently considered in business practice. Granted, what is "superior" to a manager or engineer in a company is not necessarily considered successful to the populous at large. Further, while building a superior alternative is laudable—it is not enough. It is imperative that one move beyond this myopia and adequately consider four other less-thought-through factors that might abruptly prevent an option from achieving innovation success.

Law 2: The Stability of the Existing Alternative Must Be Reduced

Isaac Newton pointed out that a body in motion will stay in motion. The momentum to continue in the existing system may be referred to as stability and may greatly impede the ability to change, even when a demonstrably better alternative is present. Stability itself may be influenced by a broad host of factors, including contractual obligations, time since last purchase, the cost of removing the old system, or affinity programs and discounts. Given that high stability translates into the existing option having a much higher pull relative to the new option, it is crucial to identify key factors contributing to both the existing system's stability (factors you will have to contend with) *and* instability (factors you can use to your advantage).

Law 3: Fear of the New Alternative Must Be Reduced

Consider something as simple as the purchase of a vacuum via the Internet and a few of the issues that may be present. Will it actually perform the way the description promised it would? Will the merchant actually send the right product, or, for that matter, any product at all? If you do not like it, will you get your money back? Is the information you are sharing with the merchant safe? Is this one going to be replaced with a better model soon, leaving you with the outdated unit? Is this the best price? Will it fit in your closet? As questions mount, uncertainty grows. Any new system is associated with a level of uncertainty and fear. This is true for vacuums, and it is true for new government policies.

Some common causes of anxiety regarding a new alternative include specifics regarding a product or service (whether it will live up to expectations), as well as other factors such as start-up costs and compatibility with existing procedures and technology. It stands to reason that if change to a new alternative is to successfully occur, uncertainty and fear associated with this option must be reduced. Uncertainty may effectively deplete the potential success of even great innovations.

Law 4: Outside Independent Influences Exert an Impact

Independent influences are external and dynamically changing forces (e.g., legal, technological, and social) that are usually beyond the control of the person or organization seeking change. To illustrate, suppose you are a manufacturer and have a production process using a particular chemical derived from a plant that calls the Ecovarian rainforest home. You like this chemical a lot—it is easy to use, safe, and very efficient. As well, you also find yourself being able to acquire this chemical at a remarkably low price.

Now suppose the government of the country in which you are manufacturing your product develops an issue with the human rights policies in Ecovar and prohibits trade with this country. Your thoughts regarding the value of this chemical now mean little, as its use in your product will no longer be viable. Imagine further that the plant used in the production of the chemical is suddenly placed on an endangered species list, inciting a great deal of media and social pressure to save the Ecovarian rainforest and not use plants from this region. Maybe your spouse is a committed environmentalist and he or she does not approve of you destroying such a precious earth resource. Your personal preference would still be to continue to use the chemical derived from this plant, but you fear social reprisal if you decide to do so. One thing is apparent: there are many independent influences well beyond your control that have a large impact on how you do business. How one leverages these they may either enhance or impede innovation success.

Law 5: One Must Overcome Bias in Search and Choice

Our brains are often likened to computers. We take in data from our environment, use "software" in our cerebral cortex to mentally operate on the data, and finally spew out an answer. This process could involve a numerical calculation, a decision regarding what we want for dinner, or a thought regarding a movie we just watched. On the surface, this analogy seems reasonable. Reality presents a very different perspective. Let me ask, when you are looking for a new car, do you look at *every* vehicle available on the market? For each vehicle, do you look at *all* the features? And after you have considered all the features, do you arrive at an overall value for each product? Finally, based on your utility calculations for 1,574 vehicles, do you select the one with the highest computed score?

Biases in search and choice arise in a number of ways and usually result in the consideration of only a small subset of the alternatives and information potentially available to us. If you are like many, the last time you went shopping for a vehicle your search was not exhaustive—you only considered a few alternatives. Further, of those alternatives considered, you may have only looked at a few key elements, such as prestige and reliability, to the exclusion of many others, such as fuel efficiency, emission levels, trunk space, type of tires, and so on. We are forced to simplify this complex world. We do so through the nature of our search processes, modifying when, where, and how much data we will choose to gather. For example, when considering your next vacation, do you go to thirty-seven different Web sites or just rely on one or two travel Web sites that you are already familiar with?

Simplification may also occur through the mechanisms we use to make decisions. Even if we have collected a lot of information, we might just use one or two pieces to make the final decision. Clearly, the success of even the most brilliant innovation may be neutralized if people never come across it, or if it is automatically rejected due to some idiosyncratic feature.

SUMMARY

Business is rife with examples of products, services, and policies that did not do well, despite substantial funding and considerable management intellect—among them, Bic Parfum, IBM's OS/2 Warp, Levi's three-piece suits, New Coke, Honda's Accord Hybrid, Chemical Bank's introduction of home banking over the Internet, and government initiatives regarding gun registration as well as electricity deregulation. Each organization was a strong entity, but the attractiveness of the new option never reached a level sufficient to have a significant impact on change. In each of the cases, failure stemmed from one or more of the five laws associated with creating successful innovation: (1) the absence of a superior value proposition, (2) a high level of stability associated with the existing alternative, (3) a high level of fear associated with the new alternative, (4) the impact of independent influences, and/or (5) bias present in search and choice.

CHAPTER ONE

THERE MUST BE SUPERIOR VALUE (1ST LAW OF INNOVATION SUCCESS)

Systems do not exist in a void. They are present to serve some purpose in an environment of physical and social forces. It is within this complex rubric that we must consider what value a given innovation offers. Think about a sporting goods manufacturer introducing a new running shoe. While this new offering might technically be considered an interwoven collection of fabric and rubber, this mere physical description does not adequately convey the benefits derived by the user. Instead, the value is also a result of the shoes serving a variety of purposes, some of which might include enhancing foot comfort and affording the ability to exercise more often. At a higher level, these shoes may also send a bold fashion statement to the world and demonstrate to peers that the user is part of, if not above, the crowd.

In order to initiate change, an innovation must consider the following question: "what does this new offering have that is substantially better than competing options?" In Exhibit 1-1, the Comprehensive Change Model is presented, with this particular aspect highlighted. The focus here is on making sure that the value offer associated with the desired alternative is as large as possible. Whether one is talking about a new product, service, policy, or personal behavior, the imperative is clear—the innovation must be superior in some way. Very few with a grain of sanity would argue this point. Nonetheless, there are two fundamental reasons why this "apparent and obvious" element begs further consideration.

EXHIBIT 1-1
COMPREHENSIVE CHANGE MODEL: VALUE OFFERING

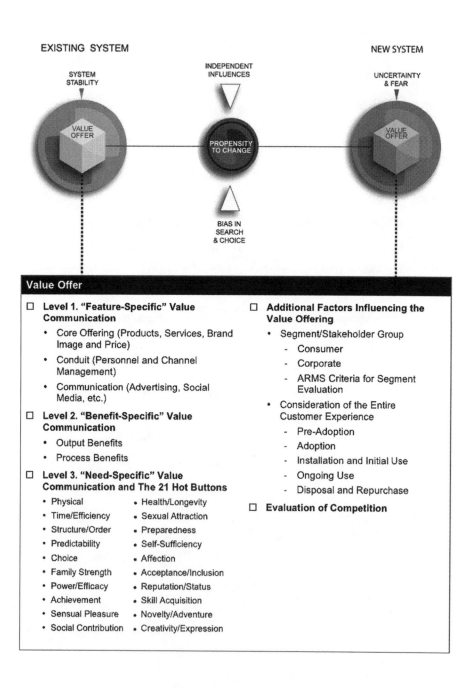

EXISTING SYSTEM

NEW SYSTEM

SYSTEM
STABILITY

INDEPENDENT
INFLUENCES

UNCERTAINTY
& FEAR

VALUE
OFFER

PROPENSITY
TO CHANGE

VALUE
OFFER

BIAS IN
SEARCH
& CHOICE

Value Offer

☐ **Level 1. "Feature-Specific" Value Communication**

- Core Offering (Products, Services, Brand Image and Price)
- Conduit (Personnel and Channel Management)
- Communication (Advertising, Social Media, etc.)

☐ **Level 2. "Benefit-Specific" Value Communication**

- Output Benefits
- Process Benefits

☐ **Level 3. "Need-Specific" Value Communication and The 21 Hot Buttons**

- Physical
- Health/Longevity
- Time/Efficiency
- Sexual Attraction
- Structure/Order
- Preparedness
- Predictability
- Self-Sufficiency
- Choice
- Affection
- Family Strength
- Acceptance/Inclusion
- Power/Efficacy
- Reputation/Status
- Achievement
- Skill Acquisition
- Sensual Pleasure
- Novelty/Adventure
- Social Contribution
- Creativity/Expression

☐ **Additional Factors Influencing the Value Offering**

- Segment/Stakeholder Group
  - Consumer
  - Corporate
  - ARMS Criteria for Segment Evaluation
- Consideration of the Entire Customer Experience
  - Pre-Adoption
  - Adoption
  - Installation and Initial Use
  - Ongoing Use
  - Disposal and Repurchase

☐ **Evaluation of Competition**

First, there is considerable evidence to show that the inability to offer a demonstrably better option is one of the key sources of failure for new initiatives.[1] In many cases, even though a person or company sincerely believes they are offering a superior proposition, the perception of the intended audience is that this "difference" is either trivial or nonexistent. Making matters worse, there is a strong tendency for managers to cling steadfastly to such erroneous beliefs. Research suggests that people will search for information to confirm they are correct and also discredit or avoid information that opposes their viewpoint.[2]

The second reason, in many cases related to the first, is that the method by which individuals such as managers, engineers, and salespeople set about developing and assessing the superiority of an innovation may differ markedly from one person to another. The reason? Some are so close to the project that they see the world at a granular level. For example, they may understand what specific wording of a technical report should be altered or what chemical should be added to improve a formula. Others take a broader and more strategic view, concentrating not so much on the details and minutiae, but rather the more global implications such as enhanced competitiveness or sustainability. The good news is that these approaches are related—separated through issues of translation.

Establishing a strong value offer and building attraction to an alternative requires reconciling, and indeed even leveraging, each of these different vantage points. The micro through to the macro. These contrasting perspectives relate to *features*, *benefits*, and *core needs*, as diagrammed in Exhibit 1-2. Features exist to provide benefits. Benefits serve to meet higher order needs. In order for value to be perceived, it is necessary to connect all three levels. For example, knowing a car tire has silica embedded in the rubber or sawtooth treadblock shapes (*features*) may mean very little to the casual observer. Consequently, the key *benefit* is not discerned until he or she comprehends that this means the car can stop quickly on icy surfaces. The ability to stop quickly, in turn, enhances one or more *needs* of the individual, such as perceived safety, and perhaps contributes to the sustained wellness of his or her family. These three aspects (features, benefits, and needs) represent the *three levels of value communication*. This may seem fairly straightforward, but you would be surprised how many people tend to speak only one of these fluently, when mastery of all three is essential.

EXHIBIT 1-2
THE THREE LEVELS OF VALUE COMMUNICATION

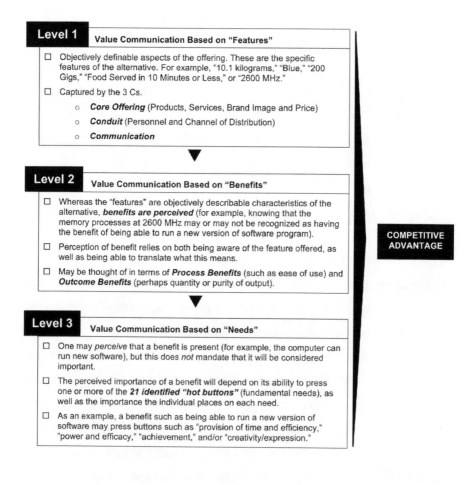

Level 1 — Value Communication Based on "Features"

- Objectively definable aspects of the offering. These are the specific features of the alternative. For example, "10.1 kilograms," "Blue," "200 Gigs," "Food Served in 10 Minutes or Less," or "2600 MHz."
- Captured by the 3 Cs.
  - *Core Offering* (Products, Services, Brand Image and Price)
  - *Conduit* (Personnel and Channel of Distribution)
  - *Communication*

Level 2 — Value Communication Based on "Benefits"

- Whereas the "features" are objectively describable characteristics of the alternative, **benefits are perceived** (for example, knowing that the memory processes at 2600 MHz may or may not be recognized as having the benefit of being able to run a new version of software program).
- Perception of benefit relies on both being aware of the feature offered, as well as being able to translate what this means.
- May be thought of in terms of **Process Benefits** (such as ease of use) and **Outcome Benefits** (perhaps quantity or purity of output).

COMPETITIVE ADVANTAGE

Level 3 — Value Communication Based on "Needs"

- One may *perceive* that a benefit is present (for example, the computer can run new software), but this does *not* mandate that it will be considered important.
- The perceived importance of a benefit will depend on its ability to press one or more of the **21 *identified "hot buttons"*** (fundamental needs), as well as the importance the individual places on each need.
- As an example, a benefit such as being able to run a new version of software may press buttons such as "provision of time and efficiency," "power and efficacy," "achievement," and/or "creativity/expression."

LEVEL 1. "FEATURE-SPECIFIC" VALUE COMMUNICATION

At some level, an innovation may be broken down to some base elements that are within the control of those trying to influence change. These are objective and concretely describable features and actions that are taken to bring about results. Consider a few examples.

Example 1. A Web site is created to help individuals lose weight. The site provides many tables pertaining to target quantities of carbohydrates, proteins, and fats. In addition to this, there is information regarding basal metabolic rates and the level of caloric burn as a function of the type and intensity of exercise a person engages in. Everything is technically accurate and, if used appropriately, would result in weight loss.

Example 2. For a government initiative, such as a new law regarding pollution control, the features of an option may be described in terms of the wording used in the document and the specific actions demanded of stakeholders. Information regarding the bill is then placed on appropriate Web sites and distributed to media outlets. Contact information is presented to permit interested constituents to call and let their feelings be known.

Example 3. A retail store selling shoes for children opens up in a mall. The sign is in primary colors and declares the name "It's Shoe Time." Careful attention is given to the lighting, displays, signage, and music in the background. Advertising in the local newspaper and on the Web presents information about sales taking place, and a graphic designer is used to present the material in a specific way.

In each of these cases, the (potential) benefits of the options were described in terms of "feature-specific" language. Features are the brass tacks. Where the rubber hits the road. The levers the change agent has at his or her disposal. Features are the key tactical elements that can be manipulated. To digress into an intensive examination of each of these feature-rich components would both detract from the purpose of this book and duplicate existing work.[3] Nonetheless, Exhibit 1-3 provides a more detailed consideration of some of these key levers. Under this organizing framework, we can think of the levers as consisting of the *Core Offering* (i.e., products, services, brand image, and price), the *Conduit* (i.e., personnel and channel management issues), and *Communication* (i.e., advertising, social media, etc.).

The terminology employed in Exhibit 1-3 is very consistent with a marketing orientation. Experience suggests that people responsible for policy development and implementation often balk at the idea that they are in some way "marketing" something. This negative reaction is likely associated with pejorative connotations associated with some forms of marketing, such as high-pressure sales or telemarketing. Despite superficial objections, similarities are typically present. For example, many policies have physical manifestations, costs, procedures that must be followed, people that must be dealt with through one or more channels, a communication strategy, and so on. The same could be said of areas where personal or organizational change is desired.

At the end of the day, the issue comes down to the specific elements a person has control over and the options associated with these elements. Wording, location(s), people, processes, pricing, frequency and content of communication, and so on—these are the features that may be directly controlled. However, does the manipulation of these concrete elements ensure that success will result or that people will perceive an alternative in the way that was intended? No. This is where the translation from features to benefits becomes critical. Going back to the weight-loss Web site example, it is possible that people who go to the site will not understand the benefit of this site relative to others and will click to something else. In the same way, the government initiative may not be looked at as life changing, and the shoe store might be perceived as odd. Without the perception of positive and meaningful benefits, all the feature manipulation in the world will not have an impact.

EXHIBIT 1-3

LEVEL 1. "FEATURE-SPECIFIC" VALUE COMMUNICATION

C1. Core Offering (The What)

▶ Products

- ☐ Typically have a tangible presence. May include items that may be converted to physical value (e.g., stocks).
- ☐ Characteristics may be *functional* (such as size) and/or *aesthetic* (such as design).

- ☐ May be *established* (quality ascertainable prior to purchase, such as with a watch)
- ☐ May be *derived* as a result of a service (like a tattoo).

- ☐ *Core goods* may be purchased on their own to achieve a purpose (as with an IPod)
- ☐ *Peripheral goods* enhance the role of the core good (such as an IPod stand).

▶ Services

- ☐ Services are often performed in conjunction with recipient. As such the client is involved in production (a co-creator).
- ☐ Some aspects often not visible (for example, ideas in the mind of a consultant).

- ☐ May exist as the core offering (for example, accounting, consulting, legal advice), or in a peripheral capacity (customer service, training, delivery, etc.).
- ☐ May include self-service or automated services.

- ☐ Services often associated with a higher level of variability than products.
- ☐ May serve as an exceptionally strong differentiator for some segments.

▶ Brand Identity

- ☐ Perceived personality of the organization as a whole and the brand(s) more specifically.

- ☐ On organizational level, trust and Corporate Social Responsibility (for employees and community).

- ☐ Common dimensions of brand identity include: sincerity, excitement, competence, sophistication and ruggedness.

▶ Price

- ☐ Financial costs associated with the item. May include the costs of acquisition, financing, operation and so on.

- ☐ Includes sales promotions focused on a temporary reduction in price.
- ☐ Volume Discounts

- ☐ Bundling – price reductions for simultaneously purchasing multiple items (for example, a computer and software).

C2. Conduit (The Who, When, Where and How)

▶ Personnel

- ☐ Number, type and training of personnel.

- ☐ Evaluated in terms of: (1) knowledge, (2) empathy/caring, (3) speed of response, (4) open and meaningful communication, (5) honesty, and (6) problem solving orientation.

▶ Channel Characteristics

- ☐ Specific location of delivery (for example, a Web site vs. a physical store).

- ☐ Characteristics of physical space, such as the atmosphere of retail environment.

- ☐ Functions of channel members for financing, distribution, research, advertising, order fulfillment, and so on.

C3. Communication

- ☐ Website, Sponsorship, Advertising, Public Relations, Packaging.

- ☐ Customer Relationship Management
- ☐ Social Media

- ☐ Messaging strategy of employees (with everyone "singing off of same sheet").

LEVEL 2. "BENEFIT-SPECIFIC" VALUE COMMUNICATION

A feature is a physical description (it is made out of titanium); a benefit is the perceived advantage of this feature (it will last longer). Benefits may be a function of the specific output (*what* is produced) as well as the system process (*how* something is produced). Exhibit 1-4 considers a range of benefits, classifying them into *output benefits* and *process benefits*.

Output Benefits

Most systems are designed to produce a specific output. Peter Drucker, in his influential article "Theory of Business," suggested that there are two questions every manager needs to ask. The first, what business are we in? The second, how's business?[4] Every system is designed to generate some output. Lawnmowers cut grass, college courses provide information, cell phones transmit voice and data. Accordingly, innovations may be judged according to their intended output. In some cases these are positive, such as increased volume, purity, or effectiveness. In others the benefit comes from the avoidance of negative output, perhaps reduced administrative/operating expenses. To parallel Drucker, what are the intended outputs of your innovation, and how are you doing in this regard?

Process Benefits

Two products may produce virtually the same benefit. For example, two blenders may equally liquefy their contents, but one may be better in terms of the actual usage experience. Of course, some of these process benefits may also lead to outcome benefits. For example, increased levels of feedback during a manufacturing process may result in a higher level of quality. Some of the more common process benefits include ease of use; enjoyment/ pride of use; the ability to control the magnitude of operation; provision of feedback; and stability of operation.

Once benefits are perceived (outcome or process), the next issue becomes whether these benefits are actually looked at as something important. In order to be thought of as such, an offering must tie in to one or more core needs.

EXHIBIT 1-4
LEVEL 2. "BENEFIT-SPECIFIC" VALUE COMMUNICATION

Outcome Related Benefits

- ☐ **Product/Service Specific Outcomes**
  - What are the key objectives of the system (for example, a lawnmower cuts grass), and how well does the system fare on these dimensions?
- ☐ **Efficiency/Volume of Output**
  - Amount of output able to be produced, or the input/output ratio, such as greater return on equity.
- ☐ **Cost Reduction**
  - May arise from the use of less physical material (efficiency), lower levels of energy, a faster process or decreased human resource requirements.
- ☐ **Quality/Purity of Output**
  - The level of purity/quality associated with a process.
- ☐ **Reduced Negative Output/Prevention**
  - The reduction of negative bi-products of a product, service or policy (such as injuries on a work site, side effects of some drugs, toxic chemicals produced by a manufacturing process, or delayed wait times as a result of a new healthcare policy).
  - In some cases, prevention means an increased life-span of something positive (perhaps special packaging to preserve the freshness of fruits and vegetables).

Process Related Benefits*

- ☐ **Ease of Use**
  - Access to Service
  - Convenience
  - Ergonomics
  - Comfort
  - Automation
  - Portability
- ☐ **Magnitude Related**
  - Speed of operation (faster, slower, variable)
  - Level of power (gentle vs. powerful).
- ☐ **Ability to Customize Production/Process**
  - Product or service able to be tailored to specific needs of customer.
- ☐ **Feedback**
  - Provision of information, such as signalling about the process (for example, the temperature or stage of completion).
- ☐ **Enjoyment/Pride of Use**
  - May arise through a connection to aesthetic or brand elements beyond the physical performance of the product per se.
- ☐ **Stability**
  - Stability of operation may be enhanced through increased reliability, sustainability, durability or periodicity of maintenance.
- ☐ **Safety**
  - The ability of a product or service to enhance safety during production.

* Process benefits are those that transpire *during* the use/implementation of the product, service or policy. The goal of distinguishing between process and outcome benefits is to encourage thought regarding the importance of the entire customer experience.

In many cases the process related elements are directly linked to the outcome benefit. For example, the ability to enhance "feedback" may influence the "quality of the output", or increased "safety" results in "prevention".

A process benefit may have an enduring impact long after the process has been completed (e.g., enjoyment/pride of use may continue as a perceived benefit months later).

LEVEL 3. "NEED-SPECFIC" VALUE COMMUNICATION (HOT BUTTONS)

Once features are understood in terms of what benefits they provide, the next critical level of communication arises: the perceived benefits must resonate with the individual and scream, "this is important!" Suppose you introduced a product that would allow customers to save 20 percent of the time relative to their current product. Is this perceived as something that changes their world or something that they couldn't care less about? Ideally, such an improvement would push one or more of the buttons representing core needs. Core needs, in this case, may be thought of as basic drives integral to human existence and possessed by all individuals to varying degrees.

While appealing to deep-seated needs through such "button pushing" might sound rather Machiavellian, and may be so on some occasions, one would hope most actions we take are sincere and serve to meet the needs of those with whom we interact on a personal or professional basis. By keeping an eye on what needs are targeted, a reality check is present during product, service, and policy development. What are the key needs we are trying to meet? How well do the proposed changes address the specified needs? Are there additional needs we should try to meet as well? Which needs are not being served to the fullest extent? Are any needs particularly acute right now?

Based, in part, on the work of Abraham Maslow[5] and expanded on by others,[6] a number of "hot buttons" have been identified to understand what factors may be used to really motivate people and organizations. A spectrum of twenty-one different "buttons" is summarized in Exhibit 1-5, ranging from base physical needs through to those of a higher order. These buttons operate through both *emotional* and *intellectual* mechanisms to motivate individuals into action. Although these are typically expressed in terms of the needs of an individual, corporate equivalents may also be made. For example, to an individual, meeting "physical needs" might be expressed as living without the fear of attack, with access to elements required for basic survival. On the corporate level, this need might be expressed as having the ability to make a profit, retain productive employees, and guarantee required input resources.

To review, consider a bank. Interest rates, loans, savings, credit cards, annuities, operating hours, and technical aspects associated with the Web—these are some of the objective *features* that may be offered. These, in turn, may translate into *benefits* such as convenience, ease of use, and increased return on income. While some may appreciate the implications of such benefits, others may not fully grasp their significance (the "what's in it for me" factor). This is where understanding the core needs/buttons comes in. It is not until the buttons are pushed that motivation erupts. While a bank is unlikely to be particularly successful trying to push "sexual attraction and expression," there are a host of others listed in Exhibit 1-5 that would seem to be open for pursuit: physical needs, provision of time, preparedness/versatility, predictability, self-sufficiency, increased strength of family, reputation and status, power/efficacy, and achievement would all seem to be potential candidates for pursuit. Should they pursue all? Probably not at one time. Moreover, some of these will have a greater impact on some people more than others. This is where understanding additional factors influencing core utility, such as segmentation, becomes incredibly important.

EXHIBIT 1-5
LEVEL 3. "NEED-SPECIFIC" VALUE COMMUNICATION
(THE 21 HOT BUTTONS)

	Button	Description
Basic	1. Physical Needs	• Basic food and shelter requirements. • Basic levels of safety and security.
	2. Optimal Health and Longevity	• Optimal/enhanced functioning of body. • Prevention of illness/decline. • Strength, youth and vitality.
	3. Self-Sufficiency	• Independence and autonomy. • Control over uncertainty imposed by others.
	4. Acceptance and Inclusion	• Sense of acceptance and/or belonging. • May be a formal or informal affiliation.
	5. Affection/Emotional Relations	• Sense to true emotional connection. • May be platonic or romantic.
	6. Sexual Attraction and Expression	• Enhanced sexual attractiveness. • Increased ability to engage in sexual acts.
	7. Increased Strength of Family	• Enhanced unity of family as a whole. • Benefit to one or more members.
	8. Provision of Time and Efficiency	• Increased productivity and efficiency. • Increased ability to pursue leisure activities and other tasks that would have otherwise not been possible.
	9. Structure and Order	• Sense of precision with things in "right" place. • Stability and understanding of how things work.
	10. Preparedness/Versatility	• Increased ability to cope with or benefit from one or more possible future realities.
	11. Predictability	• Ability to predict future environment or outcomes.
	12. Availability of Choice	• Sense that real alternatives are present. • Ability to keep options open.
	13. Skill/Knowledge Acquisition	• Skill acquired for personal or professional goal. • Intellectual growth/curiosity reduction. • Enlightened sense of understanding.
	14. Reputation and Status	• Formal recognition for achievements. • Sense of superiority over others.
	15. Power and Efficacy	• Confidence in ability to handle demands. • Legitimate ability to control situations.
	16. Achievement	• Ability to attain certain goals and milestones. • Overall quantity of output. • May or may not be publicly recognized.
	17. Aesthetic/Sensual Enjoyment	• Beauty along one or more physical dimensions. • Sensual indulgence with goal of hedonic fulfillment.
	18. Novelty and Adventure	• Exploring/experiencing new things. • Engaging in unique experiences.
	19. Contribution and Compassion	• Ability to make a difference in lives of others. • Ability to demonstrate selflessness.
	20. Creativity/Expression	• Ability to present one's inner thoughts, feelings and sense of self in a tangible manner.
Higher Order	21. Spiritual Connectedness	• Ability to connect on a spiritual level with God, nature or other entity.

ADDITIONAL FACTORS INFLUENCING THE VALUE OFFERING

There are a number of unique factors that deserve special attention given their impact on the value offering. In addition to independent influences (dealt with in the 4th Law of Change) and bias in search/choice (dealt with in the 5th Law of Change), we need to consider: (1) differences by segment/stakeholder, and (2) the stage of the customer experience.

Differences by Segment/Stakeholder Group

Not all people see the world the same way. This ties into the concept of segmentation, one of the cornerstones of effective business strategy. Methods to segment the consumer and business markets are presented in Exhibits 1-6 and 1-7, respectively. While some segmentation strategies might be more readily apparent, such as an expensive day-care center segmenting on the basis of income and targeting their advertisements toward residents in an upscale community, there is rarely a "right" way to divide the market up. One company might segment on the basis of demographics and another on the basis of psychographics, and both might be successful. For example, a watch manufacturer may wish to target a segment on the basis of a benefit such as durability (useful in a wide range of environmental conditions), on the basis of a demographic dimension (individuals participating in sports), or on the basis of a psychographic element (adventurous individuals with a strong need to dominate).

Should the situation merit, one is able to combine elements from within a category. For example, demographic elements of marital status and age might yield a target segment of "single males between twenty-five and thirty-five years of age." It is also possible to combine traits from different categories. A graduate program in a college might target individuals in the Pacific Northwest (geographic) between the ages of twenty-five and thirty-five (demographic) with strong aspirations for business success (psychographic). The caveat here is that at some point in time, the number of criteria used explodes to a point where the segment is overdefined. For example, it might be possible to target industrial clients who have over one thousand employees (corpographic) and purchase high volume (behavioral) in the South (geographic) with purchasing managers who are very concerned about the environment (personal). This may reduce the segment down to one person! How detailed is too detailed is a judgment call—the idea is that when one uses too fine of a method to segment the market, strategic power is lost.

Simply dividing a marketplace up for the sake of dividing it up does not make sense. Any successful segmentation strategy must ensure that targeted segments are viable. Viability is affected by the extent to which the segment meets the ARMS conditions laid out in Exhibit 1-8, by which we can evaluate whether a segment is attractive to pursue along four lines:

- Aligned—Is the segmentation strategy aligned with the resources and strategies of the organization?
- Reachable—Is it possible to communicate efficiently with the target segment(s), or is the segment really difficult to access with your message?
- Moveable—When you do get through to this segment, do they want to act on your message?
- Sustainable—Is this segment large enough, with strong prospects for the future?

EXHIBIT 1-6
SEGMENTATION OF THE CONSUMER MARKET

Method	Description	Examples
Demographic	• Demographic segmentation divides a population according to physical (e.g., age, ethnic background or gender), employment (type of profession, income level), and/or social (e.g., religion, language spoken at home, family size, type of housing) characteristics.	• A good example of this would be razors designed for men. The "man's" razor is likely either metallic or a dark color. The advertisement probably features a chisel faced man shaving to high tempo music with an exotic car or fighter jet featured at some point. The "woman's" razor is likely a pastel color, is shown in a bubble filled environment and soft music wafts in the background. • Alcohol manufacturers have been chastised for targeting lower income groups with less expensive, high-alcohol malt beverages.
Psychographic	• Psychographic segmentation pertains to the division of the population according to personality characteristics. These might include extraversion, need for uniqueness, or need for social approval.	• Advertisements in fashion magazines often use personality type to segment ("sophisticated," "athletic," or "bad boy/girl"). Common product categories using psychographics would include watches, perfumes/colognes, and eyewear.
Behavioral	• Behavioral segmentation focuses on the characteristics of each purchase and/or use. Different aspects include: frequency of purchase, average size of purchase, timing (day, week, season), and purchases based on special occasions.	• Some people go grocery shopping on a near-daily basis; others might go grocery shopping only once or twice a month. The two groups likely have very different needs. • Resorts might cater to guests based on time of the year (e.g., skiing in winter and hiking in summer). • Restaurants may have different menus depending on the time of the day (breakfast versus lunch), day of the week (Sunday brunches) or time of the year (at Christmas).
Benefit	• Benefit segmentation focuses on a specific performance or image characteristic sought after by the segment. Issues pertaining to usage context can be particularly relevant here.	• Chairs provide an excellent example of benefit segmentation. Easily stored (foldable or stackable), easily sterilized (for physicians' offices), comfortable (a lounge chair), weatherproof (for outside), durable (for restaurants), beautiful, and so on. • *Usage context may also influence the value of the perceived benefit.* The brand of beer one prefers to drink may differ depending whether one is with clients, friends or alone. • A given product might have different types of customers depending on the benefit. Some purchase a cell phone mainly for back-up, whereas for others it is their only phone.
Geographic	• Geographic segmentation divides the population based on location. This may be a map/coordinate-based element (a street, city, region, country, etc.), or other mechanisms for classifying a geographic location (climate, or types of insects present).	• Hardware stores may adjust the products they carry depending on whether the store is located in an urban versus a rural area. • Some countries may have different packaging, labelling and/or component requirements. • Remote car starters tend to be popular in regions with extreme temperatures (very cold or very hot).

EXHIBIT 1-7
SEGMENTATION OF THE INDUSTRIAL MARKET

Method	Description	Examples
Corpographics	• Corpographic segmentation divides companies into groups based on physical dimensions of the company or factors related to the nature of the business they engage in. Such factors include: (1) industry type/classification, (2) size of the company along some dimension such as number of employees or revenue, (3) type of technology used, (4) type of input materials required.	• Companies are often grouped into small, medium and large, based on number of employees, income, growth or some other measure. • Beyond size, examining the nature of the industry, type of technology or type of input may be valuable. For example, a company selling fire-protective clothing may focus on manufacturers where heat/flames are present.
Behavioral	• Behavioral segmentation focuses on the characteristics of each purchase and/or use. Different aspects include: (1) frequency of purchase, (2) average size of purchase, timing (day, week, season), and (3) purchases based on special occasions. The purchasing approach of the organization may also be a distinguishing characteristic.	• Some organizations will review their requirements with a certain periodicity (perhaps once per year, software needs are considered during the strategic planning process). Similarly some companies may concentrate their purchases during select periods of the year (fall, quarterly, monthly, etc.). • Customers are often sorted into tiers based on total volume of purchase (heavy, moderate, light, and nonuser).
Benefit	• Benefit segmentation addresses some focuses on a specific performance or image characteristic sought after by the segment.	• Some organizations will seem to have little in common at first, but may have a common benefit that they require. For example, both photographers and mobile medical units need cases that are light, secure and durable. • Some companies may purchase accounting software for purposes of regulatory compliance; others maximize operating efficiency.
Geographic	• Geographic segmentation divides companies based on location. This may be a map/coordinate-based element (e.g., a city, region, country) or other mechanisms for classifying location (e.g., climate, or types of animals and trees present).	• Many larger companies already segment markets into regions and subregions (e.g., the Western Canada region of the Canadian division). This may be for organizational structuring and/or regional differences in requirements or demand.
Personal	• Companies may also be segmented by characteristics of individuals making and/or influencing decisions.	• Demographic and psychographic variables associated with the purchasing manager might also be the basis for segmentation. • A company selling environmentally friendly products might search out purchasing managers with a strong sense of ethical responsibility.
Value Chain Contribution	• Value chain contribution seeks to indicate the benefit(s) of the offering to one or more specific elements of an organization's value (production) chain. These include support functions (e.g., firm infrastructure, human resource management, technology development or procurement), as well as primary activities (e.g., inbound logistics, operations, outbound logistics, marketing and sales, services, and so on).	• One possibility is to recognize what aspect(s) of the organization's value chain you are targeting and make it clear how improving those aspects will benefit the organization as a whole. • Typically, the more elements of the value chain that are benefited (with none being harmed), the greater the level of acceptance will be.

EXHIBIT 1-8
CRITERIA FOR EFFECTIVE SEGMENTATION (ARMS)

Element	Description	Examples
A Alignment	• The extent to which the segmentation strategy is aligned with the current brand identity, strategy and resources (for example, skill sets, distribution, etc.) of the organization.	• For some educational institutions, the ability to offer distance delivery via technology is straightforward (personnel and technology are already in place), whereas for others, this would require a significant acquisition of equipment and retraining of personnel. • A building supply store might believe they could expand their space and target commercial roofers, but this may determine that this service would divert too many resources (dollars, equipment and personnel) in a nonstrategic direction.
R Reachable	• The ability of the organization to communicate with and deliver required products and services to the targeted segment(s).	• Is it straightforward to send messages to this segment (perhaps via email, advertisements or media)? Are there any large impediments to delivering the product and/or services? • If you wanted to reach 20-30-year-old males, where would you advertise? The bar, MTV, football games might all be good choices. On the other hand it may be difficult to communicate with 50-60 year old females.
M Moveable	• To the extent to which this segment is likely to adopt the suggested action (for example, actually buy the product).	• Some groups will be easier to "move". Others may hear the message but be slow to act. • It might be straightforward to communicate with 18-year-olds, but it is likely going to be difficult to convince them to purchase life insurance. Similarly, anti-smoking advertisements may be more effective for teens who have never smoked than for 70–year-olds who currently do.
S Sustainable	• The extent to which the targeted segment will represent a viable income stream for the foreseeable future.	• Is this segment currently large enough? What are the growth prospects for this segment (size, share and amount)? What are the competition levels like? The largest segment is not necessarily the best segment. • Snap-On Tools has found success by targeting the niche market of professional mechanics. This loyal segment appreciates the quality of tools and the ease of acquisition via delivery vans. • During an economic boom, certain luxury products may experience heightened demand from some segments, however, demand may fluctuate greatly with the economy • Some sectors of the economy may be growing and some may be shrinking. Targeting one may be far more profitable than targeting the other.

Think about retirement investing. We know that it is important to start young, given the time value of money and compound interest (Einstein called this the greatest force in the Universe). Suppose you are an investment firm. Clearly, selling financial products would be *aligned* with your strategy. It would also seem reasonably easy to *reach* males ages eighteen to twenty-five through media related to sports programming or music videos. This group would also seem to be large enough and *sustainable* on a long-term basis (they will continue to be a sizeable group). Would you like the job of selling retirement investment products (something that they will not actually benefit from for forty-plus years) to someone in this age range? Beer, pizza, clothing, and cars will likely be ahead of you in the line. Not looking good. This group, as much as they could use your product, will be extremely difficult to *move*.

Consider the Entire Customer Experience

The customer experience consists of multiple stages: (1) preadoption, (2) purchase, (3) installation and initial use, (4) ongoing use, and (5) disposal/repurchase. These are represented in Exhibit 1-9. A given attribute might be particularly salient during one stage but not during the others. For example, when a buyer thinks about adopting a firm's product, he or she might consider the type of personnel provided during the preadoption phase (for example, the caliber of engineers to assess structural requirements); the financing terms available during the purchase phase; the fit with existing components during the installation phase; the performance efficiency, output quantity, ease of use, and so on during the operation phase; and the environmental friendliness of the product when the disposal phase eventually rolls around. For some products and services, a specific benefit such as safety may be thought of as critical for multiple stages of the customer experience, including installation, operation, and disposal.

Consider an office furniture supplier. While a characteristic such as brand image should remain consistent throughout the ownership process, the types of services offered may vary considerably. At the prepurchase phase, services might include consultation regarding interior design as well as education regarding ergonomics. During the purchase phase, it might be possible to present a proposal to the board, offer financing, or provide "buy-back" insurance in the event that business slows. Delivery, set-up, and instruction regarding furniture use and cleaning may occur during the installation phase, followed by an annual inspection of wear and tear. Finally, when it is time to replace the furniture, is it possible to offer free removal and recycling? True, some customers just want furniture at a low price and loaded on a truck. However, in cases where continuous interaction is possible, this infusion of service will increase the likelihood that a long-term relationship is fostered.

EVALUATION OF COMPETITION

Rarely does an innovation exist in a competitive vacuum, devoid of opposing forces. In some contexts *direct competitors* are easy to identify. If you sell accounting software, you are probably aware of a number of different accounting software products on the market and where they differ from yours, feature by feature. Sometimes part of the battle is dealing with *indirect competition.* In such cases your combatants are not quite as well defined, but they still have the potential to draw people away from your cause. Suppose you operate a movie theater. Some of your direct competitors might be described as other movie theaters within a ten-mile radius. Indirect competitors might include restaurants, sporting events, live theater, opera, museums, and so on. Finally, and in many situations, the key competitor of primary importance is *nonbehavior.* Such would be particularly acute in the case of charities seeking people who currently do not donate, medical agencies needing blood from people who currently do not give, investment firms trying to help people who do not currently save for retirement, and so on. This nonbehavior alternative (nonpurchase) is pervasive—present in any situation where a person has the option of walking away. For example, a person might be actively considering Car A vs. Car B, but a very real option is to leave and make no purchase whatsoever.

EXHIBIT 1-9
CONSIDERATION OF THE ENTIRE CUSTOMER EXPERIENCE

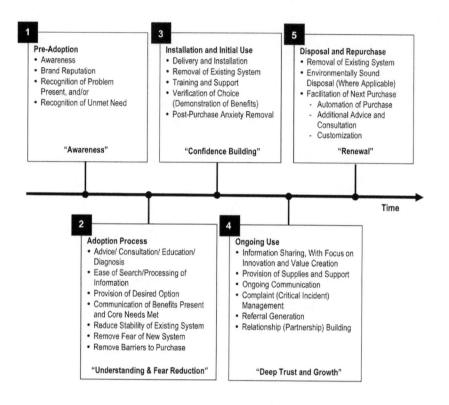

1

Pre-Adoption
- Awareness
- Brand Reputation
- Recognition of Problem Present, and/or
- Recognition of Unmet Need

"Awareness"

3

Installation and Initial Use
- Delivery and Installation
- Removal of Existing System
- Training and Support
- Verification of Choice (Demonstration of Benefits)
- Post-Purchase Anxiety Removal

"Confidence Building"

5

Disposal and Repurchase
- Removal of Existing System
- Environmentally Sound Disposal (Where Applicable)
- Facilitation of Next Purchase
  - Automation of Purchase
  - Additional Advice and Consultation
  - Customization

"Renewal"

Time

2

Adoption Process
- Advice/ Consultation/ Education/ Diagnosis
- Ease of Search/Processing of Information
- Provision of Desired Option
- Communication of Benefits Present and Core Needs Met
- Reduce Stability of Existing System
- Remove Fear of New System
- Remove Barriers to Purchase

"Understanding & Fear Reduction"

4

Ongoing Use
- Information Sharing, With Focus on Innovation and Value Creation
- Provision of Supplies and Support
- Ongoing Communication
- Complaint (Critical Incident) Management
- Referral Generation
- Relationship (Partnership) Building

"Deep Trust and Growth"

All alternatives, yours as well as competitors', may be described in terms of their features, benefits, and needs met (see Exhibit 1-2). Given the diversity of competing options, a potentially confounding problem comes down to making meaningful comparisons between yourself and competing options. Direct competitors can usually be compared explicitly on the same attributes (aspects covered in the *feature level*, as in Exhibit 1-3). For example, a person comparing different laptop computers may make side-by-side comparisons in terms of price, length of warranty, size of screen, and so on. Given the physical nature of most of these attributes at the feature level, it is usually straightforward to create a matrix listing your alternative relative to the competition on each of the dimensions. Of course, this alone does not accomplish much until the actual importance of each of the dimensions is taken into account (a three-year warranty is better than a one-year warranty *only* if people actually care about warranties). Once this is taken into consideration, it becomes possible to directly assess where you stand relative to direct competitors.

Comparing indirect competitors becomes more difficult in that features do not align completely (e.g., both may have a price, but beyond that they are substantially different). In these cases it is beneficial to compare the options in terms of the *benefit level* (see Exhibit 1-4). For example, in addition to a feature such as price, both the theater and the baseball game can be compared in terms of some overarching benefit such as entertainment value. As per Exhibit 1-5, they could also be compared in terms of *need* level, such as strengthening of family, predictability, or achievement. In a similar way, even nonbehavior serves some benefit(s) as well as some needs. For example, in terms of benefits, not donating blood (covered extensively in Chapter 6) serves to make life easier (no effort is required), and it also reduces negative outcomes such as pain or possible fainting. Needs served by not donating might include the maximization of optimal health as well as an increased provision of time.

SUMMARY

This chapter commenced with an exhortation to remember that an innovation does not occur in a vacuum. It exists in a complex atmosphere and often serves to meet multiple objectives. With respect to the purpose of an innovation, caution was placed on understanding that while features may produce benefits and benefits may satisfy one or more needs, for some individuals there may be limited ability to interpret how the features translate into benefits or how the benefits translate into meeting core needs.

Accordingly, there are three different levels of value communication. For example, a person may know that a cleaner has a certain chemical but may not know what it actually does. Once he or she knows that it reduces bacteria (a benefit), does he or she understand that this will reduce the likelihood of a family member becoming ill (meeting the need of promoting the strength of the family)? In such cases, emphasis must be placed on helping the customer be able to make the translation from features and jargon to the explicit realization that important needs are being met through these features. When needs are met, buttons are pushed.

Additional factors impacting core utility were also considered. It was stressed that one needs to be aware of: (1) idiosyncrasies of the segment/ stakeholder group and (2) the stage of the customer experience, including pre-adoption, purchase, installation and initial use, ongoing use, and disposal/repurchase.

CHAPTER TWO

THE STABILITY OF THE EXISTING ALTERNATIVE MUST BE REDUCED (2ND LAW OF INNOVATION SUCCESS)

The existing system usually has an upper hand over the innovation. The tendency to continue using the alternative in place may be particularly strong, even in cases when a better option is available and/or substantial opposition to the current system is present. In such cases, for one reason or another, the attraction to the existing system remains solid.

People tend to switch marital partners with a greater frequency than they switch banks. It is doubtful this is due to an overwhelmingly positive sentiment toward banks. Rather, for many it likely stems from the perception that leaving a bank would be far too difficult. It is this perception that keeps the stability associated with the bank at a high level. A bank trying to be innovative and provide a truly better offering will need to contend with this.

Think of some instances where you might find yourself less than pleased with a product or service, but you continue to avail yourself of it—sometimes with the full knowledge something better is out there. Maybe it is a family physician who is rather unfriendly, a software package that is particularly slow, a television that is outdated, a procedure at work you think is inefficient, or a personal behavior such as smoking that you would rather live without. Perhaps it is a bank. Perhaps it is a spouse.

There is no question it can be frustrating to find ourselves stagnating in circumstances where we believe better options may be available but, for one reason or another, we choose to stick with the status quo. It can be equally exasperating to watch other individuals in this type of situation. Within a personal context, you may have examples pertaining to someone you care about very deeply—maybe you want your mother to move from her current residence into a nursing home, but she strongly opposes the prospect. Within a business setting, you see people who you believe would be much better off if they would only switch from their current system to yours. You hold a solution, but they seem to want no part of it.

The purpose of this chapter is to explore conditions promoting the stability of the existing system, as well as those that result in destabilization. If you are currently trying to capture market share, you will want to consider approaches that may serve to (further) destabilize an adversary's existing system. Conversely, if you are seeking to promote the stability of your system and maintain brand loyalty, your focus should be on understanding and effectively removing existing Achilles' heels. The ten factors influencing stability, covered in this chapter, are outlined in Exhibit 2-1.

GENERAL MOMENTUM DUE TO PSYCHOLOGICAL FACTORS

Complacency Due to Ignorance, Habituation, or Priority Setting

A number of psychological factors may influence the general momentum of the existing system and ultimately foster "doing what has always been done." One such possibility is that *complacency* has set in—the issue at hand is not even on the radar. Sometimes this is because a person is not aware that a system even exists. Think of all of the parts of your car engine that you know absolutely nothing about.

EXHIBIT 2-1
COMPREHENSIVE CHANGE MODEL: STABILITY

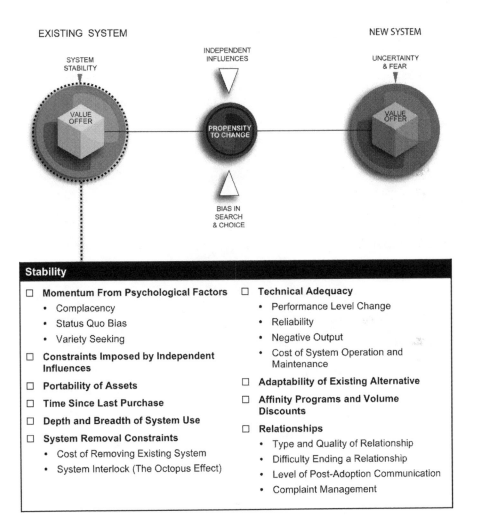

EXISTING SYSTEM

NEW SYSTEM

SYSTEM
STABILITY

INDEPENDENT
INFLUENCES

UNCERTAINTY
& FEAR

VALUE
OFFER

PROPENSITY
TO CHANGE

VALUE
OFFER

BIAS IN
SEARCH
& CHOICE

Stability

☐ **Momentum From Psychological Factors**
  • Complacency
  • Status Quo Bias
  • Variety Seeking
☐ **Constraints Imposed by Independent Influences**
☐ **Portability of Assets**
☐ **Time Since Last Purchase**
☐ **Depth and Breadth of System Use**
☐ **System Removal Constraints**
  • Cost of Removing Existing System
  • System Interlock (The Octopus Effect)

☐ **Technical Adequacy**
  • Performance Level Change
  • Reliability
  • Negative Output
  • Cost of System Operation and Maintenance
☐ **Adaptability of Existing Alternative**
☐ **Affinity Programs and Volume Discounts**
☐ **Relationships**
  • Type and Quality of Relationship
  • Difficulty Ending a Relationship
  • Level of Post-Adoption Communication
  • Complaint Management

In other cases, a system can be technically in the foreground, but functionally invisible. In such situations, it is not that people are happy or unhappy with the current system; it is simply that they pay it little thought. The system has become so ingrained in "the way of doing business" that without some degree of outside prompting, it is highly improbable it will ever be changed—nobody questions why something is present or why a particular process is followed. Think about some of the elements in your life that you repeat daily without question: the route you take to work, the procedures by which expenses are approved, the software you use for specific tasks, and so on. These processes become second nature. This is not necessarily a bad thing. If you changed every system in your environment on a daily basis, your sanity would be short-lived. Nonetheless, this state of reduced vigilance for noticing different systems in our environment may result in the inability to detect that changes might be necessary or beneficial.

Complacency is also inherent when there is some dissatisfaction with the system, but this level of displeasure has not yet risen to a level where it is perceived to warrant action. That is, it is registering on the conscious level, but it is low on the priority list—there are other fires casting hotter and higher flames at present, and they have to be put out first. In such contexts, extra effort may be needed to communicate why your product, service, or program should be considered more urgent than it is currently perceived to be. This might be somewhat like a car mechanic pointing out the strange but not incredibly annoying noise coming from the transmission could be indicative of a much bigger problem that, if not taken care of shortly, could result in the need to replace the entire drivetrain.

When considering the impact of your product, service, or policy, what can you do to point out, in concrete terms, what the long-term impact of not adopting your system will be? For purposes of salience, how can you more strongly position this relative to other decisions people are making, and therefore increase its priority?

Status Quo Bias

Why does an existing option have an inherent advantage over a challenging one, even if all the information about the challenger is known and there are few costs to switching? Researchers examining the status quo bias have put forth a number of explanations involving mental constructs to explain this barrier.[1] In general, people desire to act in a consistent manner. After we have made a decision, we want to believe we have made the right choice—or at least we did not make a poor choice. To believe we should have selected something different may well invoke cognitive dissonance. This is the lousy feeling we get when an action taken and a belief regarding that action do not align, as would be the case if a person who is opposed to alcohol consumption drinks a beer. People do not want to wilfully place themselves in a position where their existing beliefs will be challenged. A devout Buddhist is not going to actively seek out a Catholic mass. We are not prone to challenging the wisdom of our previous decisions.

In a similar vein, the need for consistency can be observed in the "sunk cost effect"[2] that spurs the tendency to spend more money on an initially chosen alternative if a large investment has already been made. In many situations, this results in escalation of commitment and good money being thrown after bad. In a sense, the attitude is, "Hey, if we paid that much money on this, we *must* have made the right choice." Suppose a company spends a considerable sum on some element of infrastructure that does not quite work out as planned (large software "solutions" frequently fall in this category). Even though the best move might be to admit defeat and move on to another solution, there can be a propensity to put more money toward it.

Variety Seeking

Some product categories are inherently unstable, even to the extent that active variety-seeking directly follows a given purchase. While you may have some loyalty to a given restaurant, there are probably few occasions where you would want to go to the same restaurant back to back. Yes, you could get an entirely different meal from the same restaurant and therefore meet some variety requirement, but you would probably prefer to get an entirely different meal from an entirely different restaurant.

Novelty is also often desired in many clothing and jewelery selections. Rarely would you see a person buy two of the same necktie, scarf, ring, pendant, and so on. Variety-seeking is also common in purchasing grocery items, furniture, and cars. As a matter of course, some business opportunities may be developed around strategies that present additional variety to patrons. A spa could offer new treatments; a floral shop could offer new varieties of flowers, and so forth. Consider Lacoste polo shirts; the company is able to enhance sales by providing the same basic shirt in a broad range of colors and patterns.

In some cases there is a downside to offering variety. First, it may significantly increase the expense of operations. New production, distribution, and advertising expenses may take a considerable toll on the bottom line. Second, though providing variety may increase the novelty associated with the offerings, it may also increase the amount of effort needed by the customer to process the offerings and ultimately make a decision. So, while offering variety can provide opportunities to grow, at other times offering a high level of stability and predictability may be preferred.

Similarly, many businesses have tried to execute mass-customization strategies. For instance, through the Nike Web site, customers can design a sneaker that is unique to the world. However, some have found that not as many consumers as anticipated will spend the extra money required to achieve this level of uniqueness. This was the experience of Proctor and Gamble after a seven-year run with reflect.com starting in 1999. Through this site, customers could customize their makeup, creating their own lipstick, body lotion, and more. The execution by all accounts was sound, but the demand for this level of tailoring simply was not there.[3]

CONSTRAINTS IMPOSED BY INDEPENDENT INFLUENCES

Independent influences are forces beyond the direct control of the organization, and these will be expanded on considerably in the 4th Law of Innovation Success. These include: (1) legal and regulatory forces, (2) government programs and initiatives, (3) technological innovations, (4) media and popular culture, (5) macro social trends, and (6) reference groups and significant individuals. Any of these may influence the stability of the existing system. For illustration, consider constraints to switching that arise from legal and regulatory forces.

I might want to drive a car without insurance or refuse to pay income taxes, but my ability to do so is expressly forbidden by the government. In cases where we do have legitimate volitional control over options, formal constraints can still emerge from legal implications that would result from breaking a contract. Have you ever signed up for a service having a time length associated with it? Maybe it was a one-year monitoring package with a home security company, a three-year plan with a cellular provider, a forty-eight-month car lease, or a thirty-year mortgage. Then, prior to this time lapsing, you want out. Good reasons may abound. Six months into the security-monitoring contract, you take a job in a different city. When you receive your first cell-phone bill, you gag at all the extra hidden costs this provider apparently considers standard, and you no longer want to use their services. After twenty-four months of your car lease, you are fed up with the constant repairs and you realize this model is really no longer the "cool one." Four years into your thirty-year mortgage, interest rates are now significantly lower than when you signed up. Sometimes, the penalties for getting out are minor—a negligible administration fee, for instance. However, in more extreme situations, there is no escape hatch and you are expected to fulfill the payments for the life of the contract.

It may be very hard to move people to your system if there are severe penalties (social, legal, or economic) in place if they switch from their existing provider. Does this mean you should not waste your time on these people? Possibly—you only have so many resources, and there is no point chasing down those who are highly unlikely to take advantage of your innovative offering. Or, you may wish to work with them on a more casual basis, providing information and indirect support until such time as they are released from their contractual obligation. On occasion, it may be advantageous to assist in paying for extra expenses incurred if they make an early break from the existing contract. This tactic can be especially useful if this does not mean an actual financial outlay on your part. For example, a cell-phone service provider may offer three months of free service to entice people to switch early and start a long-term contract with them. The consumer might still have to pay the penalty but can mentally and financially offset this by the money saved because of the "bonus" offered.

What are the independent influences providing stability to the existing system you are trying to compete with? What can you do to offset or exceed the benefit that these provide? Are there any independent influences that may work against/destabilize the existing system? For example, are there new pollution laws making the current option less attractive?

PORTABILITY OF ASSETS

It is impossible not to be touched by stories of immigrants who gave up their homes and all of their belongings in order to move to a place of greater opportunity. Making a change meant leaving something behind. Far less dramatic, but still impactful, some of the changes we make require we leave something behind. Sometimes these are relationships. This is a special class of "asset" and will be discussed in a separate section. For now, we will talk about other tangible and intangible items.

If you want to switch banks, you can, but you cannot take your "fifteen years of good history" on file with the bank, or the home-equity line-of-credit agreement you have in place just in case you need it. If you leave your physician, you might be able to get your file transferred—but even if the file is sent, you have no way of knowing if all key information is still there or if the new physician will be able to understand the records. Something may be lost in the transition. The same would hold true of accounting documents, legal records, and so on.

What are you asking people to leave behind? What assets will not carry over to the new system? What tangible and intangible assets and skills have they invested in that they cannot take with them? This is an interesting point. Even if there are no financial penalties in place, leaving behind something we have invested money, time, or emotion into, such as skill development, may increase the perceived switching cost.

Imagine that you work in a given industry for ten years and acquire detailed knowledge about products and competitors. Switching employment to a new industry may be exciting because it is something novel, but you may feel like you have to give up a large part of "who you are" and what you have become good at.

TIME SINCE LAST PURCHASE

This issue is somewhat complicated, as it may vary considerably with the product class. Consider the acquisition of a motor vehicle. In such a situation, there is incredible stability immediately following the purchase. In most cases a replacement for the vehicle will not be considered for several years. Other products tend to be more cyclical in nature. Home and car insurance tend to be renewed on a yearly basis, while other items, such as utilities (gas, electricity, and telephone), tend to be examined on a monthly basis.

I know of an exceptionally successful salesperson who has based his achievements on understanding when the optimal striking point will occur—the window of time when stability tends to be very low. For many, home insurance is a good example. If you generally renew in May of each year, you probably receive your renewal notice in April. It is very possible

that each April you have a small conniption, shake your head in disbe-
lief, and think to yourself there must be something better out there. If
the phone rings at that moment and the person on the other end suggests
some possible home insurance options, my guess is that you listen conscien-
tiously. However, if this same phone call comes in June, you will probably
be less receptive...until next April. The key takeaway from a competitive
perspective is that there are some times to act that are better than others.

BREADTH AND DEPTH OF EXISTING SYSTEM USE

To what extent is the existing system used for a large number of purposes by a large number of individuals? Let us suppose only one administrative assistant briefly uses an accounting system each week. Switching
accounting systems would not pose a great problem—even if there were
major glitches in the implementation of the new system, few people would
be directly impacted. Suppose now, everyone in a one-hundred-person
organization uses this accounting system to enter his or her expenses—
nothing complex, just the recording of receipt amounts. The *breadth of
use* now makes change that much more difficult. All users will have to be
informed of the change and the new procedures explained to them.

Where *depth of use* is high (many features are used), the task of switching becomes potentially even more difficult. Suppose the accounting system also includes an elaborate cost tracking system. In addition to entering
expenses, it is used to record the amount of time and material required
for specific projects, view progress and coordinate schedules of other
team members, and provide feedback regarding performance objectives.
Changing this kind of system is a far greater organizational challenge—
many people will have to be retrained on many different elements.

Make sure you have an accurate understanding of the *actual* level of
depth and breadth of system use, not just the *potential* for such breadth
and depth to be present. I am familiar with a large telecommunications

provider that sold integrated systems aimed at medium to large companies. This system allowed every member of the organization to have a unique user code, specialized voice mail, different calling card features, and the list went on. The features were great in number and admittedly impressive on paper. Research with people who had adopted the system even revealed a high level of satisfaction with the calling features.

Despite this apparent level of contentment, the users were still very price sensitive and willing to switch systems if price expectations were not met. This puzzled the telecommunications company. The explanation was fairly simple. Reported satisfaction with many features was high, but *actual use* of the features was remarkably low. In addition, people had never been adequately trained in how to use all the different features. So, while all people had access to a number of powerful add-ons, the only feature they tended to use extensively was voice-mail, and this was easily duplicated by competitors.

From the perspective of the incumbent, you want to ensure many people are using multiple features of your product regularly. This has a number of implications. First, you must demonstrate and promote many features and opportunities for meaningful interaction while jointly minimizing the real or perceived level of complexity. Second, where training and support is needed to use more advanced features or applications, be sure this assistance is present. Finally, make the features sufficiently different from those of competitors so they will be hard to copy. Granted, this has to be approached wisely—if you are perceived to be too different from the outset, you might never be adopted.

If an existing system is used pervasively, there may be concerns about down time and inefficiencies incurred if the system is switched. Apprehension may also be present regarding the general frustration of employees at having to learn a new system. Potential solutions from a competitive perspective include having a crossover period where both systems could be used; taking steps to make sure the new system has a similar interface/usage characteristics to the old one; making sure adequate training is in place; and/or having a limited rollout to a select number of customers so implementation problems can be identified early on.

SYSTEM REMOVAL CONSTRAINTS

On occasion, the biggest barrier to innovation and change is not an emotional or financial commitment to the old system. In these cases there may even be a strong desire to move to a new system, but the inescapable reality is that in order to put the new system in place, the old system has to be removed first. This brings with it the costs of physically removing the specific system and the costs of repairing systems it was linked to.

Cost of Physically Removing an Existing System

Imagine you want to develop a new office building in the heart of the city. The location you have the opportunity to purchase has the advantage of being situated close to shops, theaters, and housing. However, an irreparable five-story apartment complex, built using asbestos insulation and pipes containing plutonium, currently occupies the location. You face a number of costs just to clear the site, some of which might entail obtaining a demolition permit, hiring a wrecking crew, taking out additional insurance in case the destruction impacts surrounding buildings, and employing people to haul away the debris. There will be extra costs due to the presence of asbestos and plutonium. On the positive side, the glow from the plutonium may be bright enough to permit work to continue throughout the night unimpeded by darkness.

You do not need to be a large real estate developer to appreciate the costs associated with removing existing elements. Anyone who has taken on even a modest renovation project in his or her house can attest to the challenges of just removing work completed by previous owners. Gouges in walls and torn drywall following a snap decision on a Saturday morning to remove the old wallpaper are often evidence of this. After what seems to be hundreds of hours of toil, frustration, and mess, you still have not done anything new. You have only removed the old.

If you are proposing a new system, what elements of the old system will have to be removed first? If you want people to adopt new software, will this require a substantial reprogramming of their existing system to ensure compatibility? Will you take on part or all of this expense? If you are a retailer and want an individual to buy a new appliance or mattress, are you going to offer to remove the old one for free? If you are a city looking to foster downtown revitalization, are you willing to assist a developer with some of the demolition costs and work to facilitate necessary rezoning? When considering the cost of removing a system, it is also necessary to consider what other systems are affected. Typically, as the number of other systems affected increases, so too does the cost of removal.

System Interlock (The Octopus Effect)

When considering breadth- and depth-of-system use, the major concern centered on how *frequently* how many *people* are using how many *features* for how many *purposes/applications* (the extent to which the system is interwoven with significant aspects of the user's life). Consequently, if many people use the incumbent system in many different types of applications, its stability can be very strong. A system may also achieve considerable stability by forging strong interlocking connections with other systems, such as other products and services. I refer to this as the Octopus Effect to denote how a system may latch onto multiple systems in a binding way. It might be conceivable to unbind one of these connections, but having to sever all of them may be particularly challenging. What other systems/facets of life have to be changed in order for the system to be changed over to yours, and how can you minimize this burden?

As an example, it would probably be fairly easy to replace a chair in a room without considerably disrupting other physical systems. However, replacing the foundation of a building will not only have an impact on the frame, but will also affect the heating, plumbing, and electrical systems. Suppose that a project management system exists that not only provides information about supply levels, but also alerts users to critical levels at multiple sites, tracks project costs, sends out bid requests to qualified suppliers, and links into shipping for quick and efficient transportation. Changing this automation would result in other systems in the organization being negatively impacted.

The previous example looked at how deeply woven an application was with other technology. Such changes can be just as complex with "soft" systems—social, legal, economic, and political dimensions. Moving from one house to another within a city is fraught with a number of administrative hassles, but moving from one country to another has far-reaching implications that include more than just transportation logistics. Among other things, there are changes in political structure, taxation, economic status, social circles, employment stability, health care coverage, and the education of children. The point to be made is this: in many cases, "softer" less tangible elements dwarf any of the material consequences of "hard" physical systems.

Companies that grow through merger and acquisition routinely face this issue. Yes, merging software systems and databases can be difficult. However, merging organizations with two distinct cultural systems (the language used, attitudes toward structure, reward systems, and general personality) also poses a problem. Consider mergers between corporate giant Unilever and the playful Ben and Jerry's; or the aggressive Merrill Lynch and the more conservative Bank of America. Culture clashes can even happen when two units from within an organization are brought together, as was the case when two different acquisition offices with the United States

Army were merged. In this case, hard system integration was conducted with expediency and military precision. However, conflicts were reported because of differences in cultural values, also known as "the way we do things around here."[4]

TECHNICAL ADEQUACY

Systems often become obsolete over time, sometimes due to their inability to withstand the physical demands placed on them and at other times due to factors beyond their control, such as changes in fashion or technology. Obsolescence also carries with it a reduction to system stability. The following factors associated with technical adequacy are considered: performance level change, reliability, negative output, and increasing costs associated with operation and maintenance.

Performance Level Change

A number of things may happen to the utility associated with the system over time. One possibility is that the level of an attribute decreases. Perhaps the 500 horsepower engine diminishes to 450, or the reliability of the system declines unexpectedly. In such a situation there is a *performance level change*, causing concern about what the future may hold. Another possibility is that the output level of performance on the attribute does not change, but there is a change in the environment that has an impact on the value of the system. In these cases there is a change to the *relative performance level*. Personal computers frequently fall into this category—adopting the newest software often renders the processing ability of the existing unit too slow and the storage capacity too small.

A different case would be where the importance level associated with the attribute is altered. That is, some aspect has typically been considered, but due to some change in policy or mind-set, performance on this dimension goes from being trivial to incredibly important. An example of this in more recent years is an increased focus on corporate ethical standards when selecting a company to do business with. It is not that there was previously no concern about such conduct, but it would seem we give it far greater weight in our decision making now.

Reliability

Reliability refers to the extent to which you are able to consistently get the expected result with each experience. Ideally a product functions in the same manner each time it is purchased, and the experience from a service provider is always stellar. Life is good and, just as important, predictable. Such reliability is not always present in every aspect of our existence. Have you ever seen a quarterback in football who is incredibly strong one game and incredibly lame the next? Maybe you have experienced something similar in your own game of golf or tennis. One day you are within striking distance of Tiger, the next day you play like you have been attacked by one. Any time our expectations are not met (assuming they were positive), this can be frustrating.

Reliability can be particularly important when personnel form the basis for competition. In brief, humans have a wonderful way of adding variability to the mix. On one occasion the food in the restaurant is great, on the next it is burnt. The airline I tend to fly with is like this. I will catch the flight first thing in the morning and will be overcome with the great service improvements that have been made within the airline. Then somewhere between this flight and the connecting one, the company seems to have issued a policy change that requires passengers be beaten. Decreasing variability in human performance may be achieved several ways: by setting clear performance standards and identifying how this translates in terms of behavior, not simply telling people to "achieve high levels of service"; by careful selection of individuals and providing adequate training; by actually monitoring and rewarding these behaviors;

and by employing facilitating technology, such as computer programs or databases.[5]

Negative Output

Systems frequently have unintended or unwanted by-products that become apparent over time. A chemical process may have certain elements that are potentially harmful to employees and/or the world at large. These by-products may emerge during the manufacturing process (noises and smells from a manufacturing plant) or some time afterward (chemical off-gassing from carpet and furniture we put in our homes). In addition to chemical hazards, some processes may be dangerous (work around high voltage cables) or just downright bothersome (noise created in the workplace).

Perhaps there are some elements of the existing system that perennially lead to annoyance and frustration. This might come in the form of wait time associated with a service, difficulty accessing some types of information from a computer program due to an unintuitive interface, or lost time because the system in question malfunctions every time it is overloaded. A critical point of collapse exists for most systems. If you are the incumbent, what can you do to protect against this? If you are the challenger, how can you build a more robust solution and therefore exploit this?

Cost of System Operation and Maintenance

Whereas negative output may be considered a by-product of the system when it is operational, the cost of system maintenance pertains to the costs associated with keeping the system running, including ongoing training costs, replacement costs, repair costs, monitoring costs, compliance costs, space costs, and upgrading costs. These fall into two general categories: the cost of keeping the gears of the machine turning and the cost of the feedstock. If the cost of maintaining the system increases or if the price of input variables such as labor and materials increases, the stability of the incumbent system is likely to decrease.

While routine maintenance costs may be burdensome, unpredictable costs associated with system upkeep, such as the breakdown of manufacturing equipment resulting in unexpected productivity decreases, may greatly diminish system stability. For example, when a car starts to break down on freeways, with costs ranging from $500 to $5,000 to fix, it is probably time to get a new vehicle...or take public transit. Similarly, when the consultant you have been working with starts hitting you with a greater number of unexpected costs, the days of using this firm are limited. Unanticipated critical incidents can be particularly destabilizing.

ADAPTABILITY OF THE EXISTING ALTERNATIVE

Some systems are relatively rigid—they "are what they are," and they are more likely to be replaced than modified. Other systems possess the advantage that they are able to meet an anticipated or possible event and are created with the knowledge that adjustments will be required over time to deal with changes to the external environment. Adaptability permits a system to overcome issues of technical adequacy by meeting new demands placed on it, and often provides a lower cost solution. How adaptable is your systems to potential changes?

AFFINITY PROGRAMS AND VOLUME DISCOUNTS

To confess, I am a "loyal" customer of an airline I do not particularly like. I actually prefer a competitor in a number of key areas pertaining to the actual flight experience. The trouble is, I have a frequent flyer account with the one and not with the other. As a result, I receive flight upgrades, access to a comfortable lounge, special travel offers, and free merchandise with one but not the other. Similarly, I have "sold out" to two different hotel chains. I also tend to use only one credit card due to the reward points that accumulate. These types of loyalty programs have become pervasive. Department stores, grocery retailers, gas stations, bookstores, hair salons, and even local coffee shops have joined in as well.

For the vast majority of these programs, enrollment is free to the customer (some might even offer a promotion or incentive for joining). Other programs will actually have an up-front fee (yearly or lifetime) providing members a discount on products and services. Still others have a certain threshold amount to be spent in order to become a member, and successive amounts required to climb to different tiers of membership (e.g., bronze, silver, gold, and platinum). The downside to programs requiring some form of initial commitment is that it may be more difficult to get people to join. On the upside, once these people have actually signed up, they are more likely to be committed.

Research has demonstrated that if these programs are designed properly, they can be very effective at decreasing defections and increasing the customer lifetime, fostering additional purchases, improving share of wallet, and yielding insight into the buying behavior of the member.[6] The impact of the program may differ depending on the pre-existing loyalty. For individuals who display a lower level of patronage, these programs have been found to increase the amount and type of sales. However, for those who are already dedicated customers, such programs act in a maintenance function, keeping spending levels consistent and increasing the length of time they remain customers.

These programs have a potential downside if improperly executed. Upfront one must consider what purposes the loyalty program will serve and what goals one seeks to meet. The best and brightest of these programs result in a more extensive relationship with the customer. In line with this, they should generally be geared toward those who will purchase more, not just those looking to save a few dollars. Moreover, it is important to realize there are different types of incentives that may be put in place to deal with different consumer motives: (1) economic rewards that foster monetary savings, (2) hedonistic rewards that provide gifts and luxuries, (3) social-relational awards that provide people with information about events and make them feel like they are part of a group, (4) informational advice that gives access to specialized material, and (5) functional rewards such as priority service—phone numbers, lineups, and so on.[7]

The signals sent to nonmembers should also be considered. The over-riding goal is to reward an individual with benefits he or she has accrued due to membership, *not* to make nonmembers feel penalized, hurt, or mistreated. This is often a perceptual issue (e.g., did the other person get a discount off the normal price or am I paying more than I should?). At least one major grocery store chain I am familiar with has done away with member pricing, perhaps for this very reason.

Volume Discounts. Some organizations structure their charges so that giving them more business means getting more savings. Sometimes this is structured in tiers (you will get a 5 percent discount after 100 units, a 10 percent discount after 220 units, etc.); at other times it is based on past or anticipated behavior. In these cases there may be a lower per-unit cost (professional house painters pay about half of the retail price for paint); a reduced commission (if you frequently buy and sell houses, a real estate agent may offer you a lower commission than she would a one-time customer); or the waiver of certain fees (a bank may waive certain transaction fees and provide a free safety deposit box to valued customers who have multiple accounts or banking products). Once an individual or organization is locked into this type of incentive structure, stability is increased.

RELATIONSHIPS—BREAKING UP IS HARD TO DO (SOMETIMES)

Recall from the last chapter in Exhibit 1-2 that one of the critical ways organizations may differentiate themselves is on the basis of the skills of personnel. These include knowledge, empathy, responsiveness, open and meaningful communication, honesty, and problem-solving orientation. Likewise, it was indicated that members of the supply chain could offer a number of utilitarian benefits such as financing, market and technical information, advertising, promotion, and processing of orders. Switching from one system to another may mean the termination of a relationship. This, in turn, may have social and pragmatic consequences. In light of this, an important question becomes: what are the key relational benefits you are providing that would be difficult for your competitors to duplicate? Likewise, what are the key relationships with an existing alternative that you are going to have to overcome in order for your innovation to be a success?

Type and Quality of Relationships

To complicate matters, relationships exist on multiple levels, with four key distinctions being the *product/service,* the *company*, the *brand*, and the *individual*. On the first count, the relationship may be with the product or service: some people want coffee in the morning, opera for entertainment, and a car for transportation. Yes, there may be preferences for brands within each of these categories, but this does not mitigate the fact that there is an overarching preference for a general type of product or service.

Sometimes the relationship with the company and the brand are virtually one and the same. For example, many people would not make a distinction between Bayer the aspirin and Bayer Healthcare. Other times, the relationship with the brand and the company might be quite different. For example, a person might have a positive relationship with Betty Crocker, Green Giant, and Häagen-Dazs, but not necessarily with their parent company, General Mills.

On occasion, the level of identification with the brand can be extreme. As Harley-Davidson jackets, shirts, key fobs, hats, and tattoos on nether regions would attest, the relationship a person has with a brand can be a fundamental part of who they are. This was the key issue in the New Coke fiasco of 1985, discussed earlier. Fundamentally, the reaction from Coke drinkers was not about a change in taste, but rather a change in brand.

From an organizational perspective, the personal relationship established by employees can be a double-edged sword. Companies undoubtedly want positive behaviors of representatives to be sincere and positive—not something they are faking to just abide by company policy. However, a common lament in many professions, such as law or sales, is that when a key person leaves, he or she takes the business with them. Ideally, through hiring and training, a company may try to ensure that the various positive elements associated with personnel are standard across the organization. This serves to make the expected behavior "company related" and decrease the likelihood of customers switching just due to a personnel change. Another option is to build relationships through mechanisms that are not as personnel dependent, such as advertising or customer relationship management (CRM) software.

Difficulty Ending Relationships

Ending relationships can be difficult. While it is sometimes difficult to reject people from the outset (e.g., when you have to select one supplier and notify five others they did not get the contract), ending a relationship can become substantially more difficult when a strong working association has been developed over time. However, even with solid relationships, negative experiences can occur and result in the decision to discontinue patronage with a company. Sometimes the relationship is ended abruptly due to some critical incident. Frequently, though, the degradation occurs over a period of time as one witnesses chronic apathy from a provider or experiences a general level of dissatisfaction on one or more product/service dimension. To this end, it amazes me that frequently the level of ongoing communication following the adoption of a product or service is nonexistent. In these cases the relationship does not end through any real volitional choice; the change in stability to the existing system is not abrupt, it just fizzles out.

Level of Postadoption Communication

Communicating with a customer following the adoption of a new product or service may serve a number of purposes. First, if structured properly, the communication may reduce any dissonance associated with the choice that was made. This is important because there are very few purchase decisions where one alternative clearly dominates all others. For example, one choice option might be less expensive but has fewer features and/or lower quality. Even just the act of spending money can have people wondering if they have made the right choice—perhaps they should have spent the money elsewhere or waited until a later time to make this purchase. Communication following the purchase can often reduce this postpurchase anxiety through offering comfort that a wise choice was made.

Second, postadoption communication may signal the relationship is based on more than "just making money." A follow-up phone call without any hooks (there is no apparent attempt to sell something more) may give the impression the organization truly wants a satisfied customer. Related to this, a third potential outcome of postadoption communication is identifying any dissatisfaction because the product, service, or policy innovation does not seem to be working as well as it should, or there is confusion regarding use. Once recognized, actions can then be taken to remedy the problem. Even if a product comes with a manual or instructional DVD, some objects can be hard to assemble, configure, optimize, etc. A couple of words of advice and assurance can go a long way to reduce stress. Granted, not every purchase calls for an intensive postadoption follow-up. A clothing store contacting a recent customer to inquire how his or her latest sock acquisition was working out would be strange, if not downright creepy.

Complaint Management

The mechanism to complain should be readily apparent to the customer. Life is life. Things go wrong. However, often only a minority of people will actually complain to the offending company. This does not mean the remaining majority will stay inert and inactive. From that point forward, they may boycott the organization, tell all of their friends to do likewise, and share their frustration with the world through poisonous postings on the Web.[8] This is tragic, given that positively resolving a person's problem often results in a more loyal customer. Actions taken by a company to remedy an outstanding issue make a number of statements about how the company cares about the customer and how doing business in the future is a reduced-risk proposition—the customer is assured if something goes wrong, he or she need not worry; it will be taken care of. However, if the organization does not know there is a problem in the first place, it stands to reason that it is going to be difficult to fix.

Beyond being transparent, the complaint process should be relatively pain free. Customers should not feel like they are on the defensive. They should feel there is a person at the organization who has a great deal of empathy for their predicament. When possible, the resolution should also be prompt. Sometimes this means empowering front-line workers with the ability to provide a remedy without six layers of managerial approval.

Often the training provided to employees is lopsided. We are usually quick to educate people about all of the technical details of a product and provide them with the authority to complete sales, but we do not seem to be as active in training them how to effectively handle difficult situations or fix typical problems. This is not to suggest all front-line personnel should handle all problems. Part of the training is to recognize that when issues are sufficiently complex and/or the clients are exceptionally important, someone with greater background and training is required.

Complaint management does not necessarily mean giving away the farm. Many times people just want an opportunity to be heard. Further, too often we are admonished, "the customer is always right." There *are* customers who are abusive, manipulative, and otherwise out to scam the system. Though the minority, such customers need to be monitored and potentially removed from the client list. There are some people you do not want to be in a relationship with, and in many cases they are not even profitable.

SUMMARY

If the stability of an existing system is extremely high, it is going to be difficult for a new system to generate a sufficient level of attraction. From a defensive perspective, the goal is to determine how the stability may be maintained or increased in order to maintain loyalty and decrease the likelihood customers will switch. However, from a competitive perspective, it is imperative to understand what factors are contributing to stability of the existing system and those that may be the weak links. What are the elements that may destabilize the system? A championship fighter goes into a match knowing where his combatant will be weak and where he will be strong. Similarly, locating both the hard shell and the underbelly of the competitor forms a necessary part of any competitive business strategy.

The stability of the existing system may be associated with a number of psychological factors, such as complacency due to ignorance of other systems, or inaction resulting from waiting for the best deal possible. Formal constraints, such as laws and contracts, as well as informal constraints, such as the depth and breadth of system use, the cost of removing the existing system, or the time since last purchase, may put very real obstacles in the way of migrating people over to a new system. Conversely, if the technical adequacy of the system weakens, the stability of the system may be eroded. This reduced adequacy may be due to the system faltering and breaking down more often or because the system cannot keep step with increasing demands imposed by the environment. Sometimes the system might perform as well as it did in the first place, but this is no longer good enough given a change in requirements.

Relationships with the brand, the company, and its personnel also form an integral part of the stability equation and may work to either stabilize or destabilize a system. Strong relationships that provide value and emotional satisfaction can generate stability and help to weather turbulence if problems are encountered during the use of the product or during the service experience. This touches on a key issue—things do not always go as planned. One key element of the relationship process pertains to post-purchase relations, maintaining contact with the customer and resolving problems that might arise.

CHAPTER THREE

THE FEAR OF THE NEW ALTERNATIVE MUST BE REDUCED (3RD LAW OF INNOVATION SUCCESS)

To this point we have considered some strategies that may be used to establish a differential advantage, and we have further examined elements contributing to the (in)stability of an existing system. Let us assume you have actually developed a new system with a strong differential advantage. Experts have even heralded your innovative solution as amazing. Congratulations. You now expect nothing but joyous celebration and enthusiasm when you present your offering to the world. Instead you are met with puzzled looks, and people seem to be more anxious than excited about the prospect of adopting your option. You shake your head and try to figure out why your offering is so poorly received.

I am reminded of a good friend who noted that a person ten yards in front is thought of as a leader, but a person one hundred yards in front is often mistaken for the enemy. In such cases their vision is cloaked in more uncertainty than most can handle. Sometimes new concepts fail not so much because they are bad ideas, but rather because there is considerable ambiguity and fear present. Consider the relatively recent move to provide teenage girls with the Human Papilloma Virus (HPV) vaccine, which serves to prevent the occurrence of some forms of cervical cancer. While the intentions have been noble, uncertainties have also been present. For one, it is unclear how effective this vaccine will be as it does not cover all strains of HPV. Some are also concerned about potential side effects. Others are afraid the vaccination serves as an endorsement to engage in sexual activity at a younger age; consequently, moral concerns arise.

When there are potential negative consequences, uncertainty may give rise to fear. Yes, fear can be a powerful motivator when the choice is either to act or to suffer great peril, as would be the case if a fire alarm was going off and smoke was filling a room. However, when the problem facing the decision maker has not yet risen to such an ominous level, uncertainty and fear may more commonly paralyze than provoke. Indecision is fostered and no action is taken. Uncertainty is a major innovation killer.

Consider something as routine as the purchase of a car. When people have strong apprehensions about acquiring a new vehicle, they may drag their feet when it comes to the search process, or they may be in a constant state of browsing, hesitant to make a decision. Some may even lull themselves into believing that if they do not deal with the problem, it will somehow disappear. Alternately, they may think that if they wait long enough, the "right" answer will magically become apparent. Regardless of the underlying belief, the end result is stagnation. This issue arises in many other contexts—a person avoiding diagnosis of a potential medical problem, a government procrastinating regarding an environmental initiative, or a corporation experiencing "paralysis by analysis"—deferring action until the problem is "sufficiently" studied.

Exhibit 3-1 presents an overview of the key elements associated with risk and ambiguity surrounding the new system, with the key elements being: (1) types of perceived risk, (2) factors associated with risk tolerance, and (3) mechanisms for reducing the perceived risk and ambiguity. Exhibit 3-2 diagrams the relationship among these variables.

EXHIBIT 3-1
COMPREHENSIVE CHANGE MODEL: UNCERTAINTY AND FEAR

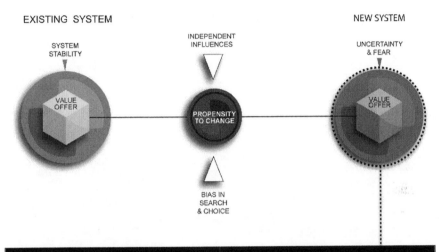

EXISTING SYSTEM   NEW SYSTEM

SYSTEM   INDEPENDENT   UNCERTAINTY
STABILITY   INFLUENCES   & FEAR

VALUE OFFER   PROPENSITY TO CHANGE   VALUE OFFER

BIAS IN
SEARCH
& CHOICE

Uncertainty and Fear

☐ **Areas of Uncertainty and Fear**
- Product/Service Class Risk
- Product/Service Specific Risk
- Transaction Risk
- Discomfort During Adoption
- Misuse of Information
- Risk of Discontinuity
- Start-Up Costs
- Payback Period
- Compatibility with Physical Systems (Barriers and Technical Constraints)
- Compatibility with "Soft Systems"
  - Independent Influences
  - Attitudes and Moral Perspectives
- Rate of Change (Social, Legal, Economic, Political and Technical)

☐ **Willingness to Take Risk**
- Availability of Resources
- Ability to Reverse Decision
- Ability to "Play" on Multiple Occasions
- Short-Term Thinking
- Time Until Final Decision
- Framing (Positive vs. Negative)
- Emotion
- Volition and Level of Control

☐ **Uncertainty Reduction Through Formal Methods**
- Guarantees
  - Money Back
  - Price Matching/Beating
  - Repair and Replacement
- Flat-Rate Pricing
- Free Trial
- Third-Party Certification and Endorsement
  - Licensing and Certification
  - Assurance of Compliance
  - Direct and Indirect Industrial Endorsements
  - Endorsements and Testimonials by Individuals
- Product/Service Support and Training

☐ **Uncertainty Reduction Through Effective Communication**
- Attention
- Understanding
- Believing
- Retention
- Action

EXHIBIT 3-2
AREA OF RISK, WILLINGNESS TO TAKE RISK
AND UNCERTAINTY REDUCTION

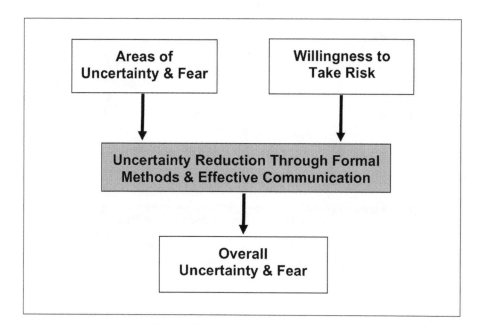

AREAS OF UNCERTAINTY AND FEAR

Product/Service *Class* Risk

A product class such as dry goods (products such as flour or salt) or a service class pertaining to warehousing probably does not give most people the willies and cause them to lose sleep. Some product and service classes do. Financial services, especially those relating to the stock market, may be looked at as particularly volatile. Accordingly, while some stocks may be more risky than others, it is generally accepted the stock market as a whole can fluctuate fairly drastically in a very short period of time. Similarly, anything associated with the energy sector these days is fraught with turbulence, and housing markets are similar. Suffice it to say, stability is present to a greater degree in some sectors than others.

Product/Service *Specific* Risk

This type of risk centers on whether or not the product or service will live up to technical expectations (stated or implied) and will actually meet the requisite needs of the user. Will the medicine work as intended? Will the golf course be as good as promised? Perhaps a promising new medical procedure comes out, but it has not been performed many times. Although the risk of surgery, in general, may be perceived as reasonably low, the risk associated with this particular procedure may be seen as particularly high since it does not yet have a track record. Alternately, even though new technologies may be perceived as a generally risky category to invest in, a person may feel secure in the selection of one particular innovative company because he or she believes it has particularly good management and a solid business proposition.

Transaction Risk

In a typical business deal, one party provides money and the other party provides a good or service in exchange. We know from a number of films involving kidnapping, drugs, and skullduggery that this swap of resources can go awry. Transactional risk exists in a somewhat less dramatic form in industrial and retail contexts as well. You know what product or service you are supposed to get because you have seen a picture and technical specifications, but it is not clear whether this will be what you actually receive—if you receive anything at all. According to a recent report, approximately 33 percent of the over seventy thousand complaints filed with the Internet Crime Complaint Center in the United States involved the nondelivery of merchandise.[1]

Transaction risk differs from product-specific risk. Product-specific risk relates to whether the product you ordered will actually produce the desired benefits. Will the dozen donuts you paid for really taste good and satisfy your appetite? Transaction risk, on the other hand, relates to whether you will actually get the product or service you paid for. Will you get an empty box instead of one filled with donuts? Some shady infomercials evoke both of these constructs. Will they actually ship me everything promised (transaction risk), and will it work as well as it does on television (product-specific risk)?

Discomfort During Adoption

People who have never gone for a therapeutic massage, colonoscopy, or purchased a fly fishing rod (among many other possibly intimidating experiences) might wonder how the process will work and whether they will look awkward, naïve, or just downright moronic in the process. These situations can be humbling, either because of some embarrassment that we think we may endure and/or our perceived vulnerability. When I went to purchase my last bicycle, I became painfully aware of how little I knew about what is, at least in theory, a fairly straightforward mechanical device. To be honest, I even felt a little embarrassed asking questions, because each one poignantly revealed what a neophyte I was. Sometimes one or more aspects of the adoption process, such as information seeking or usage, may be cloaked in some degree of mystery. Despite what characters on reality television shows might suggest, there are actually very few people who want to look stupid. One way of avoiding potential humiliation is to not engage in the process at all. Is there any aspect of the adoption process for your product, service, or policy that will make people feel vulnerable, uncomfortable, or incompetent? If so, what can you do to provide a safe environment and employees who are perceived to be more like counselors and advice providers than judges?

Misuse of Information

Beyond uncertainty regarding the mechanics of the transaction, risk can also be associated with the security of the data provided during the business process (whether the data storage system can be hacked), as well as how it will be used. One concern might pertain to additional charges placed on the credit card, or the possibility of identity theft. A second concern might relate to the sharing of information with a third party, which might bring unwanted advertisements for related products and spam. Finally, the concern might hinge on privacy issues. For example, most would not want medicines purchased for a psychiatric disorder or acquisitions of erotic lingerie to become common knowledge.

Risk of Discontinuity

If you were told you would be without something for a period of time, what would your reaction be? It would likely depend on what that something was. A coat hook or ottoman you could live without for a while. There are other items that need to be constant, at least to some reasonable level. Anyone who has gone through a home remodeling effort will still have memories of weeks or months of life not being normal. I knew one family that eked out an existence in the darkness of their basement for a year while the dust and debris rained down from above. Life was not normal for a long time. How long and how much are you asking someone to do without when he or she switches over to your alternative?

Sometimes concerns regarding discontinuity emerge from a desire not to experience discomfort, as would be the case if a person missed a television program because the cable company was not quick enough about switching the service over. Other times, the concern is truly about welfare. For example, being without water, electricity, telephone service, insurance, or the Internet may strike to the core of what the customer considers daily existence to be. Especially within business contexts, where days of downtime translate into days without income and potentially lost clients, continuity of mission-critical systems is equivalent to removing access to food and water. What steps can you take to make sure life for the person/company is as uninterrupted as possible?

Start-Up Costs

One of the factors discussed in the chapter regarding stability pertained to the (in)ability to port over assets (tangible and intangible), with the observation made that as the ability to transfer assets decreases, system stability increases. Often there is a related concern regarding the amount of resources (time, effort, and money) that will have to be expended for start-up costs necessary to get things running to the same level they were before. Consider a cell-phone plan. Many of the phones you buy are "locked," meaning they can only be used with the one provider. If you want to switch plan providers, you also have to switch phones. You also have to go through the paperwork, the credit check, become familiar with the new phone features, and learn novel aspects regarding the plan and how it fits with your lifestyle.

For those individuals who have never purchased a cell phone, concerns regarding start-up costs are real, but they know they will have to go through these costs regardless of which service provider they select. For those who already have an established provider, there may be a sense that they have already made this up-front investment, and a large psychological hurdle may be present. This barrier may be mitigated if the benefits of the new plan are readily apparent (perhaps incredible cost savings) and/or the cost of start-up is minimized (for example, if they could trade in their old phone for a new one at no cost and they are convinced there will not be issues porting over their old cell phone number).

Uncertainty Regarding Payback Period

With some investments, the goal is to put money forward and "take a loss" in the short run, with a view to saving money over the longer term.

A person might invest several thousand dollars in solar panels or a company might purchase a new piece of fabricating equipment with a view to recouping this outlay, and then some.[2] Sometimes this payback is very clear. For example, if a company acquires a new piece of software for $1,000 and this means that they will save $3,000 in fees usually given to an accounting firm, the payback is immediate. In other cases, much less certainty is present. Such would be the case with money used to explore for mineral resources or oil. Is there anything you can do to make the expected payoff that much more explicit?

Compatibility with Physical Systems

When discussing stability, we noted that a number of systems tend to be maintained because they are highly compatible with the *existing* system. We also need to look at compatibility with the *new* system as well. Some systems are advantageous because they function in an agreeable manner with other systems present, such as a television that easily connects with stereo components, or a lighting fixture that easily hooks up to the existing junction box. For the challenger, the issue is not just whether this system provides additional benefits, but also whether changes are required to any of the existing elements. Does equipment, software, policies, legislation, or something else of a significant nature have to be changed? Given a choice between two competing systems—one that is "plug and play" and one requiring a substantial reconfiguration of existing elements—the former has a decided advantage, all other things being equal.

Some physical impediments may be outright prohibitive. Consider four scenarios. First, a person wants to attend classes at the local community college, but he does not have any transportation to actually get there. Second, although contemporary design facilitates wheelchair access and many government buildings are required to make such provisions, there are still buildings that cannot be easily accessed by handicapped individuals. Third, a person thinks about purchasing a treadmill for his home, but there simply is not space available. Fourth, we want to see children from impoverished families succeed academically, but we know that this goal is impaired if adequate food, clothing, and school supplies are not available. Each example demonstrates how the propensity to change is going to be very low if physical barriers are high.

The college, wheelchair, equipment, and learning examples are nontrivial but fairly mundane in terms of physical impediments faced. There are far more intricate situations where technical incompatibilities can be an issue of micrometers. Not all laptop power cords will fit all computers; the one used for the Toshiba laptop will not work for the Mac computer and vice versa. The transmission from a Dodge Durango will not work with a Ferrari (this is just an assumption; I have not actually attempted this). Low tech and high tech, examples could be made for building materials such as bolts, computer chips, programming code, video games, and international space stations. Consider the switch from analog to digital television transmission in the United States.

As initially planned, the switch from analog to digital transmission was to have occurred in February of 2009. It became apparent, however, that many households were not prepared for this transfer, despite four years of planning. Two weeks prior to the switch, Congress voted to move the changeover by four months. At the time, Representative Edward Markey noted, "It is unfortunate that Congress had to take additional action on this issue, but the prospect of leaving millions of consumers in the dark was simply unacceptable."[3] The potential of having so many people with incompatible technology resulted in the delayed introduction.

What are the physical and technical barriers preventing or limiting the change you would like to see happen? Take a broad perspective, thinking of this in terms of the entire purchase/adoption process, from receiving information regarding your alternative through to installation. Do not just get caught up in the minutiae of the technology itself, such as the configuration of the connector pin assembly. This is not to suggest that such fine-grained technology is not critical or should not be communicated—inevitably, this information is useful. However, it is also valuable to remember that physical and technical impediments may emerge well prior to the connection of the final unit and in some cases may be very basic. Perhaps the person does not have a truck large enough to carry the new technology home.

When discussing compatibility, the tendency seems to be to gravitate toward technical or physical compatibility. Will this tire fit on that rim? Will that toner cartridge fit my laser printer? Will that truck fit in my garage? Does flange X fit with flange Y, or will this programming code link well with the code from the other unit? Obviously, technical components are important and require attention. Again, though, compatibility on "soft" dimensions (social, legal, economic, and political) must also be stressed.

Compatibility with "Soft" Systems

Compatibility with Attitudes and Moral Perspectives of Individual. A system may fit perfectly well with all of the existing technology but still be at odds with the personality and attitudes (including moral viewpoints) of the individual. For example, a given product might be ideal for a given application but be produced with an ingredient, by a company, or in a country, that a person has ideological problems with. Ideological issues, in turn, may be largely a function of the independent influences acting on the individual.

Compatibility with Independent Influences. To what extent does the new system fit nicely with the "soft" systems described by the independent influences? Often a good place to start is with the question, "So…is it legal?" An interesting example of this would be the Segway scooter. When it first came out, in some places, it was illegal to ride the unit on either the sidewalk or the street—perhaps OK if you have a really large driveway, but otherwise limiting.

Other questions of compatibility also present themselves. Does it fit well with prevailing social trends? Is it in line with the attitudes and opinions of those around you? Stated differently, legalities aside, there may also be constraints imposed by "the way we do things around here." An example would be attitudes toward environmentally responsible behavior independent of regulations, or deeply ingrained general patterns of behavior. Recall that changing the mind-set of how banking works was a constraining factor in the Pronto home banking case.

Beyond mere social convention, social judgment may also play a role. People may be very concerned about how others will react to their decision and any associated embarrassment and loss in esteem they might incur.[4] Although legal and social issues are given considerable attention in the next chapter regarding Independent Influences, at this point it is also beneficial to note how the rate of change associated with these forces may also influence the uncertainty associated with a new option.

Rate of Change (Social, Legal, Economic, Political and Technical)

Every so often I marvel at satellite images of earth, with clouds and environmental forces constantly in motion—churning and impacting the stability of a given region. A park that was an idyllic location for a picnic last Tuesday may experience rain and lightning today. The movement of independent influences presents a similarly dynamic atmosphere for different systems to exist within. Changes on social, legal, economic, political, and technical (SLEPT) fronts also affect the viability of an option. The rate of change of these influences may increase the perception of risk.

Consider changes to technology. Moore's Law was initially formulated to describe how the number of transistors that could fit on an integrated circuit would double every eighteen months.[5] The general form of this law, suggesting that technology is increasing at an exponential rate, has been evidenced elsewhere, including disk storage density and network capacity. For the customer, inadvertently purchasing "old" technology may result in a number of financial repercussions, such as diminished life span of the product due to performance limitations and/or reduced compatibility with emerging technologies.

Even low-tech items may change rather quickly with shifts in fashion and social opinion. Such cycles are associated with a spectrum of products linked with popular culture, such as music, clothing, and home décor. A number of durables, including houses, cars, sporting goods, and appliances, are also subject to trends. When high rates of change are present, making a purchase is a near guarantee you will be out of date in the future—the only issue remaining is how long this will actually take. If people feel they are at the tail end of the trend or the trend is moving too fast, they may feel it makes more sense to spend their money elsewhere.

On a macro level, sometimes apprehensions regarding the rate of change can emerge indirectly as a result of transformations in ownership structure due to mergers and acquisitions. Such instability brings fear regarding whether the consolidated company will adopt one product line over another and/or whether existing service agreements will be maintained. Consolidation may also bring concerns about what will be considered the new technical standard in the industry.

WILLINGNESS TO TAKE RISK

In the previous portion of this chapter, we considered *where* people would see risk to be present. Now we consider the *willingness* of people to deal with the risk they encounter. Although people generally prefer items they can predict with certainty, some people seem to have a greater willingness to take risks than others.[6] There are people who delight in placing retirement savings in high-risk funds, while others feel nervous just putting money into government T-bills. Some will head off without a care to try skydiving, while others will feel uncomfortable switching brands of coffee or laundry detergent. At work, some will leap with incredible zeal toward grand and outlandish projects with high stakes and the possibility of failure. Others will feel much more comfortable with incremental improvements. We differ.

Evidence suggests the odds of a person undertaking a particular behavior partially stems from a general personality predisposition, referred to as risk propensity.[7] Risk propensity tends to be shaped by the background and demographic characteristics of the individual, being greater for men versus women and for young versus old individuals.[8] The willingness to take risk is also influenced by a number of more general factors: (1) available resources, (2) reversibility, (3) the ability to "play" on multiple occasions, (4) short-term thinking, (5) time until the final decision, (6) framing, (7) the emotion experienced by the decision maker at the time of the decision, and (8) the level of volition and control the person perceives he or she has.

Availability of Resources

In some circumstances, the resources available to an individual or organization are limited, and the decision made regarding a new system may have longstanding consequences. For example, a given manufacturing company may seek to invest in new equipment. Choosing the right equipment may result in a prosperous future. Choosing the wrong equipment may result in a legacy of frustration and competitive disadvantage. This is not a candy bar purchase, where, if the one selected does not provide satisfaction, you can mindlessly shell out another dollar. If the new equipment fails, further resources to purchase a different manufacturing system may not be available.

In the same way, where the purchase consists of a large portion of the budget or the budgeted amount is allocated on a fixed-period basis (perhaps

$500 is available each year to spend on software upgrades), the perceived risk will probably be high.[9] To underscore, perceived risk is going to be influenced by available resources, not simply by the specific dollar value involved—a company with $10 billion in reserves will have less anxiety about a $1 million investment than a company with only $1 million in the bank.

Ability to Reverse the Decision

On some occasions, we are able to reverse a decision with few, if any, consequences. Think about an admittedly low-tech innovation such as new bathroom towels. Perhaps fuchsia has been deemed by fashionistas to be the color of the season—and as much as this shade of pink does not produce an instantaneous feeling of joy, you figure there might be something to this fashion statement. You feel bold at the checkout counter; however, you take the towels home and they look horrible. No, worse than horrible. You are concerned your family may abandon you and your neighbors may phone a government agency because such a color would be cruel to your children. You get back in the car, take the towels to the customer service counter, get your money back, and that night you sleep soundly.

On a corporate level, there may be business contexts where it is possible to pursue multiple paths simultaneously and the option of abandoning unsuccessful ones exists. However, some decisions can be difficult, if not impossible, to reverse. Perhaps it concerns a new business direction that will determine who you hire, the assets you acquire, and the general path will be followed for some time to come. As reversibility decreases, risk tolerance generally decreases as well.

Ability to "Play" on Multiple Occasions

There are some games we can participate in over and over, while others are played either infrequently or only once. If you do not like one restaurant, you could try another. If this office supply store does not work out, there is another down the road you could use next time. However, if the one open-heart surgery does not work out, there may be no need to schedule the second one. If you purchase the "wrong" car, it may be some time before you are able to play that game again.

Consider the St. Petersburg Paradox.[10] Imagine I offer to pay you $2n, where "n" equals the number of times it takes me to flip a coin until it lands on heads. According to this rule, if it takes me two times to flip the coin until I get heads, you would get 2^2, the product of $2 x $2, which equals $4. How much would you pay me to play this game? If you are like most people, you would probably pay somewhere between $2 and $5, even though the expected value of the game is infinite. Yes, *infinite*.[11] How can it be that you would so grossly undervalue the game I so graciously offered to you? The answer, at least in part, is that you did not think about the value of playing this game on many occasions—you plan to play this game only once. One very real possibility in playing this game is that you will get heads on the first flip and only take $2 home.[12] This example also accentuates that people are typically in the game for short-term benefits.

Short-Term Thinking

Suppose I held out a $50 bill and said you could either take this right now or wait an hour and I would give you $55 (a return of 10 percent for sixty minutes of waiting). If you are like many, you would want the $50 now. Part of this may stem from a desire for immediate gratification. Part may be due to uncertainty as to whether I would actually be there an hour from now, or whether I would take off and leave you empty handed. Although there are times when the argument comes down to "over the long term," the most persuasive and less risky arguments are those that pay dividends right here and right now. If long-term thinking is required, ensure that the benefits are concretely presented and well backed up.

Time Until Final Decision

People tend to become more risk averse as the time of an action draws nearer.[13] Think about a person who decides he or she wants to skydive. As the time of the jump comes closer, it is possible the level of risk the person perceives to be present shifts. Perhaps when the decision was first made, the risk associated with the jump was either not considered or was considered but perceived to be small. Over time, the level of risk may become more apparent. As the *perceived risk* grows, it may surpass the risk threshold existing for the person, and a decision to disengage may be made. This speaks to the need for constant communication with the client during the purchase process so levels of perceived risk regarding a given project are monitored and kept at bay. It also points to the reality that in some contexts, perception of risk may shift over time and the initial confidence witnessed may eventually give way to unbridled anxiety as one approaches the time when true commitment to a given action is required.

Framing (Positive vs. Negative)

The way in which a given problem is framed may also have an impact on the level of perceived risk. In other words, is it perceived as the opportunity for a gain or as the potential for a loss? Consider a pioneering study in this field that looked at decision making regarding a particular medical treatment for a hypothetical condition contracted by six hundred people. One group was told that a given treatment would save two hundred people, and 72 percent of the participants in this group selected this option. Another group was told that if a certain treatment were prescribed, four hundred people would die. Even though the end result would be the same (two hundred people live in both scenarios), only 22 percent of the people in this second group chose the treatment.[14] Similarly, in the case of any change environment, is the focus on the potential losses that may be incurred or on the potential benefits that will be gained?[15] Communication focusing on positive outcomes received by acquiring a product tends to increase purchase intentions.[16]

It is not surprising that, when faced with stiff competition, some companies will pull out FUD (Fear, Uncertainty, and Doubt) marketing and try to communicate not only how people might be worse off without their product or service, but also all the negative events that could occur if they dare adopt the competitor. Could this backfire? Conceivably, pointing out what could go wrong could simply be perceived as safeguarding the interests of the customer. Then again, if the information is grossly distorted, there may be a substantial loss of credibility and trust. You want to be thought of as the provider of useful information to help people evaluate the choices they are facing. Part of this useful information may be positive while other aspects may be negative. For example, in a two-sided appeal, where you acknowledge some beneficial elements of the competitor in addition to limitations, your credibility may actually be enhanced.[17] Such an appeal might sound something like, "Yes, the competitor does have lower prices and faster delivery times, but government reports indicate these benefits come at the expense of safety and quality."

Emotion

The type of emotion a person is experiencing may influence risk-taking behavior. With respect to negative emotions, evidence indicates this is dependent on the specific negative emotion experienced. Sad and angry individuals tend to be risk takers, while anxious and fearful individuals tend to be risk averse.[18] This observation is certainly relevant to the model. To the extent one wants to see movement to a new alternative, one is advised to: (1) capitalize on occasions where people are angry or disappointed with their existing provider, and (2) reduce fear and anxiety associated with the new option.

Level of Volition and Control

The perception of risk is also influenced by the level of volition and control present in the choice context. Volition pertains to whether or not a person believes he or she has an option to engage in a given behavior. On some occasions, a person may perceive that he or she does have a choice, perhaps if he or she is electing to have cosmetic surgery or not. On other occasions, a choice may technically exist, but only one option is feasible. For example, if a person is suffering from a serious disease, he or she may conceivably be able to select whether to take a particular medication or not, but it would be a foolish decision to choose the latter. If a person sees that he or she really does have a choice (volition is high), the perceived risk is higher.[19] Ironically, the highly regarded social concept of freedom of choice is not a great thing to all individuals. If you put people in a position where they have to make a choice, you also put them in a position where they are able to make a mistake. This anxiety has to be overcome with a clear and secure value proposition.

The second key element in the choice process is control. Once a choice has been made, the ability to exert control over how the choice is executed will lower perceived risk. For example, a person might agree the stock market can be risky, but due to his or her knowledge, experience, and trading strategy, he or she is able to greatly reduce the likelihood of significant losses. In light of this, there are several key questions to be considered. Is there sufficient information being given to the individuals to provide them with a sense of efficacy (the ability to control the outcome)? Are they aware of what they can do to reduce their level of risk? Are there some features associated with greater risk that you can provide greater education about? Are there additional actions they can take, such as the purchase of enhanced warranty protection, to mitigate the downside risk?

UNCERTAINTY REDUCTION THROUGH FORMAL METHODS

The phrase "caveat emptor" (buyer beware) suggests that there is a considerable onus on the person purchasing a product or service to get it right. Nonetheless, there are a number of formal mechanisms that can either increase the buyer's confidence that the decision he or she made was the right one, or, if the buyer perceives the decision was actually incorrect, can serve to fix the problem at hand. Ultimately, these formal mechanisms reduce perceived risk. The following mechanisms will be considered: (1) guarantees, (2) flat-rate pricing, (3) free trial, (4) third-party certification, (5) endorsement and compliance, and (6) product/service support and training.

Guarantees

Earlier it was mentioned that one of the elements influencing risk tolerance is the ability to do something over again. Sometimes guarantees may accomplish this, or at least reduce the likelihood the adoption of the system will have negative ramifications. Guarantees may also send signals regarding the quality of the product—it must be good, otherwise they would not offer this.[20] Three typical types of guarantees include money back, price matching/beating, and repair/replacement. In choosing which guarantee(s) to offer with a particular product or service, one should consider the potential value to the customer, the ease of communicating the benefits, and, ultimately, overall profitability.

While guarantees provide explicit signals to the customer about the willingness of the organization to stand behind its products, they may also provide equally strong signals to individuals within the organization. Some years ago, Xerox was deciding which type of guarantee to put in place for a particular product. The specific service options under consideration were a money-back guarantee, a service guarantee (for example, if the copier breaks down, a service person will be on site within one hour), and a performance guarantee (if you are not happy with the unit we sell you, we will replace it or provide a model that more adequately meets your needs).[21]

At the time, Xerox believed the money-back guarantee would be easy to implement, but it would also probably reduce the likelihood of a long-term relationship with the customer. Customers would have valued the service guarantee, but Xerox felt it would be difficult to implement in a standardized fashion. For example, the anticipated response time could vary depending on the location of the copier and/or time of day, and some accounts, such as commercial printing outlets, would demand faster response times than others. Xerox finally decided to use a performance guarantee, which would circumvent the problem associated with the money-back guarantee and could be consistently communicated to all customers. Moreover, in conjunction with customer satisfaction surveys, this type of guarantee sent strong signals to salespeople to make sure that there was a strong correspondence between the product and the needs of the customer.

Flat-Rate Pricing

Flat-rate pricing might be considered a form of a guarantee. When potential costs are unknown or highly volatile, a flat rate for a given volume or a given time period may defray concerns. Examples might include an all-you-can-eat buffet dinner for $7.99, unlimited long-distance phone calls for $20 per month, a monthly gym membership (vs. per-visit pricing), or yearly access to a database or Web resource. Talk to your in-laws in Argentina once, or all day long—the price will remain the same. Go to the gym once, or every day this month—you know how much you will pay. Such periodic payments may also reduce the time and hassle associated with frequently acquired items. A recent example of this is the United States Postal Service's Priority Mail Flat Rate Shipping, introduced in 2009. The amount you pay is a function of how big the box is, not the weight (up to a very generous 75 pounds/34 kilograms). No more guessing; you know the postal rate from the outset.

One of the downsides to flat-rate pricing is it increases the possibility for abuse. Phone lines could become jammed, gyms could become filled, and a person with a mammoth appetite could show up at the buffet. In considering possible abuses, a number of comments are warranted. First, the rate of consumption may be higher at the beginning of adoption and then trail off over the given time period. Second, the "abuse" is often confined to a small number of individuals. Experience suggests that if properly crafted and appropriate given the nature of the product, the revenue derived from such pricing, even with potential abuses, is usually higher because people are usually willing to pay a premium for this stability. Third, sometimes the overuse does not have a high variable cost. For example, if a cell-phone provider has excess capacity in the evening and on weekends, the use of this resource only nominally impacts the bottom line. Finally, if clearly communicated from the outset, it is usually possible to put usage caps in place that no reasonable person would object to.

Free Trial

All the talk in the world will not let you know how the new golf club will feel, how a new car will handle, how new software will integrate, or how new breakfast cereal will taste. While money-back guarantees ensure reimbursement if you are not happy (and *do* require up-front payment), a free trial reduces the risk even more. Not only are your financial resources unconstrained, but you need not need worry about whether or not the company will really give you the money back, charge a restocking fee, or make you fill out a form to justify why you are returning the product.

Third-Party Certification, Endorsement, and Compliance

On occasion, the reputation of the company is sufficiently strong to provide assurance the organization is legitimate. Among many, some more common ones might include Sears, Macy's, and Home Depot. However, for many smaller organizations, it is difficult to provide this type of confidence. While letters of support from previous customers might help, having direct or indirect support from one or more outside entities may serve to greatly decrease perceived risk. For example, a third-party certification from a recognized organization, such as the Better Business Bureau, will provide a higher level of confidence that the individual or organization meets acceptable standards of conduct. Four types of assurance are considered: licensing and certification; assurance of compliance; direct and indirect industrial endorsements; and endorsements and testimonials by individuals.

Licensing and Certification. In some instances, licensing and certification is gained through some form of mandatory professional membership, such as with bar associations for lawyers, a certification processes for accountants (such as a Certified Professional Accountant designation), or from a medical board in the case of physicians. In some instances this certification is mandatory. Pharmaceuticals in the United States must receive approval by the Food and Drug Administration prior to sale. At other times the certification is optional, such as the ISO 9000 stamp of approval, indicating the organization meets certain quality management standards.

Assurance of Compliance. Frequently there is no need to receive any formal recognition from a third party. Laws already exist regarding certain business practices, regulatory standards are enforced by governmental or quasi-governmental oversight bodies, and standards are often created by industries themselves. These mechanisms may all function independent of licensing requirements. Consequently, one strategy to reduce perceived risk is to educate the potential system adopter regarding these rules, regulations, and standards, all the while noting that they exist for the protection of the customer and your company strictly abides by them. As a result, the individual can sleep soundly knowing many of the potential uncertainties have already been dealt with in a structured and professional manner.

In line with this strategy, an investment company may advise potential clients of government regulations they have to abide by in order to ensure fraudulent practices do not occur (especially post Bernie Madoff). A contractor may wish to point what the building code requires and how he or she has met or exceeded this standard. A mortgage broker may make explicit the regulations he or she must now abide by to ensure the welfare of the client is maximized, and so on.

Direct and Indirect Industrial Endorsements. The mechanisms mentioned above represent measures of a more official nature. However, confidence might also be built through other less formal means, such as an endorsement from a recognized periodical (your product was rated number one by *Time* magazine); an independent organization (a procedure verified by a consultant or inspection agency); or through some other form of legitimate research ("recommended by nine out of ten hairstylists in the New York metro region" or "largest volume of sales in the city").[22] Sometimes an indirect endorsement comes by association with a third party, perhaps a company that manufactures a component of your product. For example, computer manufacturers leveraged the strength of the Intel name during the Intel Inside program to verify the strength of their product.

Yet another way to provide indirect endorsement is to list past organizations that have purchased the product or service. If clients have included Microsoft, IBM, Bank of America, and Burger King, this says something about the caliber of your company. Consider Accountemps, a firm providing organizations with temporary financial services. On their Web site, endorsements by the American Institute of Certified Public Accountants and a host of other legitimate accounting-related organizations provide assurance that work done will be consistent with required standards.[23]

Endorsements and Testimonials by Individuals. Individuals may also give legitimacy to a system.[24] A celebrity may endorse a particular product, providing some form of reassurance.[25] This tactic may be effective due to the trustworthiness associated with the individual, the attention the person may bring to a product or service, or a specific skill or attribute the celebrity and the product share in common. Ideally there is strong congruence between the celebrity and the product.[26] Examples of this agreement would include a ballerina promoting a product that is supposed to graceful, an Olympic weightlifter endorsing something strong, a race car driver associating his name with a particular brand of vehicle, a well-known economist endorsing a financial policy, or a noted environmentalist backing a green initiative.

Does the person have to be famous? In brief, the answer is no. Sometimes using a famous personality can actually be detrimental to the organization due to (1) the cost associated with hiring the individual, (2) the perception the person is just providing the endorsement to make money, (3) poor linkage between the celebrity and the product (e.g., a ballerina endorsing a financial policy), or (4) the individual's involvement in some questionable behavior post-endorsement—such as a Mothers Against Drunk Driving spokesperson being arrested for operating a vehicle while impaired.[27]

On many occasions, an endorsement from "regular" people might prove to be more effective. They may possess legitimacy either because they are credible regarding a specific topic, like an engineer speaking about solar panels, and/or they are a person many can relate to on a personal basis ("they are like me").[28] Having James Earl Jones endorse an educational program might be somewhat compelling, but having individuals who actually went through the program explain how they doubled their life happiness and tripled their income might be far more persuasive.

Product/Service Support and Training

Frequently, the risk associated with the product or service might not pertain to the quality of the offering, but rather to the ability of the user to successfully install and/or implement the new system. One particular type of service that might be especially valuable at reducing perceived fear is implementation support and training, aimed at assisting a person adopt the product. With some companies, such as credit card providers, the amount of customer assistance is unlimited and free. In other cases, the ability to contact support personnel may be somewhat restricted, unless some form of upgrade is acquired. As an example, with some software, different tiers of service packages (Silver, Gold, and Platinum) are made available at different rates, providing not only an enhanced sense of security (and decreased perceived risk) to the customer, but also an additional revenue stream to the provider. Similarly, some companies offer free training, in person or via the Web, for basic use issues and then charge additional sums for more advanced seminars.

UNCERTAINTY REDUCTION THROUGH EFFECTIVE COMMUNICATION

One of the key factors mediating uncertainty and fear is sufficient knowledge about a new system. Think of how you might finish the following sentence regarding fears your potential customers might have: "they would not be so concerned if they only understood...." Is it some feature of the good or service? Some guarantee that you offer? Comprehending what message you want to get out there is an essential first step. Then there is the task of actually getting the message across.

Consider the incredible number of messages we receive each day through hundreds, if not thousands, of advertisements, e-mails, communications via social media, voice messages (at work, at home, and on the cell phone), and face-to-face discussions. While the amount of information confronting us is increasing at what seems to be an exponential rate, our personal processing capacity is not. The net effect? The proportion of information we are using is declining. More and more information is slipping through the cracks.

When you distributed the brochure advertising your offering last week, or sent out the e-mail detailing new policy changes, was any of this information even looked at? If it was, did people actually understand it? If people understood it, did they believe it? If they believed it, did they remember it? Finally, if they remembered it, did they act on it? This general sequence of events, often referred to as a response hierarchy, is required for a desired action to take place.[29] Five main phases exist: (1) attention, (2) understanding, (3) believing, (4) retention, and (5) action.

Attention

At least at a superficial level, humans possess the incredible ability to process a mountain of information. Consider the cocktail party phenomenon.[30] There might be one hundred people talking, but if one of them some distance away uses your name, somehow you catch it. Perhaps you hear nothing else of the conversation, but you do hear your name. Alternatively, consider a playground with many children. Much gibberish is uttered, but a nasty word spouted from the lips of a four-year-old will be picked up immediately by almost everyone in the area. What are you doing to capture the attention of your target audience?

Sometimes a message is fashioned to capture our attention with a salient stimulus, such as a captivating visual or a strange sound.[31] Such devices may create an initial orientation response, which can be especially important in cluttered environments. Moreover, if attention is to be effectively generated, the purpose of the message must be clear from the outset, making it apparent what the consequences of attending to the message are. Too often the key message is buried. It may be obvious to the creator, but difficult or impossible for others to capture. Is your message clearly presented up front? Does this message press one or more of the hot buttons (Exhibit 1-5)?

Understanding

At some point in time, the focus shifts from "are you looking at me?" to "do you have any clue what I am talking about?" Frequently the benefits derived from a feature are very obvious. If a person is told a car will get seventy-five miles per gallon, most people will immediately be able to compute there will be considerable cost savings in the operation of this vehicle. Other features are not as intuitive. For example, knowing a circuit in your home has a Ground Fault Circuit Interrupter (GFCI) breaker might mean little to you. Understanding the breaker will trip if there is more than a 0.005 ampere variation between the hot and neutral wires probably does not endear it to you any further, and might even have a mild sedative effect. However, being told this will prevent electrocution if appliances or other items plugged into this circuit get wet will get both your attention and your respect.

Communications professionals are familiar with the problem of converting complexity to simplicity. I remember asking one person in corporate communications what his greatest challenge was. The response was, "Trying to get forty pages of material from a detailed, jargon-filled report down to two sentences for the media." The point is not that complicated features cannot be communicated effectively—it is that in such cases, extra effort in coherently structuring and disseminating the message will be required. Recognition must also be present that some segments will desire a more elaborate understanding than others and messages need to be tailored accordingly. The CEO might just need to know the piece of equipment will increase efficiency and therefore profit, whereas the engineering personnel may need to know all of the technical specifications.

Experience suggests most product managers, program developers, entrepreneurs, and other mentally gifted individuals tend to focus their sales pitch on intellectual , logic heavy arguments. This goes something like, "You should buy my product because it increases operating efficiency by 14 percent, while reducing N3 emissions by 2 percent and increasing worker safety by 1.1 fewer days lost per 100,000 days worked." However, many recipients treat this information like they would content on a foreign television channel. They do not know why this is important, and even if they did, they would not know what to do with it.

This serves to underscore the importance of two fundamental principles associated with the Elaboration Likelihood Model.[32] In order for an intellectually based message to be effective, success will depend on the extent to which your "rational and logical" arguments are able to persuade. In such situations, people must be both *motivated* and *able* to process the information. Generating motivation requires the presentation of one or more compelling reasons as to why someone should care—how will this person's life be different for the better or worse? Ensuring ability involves presenting the material in a manner that is readily understood by the audience, and this may mean additional education.

Believing

What if I told you I was able to drive a tractor backwards, blindfolded and whistling "Dixie," through the streets of New York City, during rush hour, and at one hundred miles an hour? You might pay attention to what I said. You would probably understand the words I spoke. However, you probably would not believe me. And you would be correct (I cannot whistle "Dixie"). What does it take to be believed?

Messages that are concrete/factual serve to enhance the level of belief in what is stated. Though the level of education you are required to provide might vary from individual to individual, at the end of the day you should have provided a concrete message allowing everyone to understand why he or she needs a product like yours and why yours is better than any competitive offering. Unfortunately, statements like, "We really are better!" sound rather hollow, especially when twenty-nine other competitors are saying the same thing. Want a challenge? Try to find a car dealership within a one-hundred-mile radius of wherever you are that does not promise, "the best price, with the best service, by the best people." Conversely, information such as "$20 lower than our competitors," "45 percent longer lifespan," and "ten minutes to change your oil" is definitive and concrete.

Messages also need to be realistic. Once people hear what you are saying, they need to be able to envision it could be true. Obviously realism is supported by concrete and factual information, but realism is something more. "We can take you to the moon in nineteen minutes" is concrete and factual, but not very realistic. While there is legal recourse to fight companies engaging in puffery and making false claims that cause material harm, airwaves and mail slots are still filled with bold assertions of superiority, sometimes so bold they are difficult to take seriously.

Retention

What key elements from your message will be retained?[33] Hopefully people will remember your brand name, differential advantage, and other information justifying why you are exceptional. The way in which information is presented can be an important consideration.

Where necessary, start broadly and provide the gist of the message before throwing a multitude of details at the target audience. People will also retain information much better if they have a way of organizing the information. Logical groupings of information are best. This might take the form of presenting information by function, such as speed or quality, or by component, perhaps elements associated with the cooling system, transmission, and so on. Additionally, unless you are concerned about appearing overly pedantic, some degree of repetition is usually beneficial.

You have undoubtedly heard it said a picture is worth a thousand words. A well-chosen image can do wonders to underscore the principal message.[34] From an information processing perspective, pictures can be comprehended in a fraction of a second, whereas text is processed at about the rate you are able to speak it very quickly. Consequently, pictures enhance both attention and understanding. Images also tend to be more memorable.[35] Perhaps this is why most memory enhancement techniques developed by experts employ a visualization strategy. Is there an image you can use to underscore your message? Can you convert some of your numbers into graphs or charts? Is it possible to employ a storyboard or animation? If you have to present the materially verbally, can you help create a mental picture for the listener? Can you use an analogy to relate your material to something that is already very well known?

Action

Have you ever heard, "We just did it to increase awareness," in response to an advertising campaign that yielded no increase in sales? In fairness, there are occasions where attention truly is the only goal. However, too often it is used as an after-the-fact excuse to justify a failed communication effort that was originally intended to attain so much more. In most cases, we want people to do something: stop smoking, start donating, buy our product, or *not* buy the competitor's product. Whether you wish to focus on the amount of store traffic, e-mail hits, or phone calls per hour, a key question becomes: what metrics do you have in place to evaluate how well you are doing on the action front? And, more relevant to this section, what are you doing to encourage this behavior?

Some people think action and encouragement are assured by simply providing a Web site or a 1-800 phone number. Fifteen years ago this might have been considered somewhat unique, but it is not really special now. Be clear as to why a customer should actually visit your site or contact you. How will they benefit if they do so? Is there a limited time to participate? What will they obtain that is particularly unique if they take your action?[36] What benefit would going to your Web site provide? Will it help make reservations, locate half-price options, and decrease travel costs through partnerships with airlines? To reiterate, have you provided clear information as to what you want people to do, in conjunction with how and why they should do it?

SUMMARY

Sometimes the level of stability surrounding an existing alternative is particularly low, but migration does not occur because the individual has uncertainties and apprehensions about the new alternative. When fear of the innovation is great, success is unlikely to follow. In essence, they perceive their predicament to be an "out of the frying pan, into the fire" scenario. From a defensive perspective, the incumbent could seek to create concerns regarding competitors by encouraging fear, uncertainty, and doubt about such options. The challenger is tasked with ensuring his or her competitive position is clearly articulated and the fear surrounding his or her option is removed.

Uncertainty and fear may stem from a number of sources. These include the product class, the specific product in question, the rate of technological change, transaction risk, misuse of information, social risk, and industry ownership. The impact of each of these risk areas is a function of the decision maker's willingness to take risk, which can be related to factors such as the resources he or she has available, the finality of the decision, the time horizon of the decision, and the extent to which there is a perception that he or she will be able to exercise control over the final outcome.

Two broad categories of uncertainty and fear reduction are proposed. The first centers on formal methods, such as guarantees, flat-rate pricing, free trials, third-party certification, and product/service support and training. The second concentrates on using effective communication techniques to provide a coherent delivery of the competitive advantage; it is premised on a response hierarchy of attention, understanding, believing, retention, and action. Both of these uncertainty-reduction categories may be used jointly to mitigate concerns that might be present and increase the attractiveness associated with the new system.

CHAPTER FOUR

OUTSIDE INDEPENDENT INFLUENCES EXERT AN IMPACT (4ᵀᴴ LAW OF INNOVATION SUCCESS)

To this point we have considered the fundamental elements associated with successful innovation and change initiatives: the relative advantage of the offering; the value offering of the challenger; stability associated with the incumbent; and the uncertainty associated with the challenger. Each of these may be affected by *independent influences*: dynamic social and nonsocial forces typically not under direct managerial control. In the chapter regarding the stability of the existing system, as well as the chapter considering the uncertainty surrounding the new system, a number of independent influences have been considered. These have included legal and regulatory forces, changes in technology, third-party influence, and compatibility with social systems. This chapter considers these in greater depth.

ELECTRIC CAR ADOPTION—A MYRIAD OF INDEPENDENT INFLUENCES

Consider the independent influences acting on the adoption of an electric car, not a hybrid but a full-fledged, 100 percent, "you have to plug it in" electric car. Even though the gas-electric hybrids have met with some degree of success, the concept of driving a pure electric car is still a novelty. And although excitement regarding recent models is present, it is not clear whether we are ready for them quite yet.

Traditionally, the key constraints to owning an electric car have been the maximum speed the vehicle may attain and the distance it can travel between charges. Maybe because of this, these vehicles have not received universal applause in all road-bearing lands. A very real constraint to ownership in some regions was that the use of electric cars on thoroughfares was either prohibited entirely or limited to streets not exceeding a certain speed limit.[1] Further, as much as people complain about the price of gas, it would seem the economic impetus for change to a fully electric system may be tempered by the rising cost of electricity. Perhaps as technological forces advance the electric cause, permitting unfettered, high-speed travel for extended distances at a lower cost, these barriers may be reduced. Oh, and there is that one other issue—can our current electric infrastructure, the power supplied to your neighborhood, or even the lines used in a house, actually withstand the incredible extra demand that will be created when everyone starts charging their cars at home?

Recent years have witnessed pressure from most civilized publics to reduce carbon emissions in an effort to improve air quality on a local level and reduce greenhouse gases more globally. In an effort to achieve these expectations, one possibility would be to create programs to fund the development of electric vehicle technologies, either through grants or tax incentives. There may even be efforts to encourage related industries to group together in a common geographic area in order to catalyze the process. Initiatives may also be developed to reward consumers for adopting new electric vehicles. These may take the form of tax incentives or rebates.

John Donne remarked, "No man is an island, entire of itself."[2] The other people we share our island with can have a strong impact on the decisions we make. Think about how your desire for an electric car might be influenced by people and forces around you. Media stories regarding the potential shortage of fossil fuels and government calls to become more independent of foreign oil push one way. Other stories regarding higher costs associated with electricity push another. The church you belong to has been stressing the importance of good stewardship of the earth, and you have been receiving a great deal of information about green options due to your membership in the Sierra Club. While most of your friends would admire the environmental stance you want to take by purchasing an electric vehicle, your spouse is adamant the extra money that initially has to be spent on the electric alternative, relative to its gas counterpart, could be better placed. Specifically, your child's education fund has not seen attention in the last number of years.

This scenario illuminates the diversity of independent influences impacting the way we choose to act. Sometimes these forces will even compel us to behave in a manner contrary to our own personal desires. Maybe you really want an electric car but you decide against it because of social pressures and other independent influences. Forces, such as those in the electric car example, may be organized along the following lines: (1) legal and regulatory forces, (2) government programs and initiatives, (3) technological innovations, (4) media and popular culture influences, (5) macro social trends, and (6) reference groups and significant individuals. These are also summarized in Exhibit 4-1.

LEGAL AND REGULATORY FORCES

The most stringent type of social enforcement mechanism is legal regulation or enforced standards. If you are going to play ball in business, you have to work within the rules set by organizations that possess *legitimate* authority to punish and reward through formally stated rules and clear disciplinary guidelines. Pragmatically, this category includes not only sitting government bodies such as legislatures, but also government agencies/ boards as well as professional organizations.

EXHIBIT 4-1
COMPREHENSIVE CHANGE MODEL: INDEPENDENT INFLUENCES

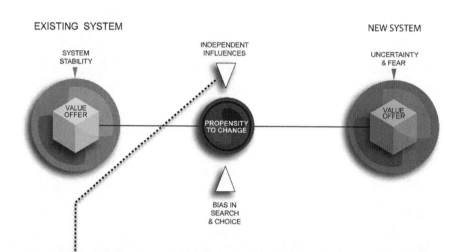

Independent Influences

☐ **Legal and Regulatory Forces**
- Government – Law Creation and Modification
- Government Department, Agencies and Boards
- Professional Associations

☐ **Government Programs and Initiatives**

☐ **Competitive Forces**

☐ **Technological Innovations**
- Product Component Innovation
- Manufacturing Process Innovations
- Business Process Innovations

☐ **Media and Popular Culture**
- News, Movies
- Internet and Social Media

☐ **Macro Social Trends**
- General Demographic Change
- Safety and Physical Security
- Financial Stability
- Health and Wellness
- Environmental Consciousness
- Knowledge and Employment
- Energy Consumption and Choices
- Globalization and Localization

☐ **Reference Groups and Significant Individuals**
- Types of Power
- Types of Groups
  - Aspirational vs. Dissociative
  - Formal vs. Informal
  - Family
- Significant Individuals Within Groups

Government—Law Creation and Modification

Federal, regional (state or provincial), and municipal governments have the capacity to enact laws within their jurisdiction. These entities have the ability to both foster and deter change. Suppose a law is enacted banning a certain production process or ingredient, thereby decreasing the attractiveness of any system using it. Such laws effectively can build or squelch the attractiveness of an alternative. Examples might include prohibiting some types of pesticides, eliminating the use of Freon in refrigerators, or keeping vehicles that are unsafe off the road. Hemp is another good example.

The ability of hemp to be used in a broad spectrum of applications (food, medicines, paper, clothing[3]), combined with its ability to grow both quickly and with far less irrigation than many plants, makes it a potentially attractive crop alternative. However, it may not be grown in the United States without a special permit because of its relation to marijuana (hemp itself contains very little THC, the psychoactive ingredient in marijuana). It does not matter how multipurposeful hemp is or how irrational the ban on growing it might be—the law makes it clear that growing it without a permit is illegal.

Society often changes faster than the legal system and, as a consequence, may inadvertently constrain what new alternatives are feasible. Apparently it is still illegal for an unmarried woman to go fishing alone in Montana.[4] On a more serious note, consider the changes that have had to be made to what is considered a "legal document" and a "signature" with the advent of the fax machine and later the Internet.

Government Departments, Agencies, and Boards

Agencies and boards are given legitimacy through government legislation but in most cases act with greater freedom than a government department, as they have separate management and an independent budget.

Examples in the United States would be the Central Intelligence Agency (CIA), the Federal Bureau of Investigation (FBI), the Environmental Protection Agency (EPA), or the Food and Drug Administration (FDA). Consider the mission statement of the latter.

> The FDA is responsible for protecting the public health by assuring the safety, efficacy, and security of human and veterinary drugs, biological products, medical devices, our nation's food supply, cosmetics, and products that emit radiation. The FDA is also responsible for advancing the public health by helping to speed innovations that make medicines and foods more effective, safer, and more affordable; and helping the public get the accurate, science-based information they need to use medicines and foods to improve their health.[5]

The FDA clearly provides a regulatory function, setting standards and ensuring these expectations are met. Having the FDA send a warning or recall regarding an existing product will likely diminish the stability associated with this item. Conversely, an endorsement from the FDA may reduce the fear associated with product use. In some food and drug categories, the impact of the FDA goes beyond a vocal endorsement—FDA standards have to be met in order for a product to be sold legally. In such cases, the propensity to legally switch to a product will be zero if FDA approval is not in place.

With some products and services, the issue is not about getting approval prior to launching the product, but rather abiding by pertinent regulations. Think about the laws administered in the United States by the Environmental Protection Agency (those pertaining to the Clean Water Act or the Clean Air Act are good examples). Note that the EPA and other government agencies have the ability to both develop and enforce regulations as they pertain to relevant laws passed by Congress. The development process often involves consultation with stakeholders. Through such opportunities to engage, participants may help in the development of regulations that influence the stability of the existing alternative(s) and/or the attractiveness of the challenger(s). Is it possible for you to get involved in the process?

Professional Organizations

Professional organizations often serve to regulate behavior within a particular vocation. Although the specific boards and agencies present will vary from state to state, it is not unusual to see membership with a professional organization required in order to receive a licence to practice. Common examples would be those established for lawyers (bar associations), physicians (state medical boards), accountants (state regulation of Certified Public Accountants), and real estate agents (real estate boards). In other cases, the associations exist to promote and support members within the profession, but membership is not required to practice. Examples would include the American Historical Association for historians and trade unions for many forms of skilled labor.

In most cases where a professional organization exists, there are stated expectations regarding professional conduct and an enforcement mechanism (perhaps sanctions up to and including expulsion) to ensure membership compliance. Which, if any, professional associations may be relevant to a system you are trying to promote? Are they required or beneficial in endorsing and/or implementing a proposed course of action?

Think about the medicinal use of marijuana. For those wishing to see marijuana available for such purposes, endorsement of research into medicinal uses of marijuana by the American College of Physicians[6] was undoubtedly considered very welcome news, as it sent signals to relevant governments regarding the potential need for such treatment. Moreover, though, it sent signals to member physicians that, where legal and therapeutic benefits have been demonstrated, support of marijuana should be considered welcome, or at least "not deviant."

GOVERNMENT PROGRAMS AND INITIATIVES

While the development and implementation of laws and regulations is one purpose of government, another incredibly important role is to shape society through programs and initiatives that, ideally, help to steer the ship in the desired direction. For example, suppose a local government wanted to encourage development of the high-tech sector. It would be impossible to legislate that organizations must become high tech. However, the government could encourage such actions in a number of ways:

- Funding of programs at business, technical, and engineering schools to produce graduates focused on this industry.
- Enabling government scientists and specialists to consult with the sector.
- Providing or subsidizing office/lab space.
- Fostering the development of a cluster of companies in related industries in order to spur collaboration and speed innovation.[7]
- Initiating venture capital,[8] grant and loan programs,[9] or tax incentives[10] to offset capital or operating costs within the designated sector(s).
- Organizing and/or sponsoring conferences bringing key forces together.

As this example illustrates, the role of a government may encompass: (1) the supply and development of intellectual resources (training of students, recruitment of trained professionals, assistance from government employees, development of research reports, access to databases, and other intellectual properties); (2) direct funding, such as operating grants, low-interest loans, subsidies, and/or indirect financial benefit, perhaps through tax incentives, (3) the provision of necessary physical infrastructure needs, such as materials, office space, testing facilities, government-owned equipment, enhanced transportation of material and people, and (4) coordination and integration of resources through the establishment of clusters, conferences, and professional networks. Hence, while the government fulfills a regulatory role, it often brings about change through other less legalistic measures.

COMPETITIVE FORCES

Too often in the planning process, it is easy to become so engrossed in our own ideas and goals that we forget that we are dealing with cunning and deliberate competitors. The point of this section is not to go through a great discourse on competitive analysis, but rather to focus some thought regarding those who may seek to devour you. Who are your direct and indirect competitors? What segments are they targeting? Where are their weaknesses? Where are your strengths? Where are you vulnerable to attack? What strategies are they using/will they possibly use to gain ground on you? What have you done to influence your stability/instability (Law 2) with existing customers? Are competitors better poised to take advantage of some aspects of the emerging world such as new technology or shifting legal regulations? How will they react to the plans that you have made? Is it possible (or wise) to bring some of your current or potential competitors on side and build alliances? Consideration of these issues will help to keep plans realistic, identify opportunities, and also focus attention on where defensive actions may be required.

TECHNOLOGICAL INNOVATIONS

Within any area of endeavor there are technical advances that either directly or indirectly influence the progression of the field. Consider the electronic communications industry, where there have been steady advancements from the days of telegraphs and Morse code through to contemporary technology, where we can broadcast streaming video from a compact cell phone to people half a world away. While it is difficult to make even vestigial comparisons between these two technologies, today's end product is a function of millions of steady and sometimes discontinuous advancements.

The first and most apparent element would be advances with respect to *product component technologies*. This would consist of new materials, new programming code, new combinations of materials, and other elements directly related to the physical entity.

The second type of technical advance relates to the *manufacturing technologies*—new and/or faster ways of production/assembly, enhanced automation, more efficient use of labor, smaller manufacturing space requirements, reduced energy, decreased waste, and other factors associated with the process of creating the product. Much of this is typified by six-sigma processes and lean manufacturing.[11] Note, with this type of technology shift, the product itself does need not change, just aspects of how it is created.

Third are general *business technologies* related to operating efficiencies—among a multitude of possibilities, these might include communication technologies that enhance material sourcing or contact with customers; more efficient and effective delivery methods; or improved software to better track project costs and decrease personnel administration. Although these technologies have nothing to do directly with the product or the manufacturing process, they provide a facilitating role.

Consider developments in the avionics industry over the last two decades on these three levels (product component technologies, manufacturing technologies and business technologies). The advancement of lighter, stronger, fire-resistant, and more soundproof materials, computer automation, and more efficient designs have permitted increased safety, comfort, and capacity along with diminished fuel requirements. The planning and assembly process has undergone marked changes as well: 3-D computer design, virtual prototyping and testing, just-in-time delivery, and increased outsourcing of larger units (as opposed to millions of small parts all assembled at one location) have resulted in more effective and efficient use of resources. Finally, a number of elements not directly related to the airline industry or the design and production of aircraft per se have also transformed operations—Internet and mobile communications technologies have improved communications within and between firms, accounting software has improved tracking of expenses, and online leadership training of managers has resulted in more productive personnel.

MEDIA AND POPULAR CULTURE INFLUENCES

There are a number of key mechanisms by which media impact society and influence change.[12] The word "media" in this context is broad, including print (newspapers and magazines), broadcast (radio and television), Internet (including social media), billboards, and an ever-expanding number of formats, including urinal advertisements and tattoos on heads. These could be broadly divided into information-based categories, including news programs and factual Web sites, and fictional-entertainment-based categories, such as movies. Granted, the two have become blurred—often extremely blurred. Viewers of programs such as *The Daily Show* or *Colbert Report* cannot be faulted for not understanding where news and editorial content trail off and entertainment begins. Sadly this would also be true of a number of "conventional" news channels. Regardless of format, media influence the lenses through which we see the world.

Media act as a socialization agent. Sometimes abruptly, but more often through subtle messaging, we are "educated" regarding what behaviors are acceptable and perhaps even desirable to the population at large. A newspaper article decries wasting energy and not recycling. A talk show discusses the problems arising from parents not spending time with their children. A popular film extols the virtues of helping impoverished persons. Over time, these channels of communication vicariously present what we come to accept as socially prescribed norms, and, by consequence, issues that have an impact on our hearts, minds, actions, and wallets.

Beyond establishing general behavioral expectations, media also act in an agenda-setting capacity, influencing what topics and issues will receive attention on a day-to-day basis:[13] the environment, corporate corruption, the plight of the economy, conflict in a foreign nation, child labor, and so on. While the impact of *one specific* source to shape the agenda is weakened in our current of era of remarkable fragmentation, if we are bombarded with thousands of stories regarding a particular topic, such as the harmful effects of plastics containing biphenyl A (BPA), it is hard to either ignore this information or dispel its importance. The implications for business practice are apparent. Are your business practices and communication efforts aligned with contemporary values and beliefs? Do they resonate with target audiences? Are they perceived to be sincere? Rather than passively reacting, is it possible to exert a more active engagement with the media? Is it possible for you to become the media through social marketing?

MACRO SOCIAL TRENDS

Although there is a strong interdependence between media influences and social trends, the two may nonetheless be treated separately. While media may report on, influence, and increase the salience of a trend, the root cause of the trend may be very much independent of the media (e.g., demographic shifts). Eight arguably interrelated trends are discussed here: (1) demographic shifts, (2) physical safety, (3) financial stability, (4) health, (5) environment, (6) knowledge and employment, (7) energy, and (8) globalization/localization. A synopsis of these components is presented in Exhibit 4-2.

EXHIBIT 4-2
EIGHT MACRO SOCIAL TRENDS

Demographic Shifts

- ☐ Aging Boomers
- ☐ Generations X and Y
- ☐ Increased double income families with fewer children.
- ☐ Increased levels of debt.
- ☐ Increased ethnic cities and neighborhoods.

Physical Safety

- ☐ Increased fears regarding personal security despite a drop in most crime rates.
- ☐ Elevated concern regarding identity theft and improper access of information in databases.
- ☐ "Orwellian" levels of surveillance and increased reliance on security checks and biometrics.

Financial Security

- ☐ Shifting sense of role government should play in economic issues.
- ☐ Return to more conservative credit and material expectations.
- ☐ Increased notion that employment is a transactional relationship and less so a "family".
- ☐ More conservative corporate growth expectations.

Health

- ☐ Increased obsession with personal health and appearance.
- ☐ Paradoxical desire to indulge and yet appear lean, resulting in a generally overweight population obsessed with quick fix promises.
- ☐ Growing concern regarding access to health care and sustainability of the existing system.

Knowledge and Employment

- ☐ More highly educated population overall.
- ☐ Expanding opportunities for education: in-person or on-line.
- ☐ Enhanced access to information.
- ☐ Eventual return to importance of manufacturing and resource acquisition.

Environment

- ☐ Increased social and ethical concerns of individuals regarding the environmental footprint of an alternative.
- ☐ Corporate emphasis on sustainable business practice, with focus on consumer demand and employee attraction/retention.

Energy

- ☐ Increased concerns regarding fossil fuels.
- ☐ Solar, wind, biomass, geothermal and nuclear (fission and fusion), with emphasis on sources that are clean, safe and sustainable.
- ☐ Desire of nations to be energy independent and avoid energy, "hostage taking."
- ☐ Renewed focus on mechanisms to reduce energy consumption.

Globalization and Localization

- ☐ Global market for "intellectual" industries, especially front line knowledge workers (e.g., call centers) as well as back room operations (e.g., programming and data entry).
- ☐ Competition from Brazil, Russia, India and China.
- ☐ Expanded opportunities for partnerships.
- ☐ Access to markets, capital, resources and labor.
- ☐ Counter movement to, "buy local."

General Demographic Change

From 2010 to 2050, the population of the United States is expected to grow from 310 million to 439 million, and the world population is projected to increase from 7 billion to 9 billion.[14] During this time period, not all age categories will be equally represented. This takes on importance, as a shifting number of people within a given life-stage segment (young children, teens, young adults, etc.) will have predictable implications. If one knows there is going to be a surge in the number of young children, there are obvious implications for child care, basic education, immunization, pediatric care, and possibly an increased consideration of how workplaces could accommodate needs of parents.

Unquestionably the most noticeable and discussed demographic cohort in North America at present is the Boomer generation (born 1946 to 1964), which has received considerable attention in recent years as its members are now hitting retirement age. Products, services, and housing that cater to the "young" seniors (sixty to seventy-five years) and the "old" seniors (seventy-six-plus years) are already becoming popular, due jointly to market opportunities and advances in understanding regarding the impact of aging on perceptual, cognitive, and motor skills. One example of this would be the Jitterbug cell phone, which is defined by its minimal nature and the way it is tailored to seniors. There are few features and nothing complicated—there is no menu, basically just a really big, easy-to-use keypad containing the numbers between zero and nine. There is also a rubber gasket on the earpiece to block out extraneous noise, and a simulated dial tone is present to emulate a standard landline.[15]

Regrettably, focus on the Boomer generation often tends to eclipse a number of other very important demographic segments. Consider this: the much-sought-after Boomers constitute seventy million people in the United States. While one might look past Generation X (born between 1965 and 1978) given its smaller numbers (twenty million), there is reason to be watching out for the group referred to by a variety of terms, including the Baby Boom Echo, Millenials, or Generation Y (born between 1979 and 1994). This group consists of sixty million people in the United States, or roughly 90 percent of the size of the much-touted boomers.

Generation Y tends to possess a number of idiosyncrasies. Relative to other generations, they tend to be more self-loving, require a greater amount of praise, and tolerate criticism more poorly. They expect authenticity in their leaders and also expect to progress through the job ranks quickly. Although they have higher levels of self-esteem, they also suffer greater anxiety and depression.[16] They also tend to place greater value on friendship, on performing tasks with meaning (not just for money), and on work-life balance.[17]

What other demographic trends are there that could impact your change initiative? For example, how do changes to education (increasing), family size (decreasing), marriage (decreasing and at later age), sexuality (more liberal), single-parent families (increasing), debt levels (increasing), general health (increasing), and so on impact you?[18] Do these indicate emergent business opportunities, or suggest changes to communication or modifications to your distribution methods (e.g., a greater Web presence)?

Safety and Physical Security

Physical security is a perennial human issue. Primitive hunting and gathering societies struggled with scarcity of food and water as well as protection from disease-transmitting insects and ravaging animals. Highly evolved urban professionals may feel insecure if their upscale vehicle is not outfitted with GPS tracking or their apartment does not have a monitored security system. An examination of *actual* crime statistics would suggest that for property crimes like burglary and theft, rates have been steadily decreasing since 1975, and for violent crimes, including rape, assault, and murder, the rate has diminished considerably over the past decade.[19]

However, the *perceived* rate seems to be a different matter, with these values elevated and climbing since 2001.[20]

Real or perceived, there is no question our current era presents us with many concerns regarding our personal safety. Air travel is filled with multiple checks and reduced freedoms. Terrorist activities abroad and heightened terrorist warnings domestically provide a backdrop of uneasiness, fuelled by intermittent reports of an arrest of some radical involved in a plot. The possibility of a cataclysmic attack echoing 9/11 would seem to be high. Increased coverage of crimes committed by illegal immigrants creates a groundswell of support for increasing the security around the border and having more stringent admission criteria—paradoxically, at a time when the prosperity of many nations is dependent on increasing the flow of immigration.

Newspapers and television stations augment these concerns and create what George Gerbner termed "the mean world syndrome" (an overinflated sense the world is a dangerous place to live).[21] Beyond traditional issues of physical violence, theft, and vandalism, our view of the world through media reports would lead many to believe that home invasions and child abductions have increased, along with an apparent deluge of pedophiles both on the street and on the Internet. Concern regarding personal information on home computers and company databases has increased and has been accentuated by the more frequent occurrence of identity theft.

In addition to the obvious implications of increased sales of surveillance equipment, there are a number of noteworthy consequences of security concerns. First, safety procedures and policies at public institutions have increased, (e.g., methods for monitoring children at school or reporting suspicious activity). Although most, if not all, of these procedures serve a benefit, the downside has been an increase in bureaucracy and a corresponding decrease in efficiency and personal freedom. A further consequence is an increased level of Orwellian monitoring. This takes the form of information in databases, biometrics for employment and travel, cameras increasingly present in public spaces—intrusions we are, in many cases, eagerly accepting in the face of increased threats to our personal and collective well-being. At a minimum, those seeking to create change must be mindful of the (increasing) measures in place. Further benefit will be given to those who are able to enhance perceived security and/or increase the efficiency of the process.

Financial Stability

My grandmother was a participant of the Great Depression. A little girl in a small Canadian prairie town, her experiences living "without" impacted her permanently. Even later in life, long after financial burdens were removed, her spending remained frugal and she would save scrap tinfoil and other reusable items. Periods of economic constraint can have an impact on our worldview. Whereas previous economic pullbacks in the latter part of the twentieth century might be considered colds or flus, with some ephemeral changes to personal and corporate behavior, it is highly plausible the global financial crisis precipitated by the subprime loan debacle in the United States (culminating in 2008) may be considered a cancer by comparison. Such immense financial scares are akin to a large bogeyman jumping out of the closet, and while recovery will be present, the way many people think and feel about money and investing will be impacted for a considerable time frame.

Focus seems to have shifted from keeping up with the Joneses to avoiding being one of the Joneses and suffering economic collapse. Job security, the ability to pay the mortgage, medical, and sundry bills, as well as having sufficient savings, are important and top-of-the-mind considerations. Products and services that further these objectives are highly valued. These take the form of insurance products protecting against sharp and unexpected job or material losses; paring back of luxury goods and luxury brands; decreased housing expectations; and less elaborate vacations. For those who are/want to be retired and have fixed avenues of income, the provision of stability is even more greatly appreciated. The positive side to this economic tragedy is that many individuals are finding meaning and defining success in less materialistic ways. Granted, humans are humans. Greed and hedonistic desires will eventually return.

Health and Wellness

It would be unfair to suggest concerns regarding health and our medical systems are a recent phenomenon; however, specific concerns and issues do shift over time.[22] On an individual level, indications would suggest we are becoming more health focused—perhaps more so than any other period in history. Specialty prepared frozen meals, restaurant menus with healthy choices explicitly identified, health club memberships, personal trainers, tooth whitening, television shows pertaining to physical activity, stores devoted to vitamins and meal supplements: based on this information, one would think society is now composed of individuals taken from the pages of *Cosmopolitan* and *GQ*. Reality differs. On average we experience a higher level of hospitalization due to depression,[23] and we are more overweight than ever.[24] Not only are adults heavier, but childhood obesity is so great[25] we are getting athletes from the NFL to promote a whopping sixty minutes of physical activity a day to our children.[26]

For some time, many professional models were a size zero, and some reports suggest problems with anorexia may be worse than thought. It would appear the more we care, the worse we get. The cause? It possibly stems from trying to balance opulence, gluttony, and a sedentary lifestyle with a post-utopian body image. It is doubtful any real change from this will occur in the near future. We want it all—especially products and services that offer to either improve or prevent ailments with minimal personal effort.

From a medical access perspective, there is a growing reality in the United States that there is a significant portion of the population having restricted access to adequate care. In nations where socialized medicine is the norm, such as Canada or France, financial burdens are immense.[27] It would appear we are moving toward some degree of convergence across multiple systems. The trend is toward basic access for the masses for common problems, with specialty services more available to those with sufficient resources. Focus will continue to be placed on improving access, reducing wait times, and decreasing costs.

Environmental Consciousness

In the early 1990s green marketing was a big force. We embraced the earth and called her mother. Similar outpourings of devotion to our terrestrial sphere had occurred many times before, but those were the '90s and we had finally become serious. And then came the SUVs, greater urban sprawl, and a reduced focus on the health of the globe. More recently we have become passionate again. Carbon dioxide emissions have become a familiar topic in the news, environmentally friendly vehicles have garnered appeal, corporate social responsibility is a commonly bandied term, and communities are providing greater infrastructure to enable recycling efforts.

While there is a general trend toward environmentally responsible behavior, there will still be ebbs and flows. The environment seems to take the back burner to economic conditions and social status. Maslow would have predicted as much.[28] When people are worried about eating and governments are fearful of economic Armageddon, all of the sudden the carbon dioxide parts-per-million values seem secondary. When gas prices are low and alternative clean sources of energy are high, again, the motivation to be green seems to dip. These fluctuating sentimentalities noted, there are a number of reasons why companies will benefit from green efforts.

With respect to a long-term survival perspective, we are mandated to engage in more environmentally friendly practices. This is underscored even further when we consider an expanding world population base. Beyond biological necessity and ethical correctness, such behavior is merited on a corporate level for other reasons. First, it tends to foster greater creativity and efficiency that may actually *reduce* production costs through reduced input materials, greater energy efficiency, or reduced waste. Second, corporations who legitimately adhere to these values stand a better chance of attracting and retaining stellar employees. This is particularly true for those in Generation Y, as they tend to gravitate to pro-social organizations. Third, if companies remain environmentally vigilant, they will be ahead of the curve when consumer adoption of "green" resurges and less likely to be branded as fickle than if they appeared to be jumping on the bandwagon only at opportune times. Finally, with each wave of the green movement, there are elements that become irreversible parts of "the way we do business," and adhering to these practices on a day-in day-out basis may reduce periodic shock and trauma induced when companies try to update in an inconsistent manner.

Knowledge and Employment

As noted in the demographics section, levels of education are increasing. This intellectual revolution is transpiring on a global level, taking the form of programs at brick-and-mortar institutions and courses offered through Internet-based channels. One could argue that independent of formal courses and degrees, the proliferation of the Internet has served to make a plethora of informational resources accessible to an increasingly broad spectrum of individuals and thereby shrink gaps between intellectual "haves" and "have nots."[29]

More broadly speaking, given our increased acceptance and reliance on technology, geographical boundaries are becoming less and less important from many commercial perspectives. On the one hand, this is encouraging, as it suggests a more intellectually advanced global village with the potential of greater diversity of supply for intellectual resources. But this also may result in greater economic instability to the extent that providers may be quickly and seamlessly shifted. This means programmers, engineers, analysts, and others relying on intellectual capacity for their competitive advantage may find themselves continuously seeking to differentiate their offerings and maintain their customer base.

The levelling of the intellectual playing field may have another unexpected consequence. While avenues will always be present to profit from proprietary information, those wishing to achieve outstanding success will find it is no longer sufficient to simply possess or broker knowledge. Key advances will come from individuals, organizations, and nations that are able to integrate the intellectual material from broad-ranging sources and transform this into meaningful tangible and intangible end products.

At the end of the day, society needs "things." Things such as food, shelter, transportation, clothing, entertainment technology, clean air, energy, and so on. Ironically, once there is parity in the information arena, economic competitiveness may be thrown back to what we have more generally considered more rudimentary forms of competency, such as manufacturing and production. This does not negate the importance of intellectual resources; it simply underscores the need to keep them pointed in pragmatic directions.

Energy Consumption and Choices

Our reliance on renewable energy sources stemming from fossil fuels like oil, natural gas, and coal has been called into question in recent years on a number of dimensions. First, given their finite nature, world reserves have been declining in supply. Second, these forms of energy have been vilified due to their association with diminished air quality and greenhouse gases that negatively impact the ozone layer. Third, many nations have perceived an urgency to reduce or eliminate their reliance on foreign energy sources. Not having sufficient supply leaves one vulnerable to energy hostage taking by somewhat-less-than-stable nations. More and more, energy supply is being perceived as a national security issue.[30]

There are obvious implications for both energy sourcing and energy use. On the first front, we have already witnessed an increased enthusiasm for the pursuit and adoption of alternative energy sources such as biomass, wind, solar, hydrogen, and nuclear. Ideally, sources that move forward will be renewable, safe, plentiful, dependable, and affordable.[31] While these sources may increase the stability of supply, there is no guarantee they will reduce the cost of supply. Consequently, energy efficiency will continue to be a major concern for both consumers and manufacturers. This could come from two possible sources. The first and obvious solution would be to develop and adopt technology to decrease energy consumption. The second would be to adopt technologies and practices that permit/encourage change to our accustomed behaviors, such as driving shorter distances and less frequently.

Globalization and Localization

The world is shrinking. As previously discussed, technological advances have reduced, and in some cases eliminated, geographical importance for many knowledge-based industries. Whether intellectual property or machine parts, the story is generally the same: insular actions that try to contain economic activities within a nation's borders may have short-term benefits, but long-term detriments.[32] There is no question that status quo is changing and dominant players on today's global scene, like the G8 (Canada, France, Germany, Italy, Japan, Russia, United Kingdom and the United States), will have to work that much harder just to remain relevant, let alone dominant. Some suggest that collective economies from the BRIC countries (Brazil, Russia, India, and China) could be greater than the current dominant nations by 2050.[33] The balance of South America also stands to make strident gains over the coming decades. Such predictions regarding the impact of globalism are premised on a number of assumptions regarding education levels, the infusion of financial resources, reduced trade barriers and transportation costs, as well as an adequate supply of other technology, material, and labor. However, there is still no question an economic era dominated by the United States and select allies will take a different form than what has been witnessed over the past century.

For many small and midsized companies, the concept of globalization is not necessarily new, but the implications are not always clear on a pragmatic, go-forward basis. Arguably, for some businesses, such as yard maintenance, time spent dwelling on this subject might be better spent trimming a shrub. Most others would be well served to take a moment to consider potential consequences and benefits of the globalization movement. Your failure to consider global forces will not stop them from impacting you. With globalization, competition may expand monumentally. On the upside, your markets will also increase. So will the number of firms you may partner and collaborate with. This is in addition to enlarged access to labor, capital, knowledge, and technology. Using such resources effectively provides an opportunity to drive the differential advantage up and the costs down. Even if current plans do not entail world domination, flexibility for expansion should be developed from the outset. This may mean developing procedures and designs compatible with international standards.

Localization may be considered the opposite of globalization. This has been seen in an increasing desire on the part of some to purchase food from producers located close to home, popularized in various forms of the One-Hundred-Mile Diet. To this point, much of this has been driven by a utilitarian desire to obtain fresher and often organic foods. However, there are a number of substantive factors that could cause people to "retreat" from other areas of globalization further. One possibility would be that assumptions regarding the growth of globalization noted above, such as the infusion of capital, technology, education, and so on, are not met *or* reverse in direction. Nationalistic sentiment and ensuing protectionist behavior may also be expected during periods of economic downturn.[34]

REFERENCE GROUPS AND SIGNIFICANT INDIVIDUALS

Sometimes we will say something like, "I don't care what anyone says, I am going to...." However, occasions where people truly act independent of the opinions of others are rare experiences. First, our beliefs are very much influenced through a process of socialization, whether we consciously recognize this or not. Second, many of our decisions are influenced by how we believe others will react. What will my father, wife, children, co-workers, boss, or church think? Is this behavior consistent with how others I associate with would behave? Is this the way the people I admire would act?

Although such social influences might include agents of the government (police officers, the IRS, the FDA, etc.) or professional organizations having legal/legitimate authority to impose sanctions and penalties, our discussion of reference groups and significant others broadens the net to include the influence of those in our social network whom *we* choose to associate with or aspire to be.

Types of Power

Different types of power exist.[35] Some reference groups may have *legitimate power*, with clearly written rules regarding sanctions and removal from the group. There is probably no end of political, religious, special interest, or humanitarian organizations willing to revoke your membership if you violate key principles held by the group. For example, the New York Botanical Garden reserves the right to revoke membership if the person "behaves in a threatening or abusive manner toward any person, or damages or threatens to damage any of the collections," and rightfully so. While no mention is made regarding whether one would have to surrender one's watering can, it is clear up front that there is a clear mechanism to prune bad members if need be.[36]

In many cases there is the ability to reward or coerce an individual, but neither the methods nor the conditions under which they will be applied are formally stated. *"Reward power"* may fall under one of two categories. For example, at work, either a positive stimulus could be applied (a promotion and pay raise) or a negative stimulus could be removed (you no longer have to work night shifts). Alternatively, *coercive power* could come through the application of a negative stimulus (a verbal tirade regarding your performance) or the removal of a positive one (nobody will agree to play golf with you).

In line with reward and coercive power, some individuals and groups are able to exert influence due to some specific knowledge, skill, or ability they are able to provide or withhold. Examples might include your stockbroker, physician, the personnel at your organization who have the power to fix your computer and get you connected to the network, and management consultants. This is referred to as *expert power* (sometimes referred to as information power) and is a function of some specific knowledge or skill that is possessed by this person or group.

On a macro level, sometimes the power of a group comes from rather amorphous sources. For example, nobody may be explicitly stating that mauve is the color of the season, but if everyone is wearing it, surely it must be in. If everyone is eating a certain food, surely it must be safe. The inherent wisdom of an action is derived from the frequency of the behavior. We may refer to this as *normative power.* For example, most people who have been to a hotel have found a message near the towels that says something like, "In order to protect the environment and conserve precious water resources, we would encourage you to reuse your towel." Research has found that appeals to normative values, such as "the majority of guests in this room reuse their towels," tend to be more effective (they work for approximately 50 percent of the guests) than the standard environmental message (approximately 37 percent).[37]

Referent power pertains to the desire to emulate an individual or group due to a strong identification with, and a high opinion of, this person or group. Nationalistic or ethnic pride is a good example. Similarly, people with strong affiliations to a political party would fall into this category.

Types of Groups

As counterintuitive as it may first sound, on occasion we are strongly influenced by groups we are not even part of. Sometimes these are *aspirational* in nature—groups we would like to emulate or belong to (e.g., Hollywood celebrities, the upper class, or professional athletes).[38] In other cases, groups can be *dissociative*—groups we do not want to be part of or considered to be like (e.g., racist organizations such as the Ku Klux Klan).[39] What type of groups/people does your target market aspire to be like? Are there some groups that they would rather die than become a part of?

Some of the groups we consider ourselves to "belong to" are *informal*, with membership defined by some idiosyncratic description, such as, "I am an environmentalist." Such groups do not require any formal registration process. One type of group that would frequently fall under this category would be a brand community. Such communities are groups that exist to celebrate and discuss a particular brand, such as a discussion forum for people who own a particular brand of car. For example, many such groups related to the Chevy Corvette exist. These communities can also exist on a formal level as well, as would be the case with the Porsche Club of Los Angeles.[40] The advent of social media has resulted in an incredible proliferation of such groups.

Formal groups are well defined and typically require some type of membership process or deliberate action, such as becoming a member of the Sierra Club by filling in a form and paying dues, or becoming a Californian by moving to that state. One type of formal group we do not choose would be that of *family*. There is no question that the impact of a spouse or child can be profound, directly or indirectly influencing decisions that are made regarding food choices through to housing.

Significant Individuals Within Groups

Within a corporate setting, there are a number of types of individuals who can be critical to effecting change. *Gatekeepers* are those who control whether information actually reaches the person you want to communicate with or whether you will get an appointment to see this individual. Office assistants, aides, subordinates all can exert an impact. *Influencers* are people who have an impact on the decision but do not actually make the decision. Often we assume the person using the product will be the one making the decision. While frequently this may be the case, in many business contexts these individuals are, at the end of the day, merely influence peddlers (granted, they may exert a very strong influence).

While the CIO might be concerned about what employees will think about new software, this is only part of the consideration. In addition to this information, he or she has to consider budget limitations, competing priorities, the extent to which this software interfaces well with other software and hardware configurations. In this case, one can overestimate the importance of the end user. Conversely, it is also possible to overestimate the impact of the decision maker—he or she may just be the person who provides final approval. Even in the CIO example above, suppose all of the end users complained bitterly about how bad the software was—this may be equivalent to decision making. This is important. Although there may be few people who can actually approve a decision and see it come to life, there are often many who are able to kill it along the way.

From a pragmatic perspective, all of this boils down to a number of key questions: Who is/are the decision maker(s)? How is the decision to be made, autocratically or in committee? What will be the key decision variables? Who are the influencers and what type of influence do they wield? Can this influencer "kill" the decision? In a case where there are multiple influencers of differing opinion, what can be provided to those who favor you to make your case stronger? Who is keeping information from the decision makers and key influencers, and how can one either get past them or win them over?

SUMMARY

Many systems are in a constant state of flux, and one or more of the critical components (the value offering of the existing system, the stability of the existing system, the value offering of the challenger, or the fear and uncertainty associated with the challenger) may be impacted by independent influences. In some cases, governments may actively encourage or discourage certain behaviors through the enacting of new laws. In other contexts, existing laws and mind-sets impede progress. Government agencies, boards, and professional organizations may also have formal rules that influence what new behaviors are accepted, if not welcomed.

The role of government extends well beyond policing what activities are permissible. Government programs and initiatives may be used to encourage behaviors within the volitional control of individuals, including smoking cessation, choosing alternative fuel vehicles, recycling or technology adoption. Technological advances may also have a significant impact on a number of fronts by influencing the form and function of products created, the method by which products and services are created and delivered, as well as general business efficiency, such as new software to more effectively cost projects.

Social trends exert a large impact on behaviors that occur. They include: (1) demographic shifts, (2) physical security, (3) financial stability, (4) health, (5) environment, (6) knowledge and employment, (7) energy, and (8) globalization and localization. In addition to these factors, the impact of reference groups and significant individuals must also be factored in.

CHAPTER FIVE

BIAS IN SEARCH AND CHOICE MUST BE OVERCOME (5TH LAW OF INNOVATION SUCCESS)

Humans are an enigma when it comes to rational information processing. On the one hand, there is no question we are logical beings, seeking to make sense of the world around us and act in a manner that will effect change in our surroundings for our betterment. We are able to diagnose and solve problems, abide by rules, search for information, and make what we consider to be good decisions based on the material we have uncovered. However, and underscore this, we fall far short of the logical consistency of our electronic creations.[1] Consequently our desire for an innovative option may be elevated or completely dissolved as a result of our information-processing shortcomings. Sometimes all it takes is one piece of information to completely break a deal.

Think about the impact of search and decision making on a couple who are living in an apartment but considering the purchase of a house—an innovation that most of us have gone through at some point in time. While they realize there are houses on the market, there are a number of reasons why they may not commence the search. Perhaps they do not see any real benefit to living in a house, or, given their first-time-buyers' status, perhaps they have too many questions *or* do not know which questions to ask, and one way of forestalling the effort of reducing their ignorance is to avoid searching altogether. Or, it may be they have no clue what Web site to go to or which real estate agent to contact, even prior to commencing the search process. There may be a number of hurdles to overcome prior to the search itself. Suppose, however, that they actually do begin to seek out information.

One would assume the end goal of these home seekers is to maximize the utility of their purchase. This, in turn, might call for a very thorough scouring of the marketplace. However, touring every single available home may be more than a little burdensome. In order to deal with this excess of information, it would not be unusual to put simplifying rules in place, such as, "the house has to be under $120,000, be less than ten years old, and be over one thousand square feet." Regrettably, the rule also would have eliminated the $121,000 house that was nine years old and had three thousand square feet. That is the peril of employing a simplifying choice rule—otherwise attractive options may be removed by arbitrary cutoff points. Regardless, suppose that the field is now reduced to seven houses; the task is more straightforward. Suppose further that four of the houses are eliminated because the kitchen in each is too small, and an additional one is ruled out because there is no fence and it would not be "dog friendly" in the future.

This leaves two houses, which should be the easy part—there are only two left—but somehow this is where the real agony in deciding often comes in. Both would be great, but only one can be selected...so choosing one will mean not having the other and therefore potential regret later. The larger size of the one house is traded off against the better location of the other. A thought war ensues...while a larger size would be really valuable, a great location is important. Size...location...size...location. Enough already, just flip coin and be done with it.

This rather commonplace example presents a number of biases having an impact on our search and decision-making processes. A bias may be defined as a tendency to behave in a way that violates some principle of rationality. For example, based on objective criteria, there might be a number of reasons why a person would be better off owning a home, but due to different reasons (biases) he or she does not even initiate a search process. It is also possible a person might commence the search process, but due to some artificial criteria in place to simplify the plethora of options out there, he or she might inadvertently eliminate a house that, in hindsight, would have been the best one.

A deviation from rationality does not necessarily imply an error. As much as many of the biases we employ may sometimes lead us to choose "suboptimal" alternatives, they usually have some adaptive purpose, most notably the saving of time and mental effort. As with the other aspects of the model, understanding bias in search and decision making may also help us to comprehend why producing the best product or service is hardly a guarantee it will be chosen. An overview of elements covered in this chapter that impact whether an innovation or change alternative will be attractive is presented in Exhibit 5-1.

INFORMATION SEARCH

Search Initiation

The first stage of the search process is the perception of a need to engage in search. If an existing system is stable and seemingly effective, there may be no perceived need to engage in search for a new option at all. For example, if your present physician seems competent, there is no reason to look for a new one. If you just bought a car and you are locked into forty-seven more months of payments, there is probably not much point spending a lot of time searching for your next set of wheels. Similarly, if you are incarcerated in a federal penitentiary and locked down in solitary confinement, you probably want a vacation very badly—but there is not much point checking the Internet for bargains.

EXHIBIT 5-1
COMPREHENSIVE CHANGE MODEL: BIAS IN SEARCH AND CHOICE

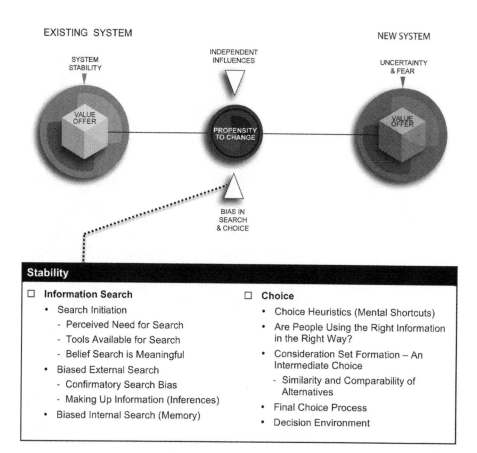

Prior to search actually occurring, multiple conditions must be present.[2] First, the person must see a need for search activities, born through a crisis with the current system or an impetus from an external influence. This may be a government mandate, advertising, social change, or some personal insight. Second, the person must have the tools and skills necessary to conduct the search. Third, the person must be in a situation where search is perceived to be meaningful. With respect to this last point, search will not be meaningful if the person knows a priori that he or she will be unable to make a choice at the end of the day (like the prisoner example above), or if he or she believes there are no alternatives that will suit his or her needs.

A Need for Search. Have you recently thought about searching for new coat hangers? What would it take to prompt you to consider such a search? Let us think about some hypothetical conditions that might cause you to stand up and take stock of your coat hanger inventory: (1) a study is released indicating there are 1,500 injuries each year attributed to the standard metal coat hanger; (2) it is announced that the local recycler is offering 25¢ for each and you figure you could buy a new car with your excess units; or (3) your latest issue of **GQ** indicated that compared to a wooden coat hanger with a broader top, the wire coat hanger caused deformations in shirts and jackets. What do the alternative you are offering and a coat hanger have in common? Perhaps people are not actively looking to change what they are currently doing, and they need additional motivation to do so.

At any given time, we are incredibly complacent regarding 98 percent of the things we have some degree of control over. Some things may rarely come into focal attention from a decision-making perspective. This could be the school our child attends, the transportation mode we take to work, the city we should live in, the word processor we depend on, or the coat hanger we employ. Simply put, most of us are not considering change on a wide number of fronts at any given time.

Search is usually initiated when we perceive an opportunity to improve our environment and/or reduce a negative experience. Along the positive front, even if nothing is wrong per se, a person might still perceive it is possible to either solidify his or her existing happiness or to take actions to extend it further. Most certainly, negative stimuli in the environment tend to motivate behavior. While we do not necessarily search out negative stimuli, we tend to be very quick to react to negative elements in our environment. Such stimuli signal something is wrong and that immediate action is required—kind of like a flashing red light or a wailing siren might do.

Compared to positive stimuli, negative stimuli are more likely to encourage action. Consequently, in order to increase search and reduce stability with the existing system, ideally one would convey that continued adoption of the existing system will lead to something bad. This does not imply that positive information about one or more alternatives would not be useful, simply that negative stimuli tend to more successfully move us into action—with search being the first stage.

Tools for Search. Does the person have access to the necessary tools, be they technological or cognitive resources, to conduct a sufficient information search? How does the segment you are targeting typically look for alternatives? What are you doing to make sure information you consider to be important to people is readily available? Should you enhance store signage, improve information on the Internet, develop a direct-mail piece, send a salesperson out, or all of the above? The central point is, if people do not perceive that they will be able to locate necessary information, they will not expend a great deal of effort to get to it.

Second, people have to believe they will be able to process the information they come across. Search will not be initiated if there is a belief that they will not be able to do anything with the information even once they have uncovered it. Suppose you were visiting Russia and you wanted to find out information about different cities you could go to. Someone points you to a computer and gestures that there are many alternatives. You glance down at the keyboard and the characters are in the Russian typeface (Cyrillic). You punch in a few characters and realize all of the information is coming back in Russian. How much longer are you going to consider the search process? For some individuals, even moderately technical information can appear to be written in Russian. To what extent do those potentially engaged in search have a *perception* that when they come across information relevant to your system, they will be able to understand both what it means and why it is important?

Belief that Search is Meaningful. In the 1960s, a psychologist by the name of Seligman conducted an experiment with dogs.[2] Some of the animals in his study were given shocks and were able to jump away from the apparatus where the shocks were administered. Others were physically constrained by a cage and therefore not able to escape. Over time, the constrained group learned that attempts to escape were useless and there was no alternative available to them. Once the cage was opened up and the alternative did exist to escape, the dogs would not actually try to escape when shocked. Seligman coined this "learned helplessness."

Some people may see some fundamental barrier(s) in place when it comes to making a change. If change is not perceived as possible, why would a person contemplate looking for information? People with lower income levels may perceive their health care, housing, and education choices are extremely limited. Children in abusive homes may see themselves as trapped without any real alternative. To the extent the existing situation seems hopeless, people may be more inclined to turn inward and try to find ways of coping with their current (lousy) condition in the best way possible, rather than looking for new options.

Biased External Search

Once search has begun, it would be naïve to think a person will try to track down all possible information about all possible alternatives. As such, one cannot fault a person for wanting to focus the search in some manner and reduce the amount of effort he or she has to put forward. Nonetheless, two fundamental biases may arise during this stage. The first is confirmatory bias, which may lead to a very focused and narrow search, greatly decreasing the likelihood that many (if any) alternatives will be actively considered for selection. The second arises from the inferences people make when they are not able to find information regarding important attributes.

Confirmatory Search Bias. Think of a controversial issue you feel strongly about or a brand name you are very partial to. How frequently do you *really* try to challenge your attitude and test whether your beliefs regarding the issue or brand still hold true (assuming, of course, they were true in the first place)? Typically we tend to do two things. First, we tend to seek out information that supports our existing view of the world, and second, we avoid/discount information that does not.[4]

Have you ever been in a situation where you have, in essence, already chosen an alternative you would like to purchase (perhaps a specific make and model of sports car) but you still perform some search in order to feel like you exercised due diligence? The goal of the search is not necessarily to find something better; it is to justify the decision you have already made.

Typically, changing a service provider or adopting a new product will require some degree of effort. As a result, many will desire to stay with the system currently in place. In these situations, people find ways to rationalize their current system, either by soliciting views confirming their position or by seeking out negative information about the alternatives. By doing so, even an inadequate existing system may be justified over a superlative new system. The logic is simple: "What we have is generally good, and while there are some flaws and shortcomings, the other alternatives also present problems. So, it just makes sense to stay with what we already have in place."

Making Up Information—The Role of Inferences. Sometimes information is not readily available. Suppose you are looking at televisions and you know the brand, the warranty, and the price, but you do not have detailed information about the quality of the screen. One possibility would be to make the decision based only on the known attributes. However, when valuable information is not present, we tend to make it up.[5] If screen quality is important and a person does not have the information, there is a tendency to approximate the value of this attribute and factor it into the decision. These are often based on implicit correlations a person has come to rely on. In this case, there may be a perceived correlation between the quality of the screen and the brand name (Sony has high quality), the price (when the price is high, the quality is good), the warranty (the warranty is so good, the quality must also be good), or all three.

The inferences drawn might actually help the company selling the product if the inferred value is higher than the actual value. On other occasions, the inferences drawn regarding a product may have a deleterious impact on choice, either because the inference results in the alternative being perceived as poorer than it actually is or because of additional uncertainty present. For example, a person might think the screen quality will be good, but in the absence of definitive information, he or she also knows he or she could be wrong. What incorrect inferences are being made about your offering?

Biased Internal Search (Memory)

To this point, we have treated search from the perspective of having to go out and acquire information from the world around us. In many cases, we also possess information in our memory that we can refer back to during the search process.[6] With a computer or other type of recording device, there is a physical representation of what transpired, and material may be accessed in a reliable manner. While humans have a memory, one key point of difference relative to the computer analog is that ours has to be reconstructed each time we try to access it.[7] Consequently, and as research regarding eyewitness testimony would attest,[8] what is remembered regarding a particular event may differ considerably among individuals and even with a given individual over time. We also fall prey to extraneous information entering in and influencing what we remember. If I told you Jeff wore a blue shirt yesterday, you could probably recreate your memory with this detail. If I said it was red, you could recall that, too. In fact, you might even be very confident about this, even if you are wrong.

Linking this back to bias arising in information search, what we search for and recall may differ considerably from one occasion to the next. More specifically, the information we tend to remember is a function of how "available" it is to us, and this, in turn, is open to bias.[9] Part of this may stem from the way we have encoded it (i.e., whether we ever put this information into memory in a way that could ever be retrieved). It can also be markedly influenced by "primes" in our environment.[10] Suppose you either: a) came across a message from a friend of yours from high school reminding you of the upcoming reunion and friends who would be there, or b) you just read a story about villagers in Bolivia who were killed in a mudslide.

Now suppose that immediately after this, you consider features important when purchasing a car. Neither the reunion nor the mudslide pertained to cars. However, if you were exposed to the reunion information, you might think about the style of the car and the quality of the sound system, whereas exposure to information about the mudslide might have you thinking about the safety of the vehicle and the traction associated with the tires. Such primes can be overt, like a salesperson telling you about a friend of his involved in an accident, or rather subtle, such as a first-aid case in view nearby.

CHOICE

In the vast majority of choice contexts, people do not consider *all* possible information about *all* possible alternatives. We know people often limit the extent of their search. Beyond this, of the subset of information examined, only a portion of this may be used when making the final decision.

Consider the last time you purchased a car. How did your decision process work? For me, I had a particular brand I was considering, I went to the dealership, and (perhaps foolishly) I disclosed my price limit. We narrowed it down to one particular model, and I was then asked what color I wanted. From start to finish, excluding the test drive I took just to reassure myself that my decision was sound, the purchase process for the vehicle took less than ten minutes.

Think about the heaping mountain of information not used. This "neglect" was not a function of access to information, but rather a result of the shortcuts I used when making the decision. Does the efficiency of my decision making come at a cost? Very possibly. There may have been a better vehicle at a better price. Does this make my decision strategy a poor one? To the extent that there was truly a better option than the one selected (based on the attributes important at the time of decision making, such as price, fuel economy, etc.), the decision would have benefited from a far more extensive collection of information. On the other hand, think of all of the time and effort saved by adopting this decision strategy.

From cars to snack food and everything in between, in order to avoid information overload we try to simplify what could otherwise be an avalanche of data. This decision-making process that uses only a subset of possible information is referred to as a choice heuristic. Choice heuristics abound.

Choice Heuristics (Mental Shortcuts)

While choice heuristics may occur in almost any conceivable decision context, they are more likely to be used when time pressure or information load is high and decision involvement is low.[11] Under these situations, there are a number of relatively common choice heuristics used to either reduce the number of potential alternatives down to a manageable number and/or select the final alternative.[12] For illustrative purposes, a number of diverse rules are considered: lexicographic, conjunctive, and maximax.

Lexicographic. A person using a lexicographic rule will choose the product that's best on the attribute believed to be most important. If more than one alternative remains, those that are highest on the second most important attribute are considered, and so forth until only one remains. Perhaps you have a migraine headache and the only thing important to you is getting it to stop. You might ask the pharmacist which drug is the best at removing the greatest amount of pain (your most important attribute). If Brand A is best, Brand A it will be...however, she indicates two have essentially the same medicinal ingredients. You ask which one will work faster (your second most important factor). She points to the one with gel caps. Done. Only two types of information were considered. There was no long, protracted decision, and attributes such as price per pill, size of bottle, and manufacturer reputation were not even considered.

Conjunctive. Sometimes an alternative is automatically rejected because it does not meet a threshold value on all relevant dimensions. Perhaps all cars above a certain price are rejected; any students below a certain grade point are not admitted into a program; or, if something contains peanuts, it will not be purchased. One of my favorite examples of this rule is seen in the "people seeking romance" ads. Two of the largest categories are "men seeking women" and "women seeking men." If you read the requests, some items are probably negotiable. A person desiring a partner who enjoys dancing might be willing to accept a partner who does not, provided the person is particularly kind and attractive. Other elements may not be open for discussion. Some people will not give further consideration to an individual who smokes. Going back to our initial gender categories, I would ask you to consider your sexual orientation. If you are an openly heterosexual male, what characteristics would have to be present in another male for you to consider him as a life partner? If he drove a nice car, had a remarkable salary, an incredible sense of humor and rugged good looks? Then would you "switch"? The answer is probably a decisive no. Sometimes the presence, absence, or value of just one attribute can cause an otherwise amazing alternative to crash and burn.

Maximax. With this decision rule, the option highest on its best dimension is chosen. A good example of this would be the process of selecting people for a sports team. Imagine you are putting together a football team. Chances are you are not looking for a person who is moderately good on a wide range of attributes. If a person can throw the ball quickly, accurately, and under pressure, do you really care if he can block? If a blocker stops everyone from getting near the quarterback, do you really care if he can kick a field goal? If the field goal kicker has 100 percent accuracy from as far away as seventy yards, are you worried about his ability to run with the ball? With the maximax rule, you want to get the person who is best at what he or she is supposed to be best at.

Cutting to the Chase Regarding Decision Rules. While the three rules above provide interesting examples of how we sometimes make decisions, many other rules have been documented. Given this, there might be a tendency to throw one's hands up and declare all of this is too complicated to be useful on a daily basis. The good news is that memorizing and identifying specific rules for each customer is rarely necessary. It is, however, good to have a general understanding of how people are making their decisions. In particular, is there something about the product or service you wish to sell that would almost guarantee it would be considered? Conversely, is there something that might cause it to be automatically rejected? Which items will be traded off against each other? Will people be willing to pay a higher price for the larger volume? Moreover, all of this goes back to consistently asking two different questions. First one must ask *"why will they buy?"* and then follow up with *"why won't they buy?"* As similar as these questions seem, they often yield very different answers and insights into the decision-making process.

Are People Using the Right Information in the Right Way?

Choice often presupposes people will understand what information is important and weigh it accordingly. For example, most would consider the price of a car and the gas mileage to be more important than the color of the carpet in the trunk. While this example seems pretty obvious, consider the purchase of something as common as a new mattress. What features should a person be looking for? Which ones are more important? Which features are worth paying extra money for? These questions would have to be answered in light of the goal the person is trying to achieve. For some people, goals are either poorly formed or, as will be discussed shortly, not even at a level of conscious awareness. Does the audience you are trying to reach have well-articulated objectives, or are these something you can help them formulate? If goals exist, do people understand what product, service, or policy features will be beneficial in achieving them? This begs a slightly different question: is there actually a linkage between what you offer and the goals that exist, or is it necessary to get people to refocus their goals?

Consideration Set Formation—An Intermediate Choice

While a heuristic such as one of the above may result in an immediate decision, it is frequently the case that a given heuristic, either alone or in conjunction with other heuristics, serves to reduce the number of potential alternatives down to a manageable consideration set. Also referred to as an evoked set, these are the alternatives actively considered for final selection.[13]

It is important to understand that variables used for narrowing the field down might be very different from those used for the final decision.[14] For example, a manufacturer might only select a supplier who can provide delivery within eight hours. Once that criterion is met, though, the manufacturer may not use this variable as part of further consideration. As such, having a shorter delivery time of one hour will provide no advantage. While heuristics may play a very important part in delimiting the number of alternatives, the similarity and comparability of alternatives also comes into play when constructing a consideration set.

Similarity and Comparability of Alternatives. People usually do not embrace a great deal of diversity in their consideration set. Research suggests the greater the feature overlap between alternatives (the more attributes they have in common), the more likely they are to be placed into the same consideration set.[15] Stated differently, people tend to include alternatives that they can easily compare with each other. This, in turn, leads to an understanding of a somewhat counterintuitive outcome of some marketing initiatives.

Sometimes, in an effort to distinguish a new product or service, the message sent out is along the lines of, "It is an incredible breakthrough of epic proportions, so much so that you cannot even compare this new system to the ones of old—it is unbelievably different!" However, the "remarkable breakthrough" may now be perceived as being too different from what people are used to, and therefore it may not even make it into the consideration set. The promoter would have been better off downgrading some of the claims, looking for areas in common with some of the more popular alternatives, and then noting some key strengths within this message. In essence, the communication would be, "It is very similar to what you have always been used to, only it is much better on a few key dimensions." By doing this, you are more likely to be perceived as a viable alternative than "interesting, but a little too different."

How many alternatives are usually in the consideration set? The answer is that this is a function of two differing objectives that are simultaneously present: (1) a desire to maximize the likelihood that the best alternative is in the set, and (2) a desire to minimize cognitive effort required.[16] The conflict is as follows—a large number of alternatives within the consideration set is unwieldy, but there is a greater likelihood of the set actually containing the "optimal" alternative. Conversely, a small set size is easier to evaluate, but may result in a great alternative not being considered.

Typically, the greater the expertise and familiarity with the choice context, the larger and more complex the choice set is *able* to become.[17] This is because experts have a greater capacity to absorb and integrate this material and, as a result, are not faced with information overload as quickly. Further, many of the alternatives will already be familiar to the expert and, as a result, a great deal of search effort is not needed to populate the consideration set. An important caveat is required here. While experts have the mental capacity to take on a greater number of alternatives, it does not mean they *will*. Experts are also able to sort the wheat from the chaff and narrow the set down very quickly.[18]

The Final Choice Process

Once the field is reduced to a manageable number of alternatives, decision theorists suggest a more deliberative decision process is often used to actively consider large quantities of information for all of the remaining alternatives, trading off one attribute against another. Accordingly, during this phase people wrestle to balance out competing objectives, and the internal argument is something like, "Yes, it costs more, but…it does have a level of higher quality." These types of trade-offs are compensatory in nature in that one attribute (higher quality) compensates for the value of another (price). For this reason, it is often this last part of the decision process that can be the most straining.

Have you ever narrowed your options down to two or three options quickly and then agonized over this rather limited set? Perhaps you do more research on the Internet, print off brochures, check out *Consumer*

Reports. Maybe you struggle to determine which features you really need given pricing differences among alternatives. This process can be labored and painful. Further, it often culminates with postpurchase dissonance— even after the selection, you wonder if you made the right choice.

Decision Environment

The importance of the decision context will vary considerably from one scenario to another, with arguably greater relevance when purchasing a product in a retail setting than when making a decision at home regarding a recycling program. Think about a time you went to a store to purchase groceries, to a mall to purchase shoes, or to a restaurant to eat a meal. On a conscious level, we often appreciate the environment and note, for example, that the store was well lit, the mall was very elegant, or the restaurant had a romantic ambience. We may even credit this environment with the reason we chose the store in the first place, but we are not fully aware of how our search and decision making has been influenced.

The mere layout of a store can affect the order in which we search for information, the amount of time we spend in the store, and the likelihood of coming across other items.[19] For example, pharmacies and grocery stores are usually organized for efficiency, with promoted items strategically placed at the end of each aisle or in other high-traffic areas. Similarly, items at eye height also tend to be seen more. Beyond layout and visibility, other physical characteristics, such as objects or colors in the store, may have an impact.

A growing body of literature indicates that within retail contexts, our behavior can be influenced by lighting, music, scent, and perceived crowding.[20] Although some differences may be present, there is also reason to be concerned about the atmospherics in Web environments as well.[21] Our judgments and actions may be influenced in ways beyond our conscious awareness. For example, people may or may not notice the tempo of music in a store or restaurant, but they are probably not aware it is influencing the way they act, such as the length of time in the store or the amount of money spent.[22] In fact, even if you could prove it to them, they might not believe you. Nonetheless, a major caveat to the research published regarding environmental factors is that the impact of a specific stimulus, such as the music played in a store, will often be a function of the type of product class and the specific consumer.[23] What is appropriate for a store targeting teenage girls may not work in a car parts store trying to engage middle-aged men.

SUMMARY

Returning to our mousetrap analogy, sometimes the reason the truly superior option is not chosen comes down to biases existing in search and choice processes. In general, for people to engage in active search for a new alternative, three conditions must be present. The person must: (1) see a need to engage in the search, (2) have the tools and skills necessary to conduct the search, and (3) believe they will be able to take some sort of action once the search is complete—the search cannot be perceived as pointless.

The search itself is rarely a study in objectivity. People frequently display a bias in the manner in which they acquire information from the world around them. Confirmatory bias may set in quickly, whereby a person will tend to establish a favorite alternative early in the process and then search for information that supports it and either avoid looking for or discredit information that does not. Further, when important information is not available, people will tend to make inferences (correct and incorrect) regarding the value of the missing information. In short, there is no guarantee people will engage in a search process that will result in an accurate perception of your mousetrap.

Choice heuristics (decision shortcuts) are frequently employed to make a decision or at least narrow the number of alternatives down to a reasonable number. These decision rules typically focus on only a small portion of the total information available, with alternatives often being rejected based on a single attribute. For instance, a product might not make it past the first cut if the price is too high—it does not matter how good it is on other dimensions. The ability of an alternative to make it to the final consideration set is further influenced by the extent to which it is perceived to be similar and comparable to other alternatives. If it seems too novel or too different, it may be regarded as an oddity or more risky. This results in the need to straddle two very different messages: yes, it is different from the others, and yes, it is similar to the others. A great product, service or policy might simply be perceived as being too unique.

While a final choice may be determined quickly through the use of a heuristic, it is frequently a more deliberate exercise with a reasonable amount of information regarding two or three alternatives being considered. For each alternative at this stage, it is not uncommon to witness people making effortful trade-offs. During this stage, people may feel torn as they try to balance out competing objectives, struggling with a decision such as, "it is more expensive and heavier than the other one, *but* it does have a higher quality." Although there is no question some of the processes involved in choice can be very deliberative, a growing body of research suggests choice can occur in an automatic manner and can be a function of factors we are not aware of, whether this be the goal we are trying to achieve, how we are using the information available to us, or some other environmental factor around us, such as the music or lighting.

PART II

CASE APPLICATIONS

Recall from the outset of this book that we defined innovation rather broadly, ranging from the mundane to the hyper-technical. While some innovations, such as robotic automation of manufacturing, involve grand complexities, many do not. Regardless of the level of sophistication, the same principles apply. Indeed, sometimes it is through the more common-place innovation contexts where the relevance of the principles becomes so apparent.

The next six chapters are presented to demonstrate how the model may be applied to a range of applications, including those of a personal nature (blood donation and becoming a vegan); energy alternatives (geothermal energy); health (nurse practitioners); and public policy (adopting the metric system). Each case seeks to demonstrate how the model components impact the attractiveness of the new alternative, thereby enabling an understanding of what has to be done to effect change within that context.

CHAPTER SIX

GIVING BLOOD

Stopping smoking, increasing charitable giving, wearing a helmet when bike riding, ramping up participation in exercise, spending more time with grandchildren, spending less time at work. Although none of these would be considered outlandish innovations, for many, each would represent a very real change to their status quo. Granted, specific components of the Comprehensive Change Model may be more relevant in some cases than in others, but it nonetheless provides a solid framework for understanding factors having an impact and articulating where efforts may be needed to bring about change.

Aside from a few individuals with strong and idiosyncratic religious reservations, one is hard pressed to find a person who carries negative sentiment toward those willing to donate blood. Aptly referred to as "the gift of life," such donations are an important part of life sustenance when blood is required due to injury or an operation. This raises an interesting question. If most people hold donation behavior in such high esteem, why is it that each year only a meager 5 percent of the population actually donate?[1]

For purposes of this example, we will assume that our target population is people between the ages of eighteen and thirty who have never donated blood before. Targeting such individuals would be *aligned* with the goals of a collection agency; reasonably easy to *reach* with conventional as well as electronic media; and, *sustainable*, providing a good stream of donations into the future. The difficulty with this segment will be getting them to *move*—to actually commit to and follow through with the behavior.

Law 1: There Must Be Superior Value Associated with Giving Blood

Stress was placed on understanding the three different types of value communication: feature-, benefit-, and need-specific. Figure 6-1 provides an overview of each of these different levels. This particular example also serves to underscore the importance of considering more than just the *feature* level of understanding. Although the process may be described in purely physical terms (the core service, location, personnel, etc.), clearly the desire to give blood is about more than just the removal of fluids from the body in an efficient manner. For most people the value of the offering is understood once one looks at the *benefits* (ease of use, feedback, enjoyment/pride of use, safety), and more specifically the underlying *needs* that are met (feelings of acceptance and inclusion, affection, reputation and status, achievement, novelty and adventure, contribution and compassion, and, for some, a sense a spiritual connectedness).

From the donor's perspective, the nature of factors considered to be important shifts substantially depending on the *stage of the donation process*. Prior to donation, key elements to be communicated with the potential donor would include: (1) knowledge regarding the mechanics of process, such as the location of the donation center, specific acceptance criteria, guidelines regarding what to eat before donating, and what medications may not be taken, (2) empathy and compassion to quell any nervousness a first-time donor may be experiencing, and (3) reaffirmation the contribution will be meaningful and significant. During the screening interview, interpersonal skills are also critical. For example, in cases where a person would not be suitable (perhaps if they have had a piercing or tattoo within the past year), it is imperative the person be "rejected" kindly but informed of his or her next donation opportunity/what he or she has to do for next time.[2]

During donation, reassurances of safety and comfort will be important, and the general atmosphere of the donation location will be central to reinforcing brand image characteristics. Personnel again play a significant role. More is required than simply Cyborg-like individuals who can insert a needle into a vein with great expediency. In addition to technical competence, staff must be perceived as clearly watching out for the welfare of the donor and helping the person feel good about his or her act of generosity.

Postdonation, recognition for the contribution made, as well as information regarding the next donation, will be important in order to encourage habitual contributions. Postdonation communication from staff seeking follow-up information regarding the visit should also echo the knowledge, empathy, responsiveness, and open communication demonstrated throughout. In light of the number of people who interact with the donor at different stages of the process, consistent training and standardized procedures are integral to attaining strong and reliable interactions.

Law 2: Stability Surrounding Nondonation Behavior Must Be Reduced

One would not expect that people have a strong affiliation with their "nondonation status." I have yet to see someone proudly sporting a button with words declaring, "I didn't give!" and a picture of a dried-up blood cell beneath it. The value offering of the nondonation option is probably not high.[3] Further, other than *complacency* due to ignorance ("I have not thought about it") and procrastination issues (the "I'll do it tomorrow" syndrome), there is probably not a high degree of stability associated with the "nondonation" option.

Some formal *barriers* may exist of a legal/regulatory nature. Some of these are temporary, such as an inadequate time period since the last donation, being too young, currently experiencing an illness such as the flu, or having taken certain medications recently. Others are permanent, such as being physically too small, having accepted money or drugs for sex, having tested positive for HIV, or having used a syringe to take an illicit drug.

EXHIBIT 6-1
FORMS OF VALUE COMMUNICATION FOR BLOOD DONATION

"Feature-Specific" Value Communication (The 3 Cs)

Core (C1)

- ☐ Products (Not Applicable)
- ☐ Price (Not Applicable)
- ☐ Services
  - Blood donation (length of time, sequence of procedure from screening to departure, etc.).
  - Distribution of blood to recipients.
  - Reward and recognition programs for donors.
- ☐ Brand Image
  - Concerned with community.
  - Professional

Conduit (C2)

- ☐ Location
  - Ease of signing up (in person, by phone or by Web).
  - Proximity of location to donor.
  - Nature of physical environment (cleanliness, décor, ambience).
- ☐ Personnel
  - Level of staffing for greeting, screening and donation.
  - Perceived level of knowledge, empathy, speed of response, communication and honesty.

Communication (C3)

- ☐ Information provided on *Web* regarding the availability of clinics.
- ☐ (Ideally) *personal communication* with potential donors regarding the process, donor requirements and concerns that may be present.
- ☐ *Public relations* to communicate to community at large regarding brand image and impact on community.
- ☐ Use of *social media* to alert regarding mobile clinics.

"Benefit-Specific" Value Communication

- ☐ **Product/Service Specific Outcomes**
  - The efficiency of the blood donation process and a clear linkage of the benefit to specific individuals or the community at large.

- ☐ **Safety and Reduced Negative Output**
  - Perception that safety is high and that pain, discomfort, embarrassment and so on will be minimized.
- ☐ **Ease of Use**
  - Convenience
  - Comfort

- ☐ **Feedback**
  - Provision of information about how the blood was used.
- ☐ **Enjoyment/Pride of Use**
  - Actual experience may be a source of pride for many individuals.

"Need-Specific" Value Communication

- ☐ Acceptance and Inclusion
- ☐ Affection/Emotional Relations

- ☐ Reputation and Status
- ☐ Achievement

- ☐ Novelty and Adventure
- ☐ Contribution and Compassion
- ☐ Spiritual Connectedness

Law 3: Uncertainty and Fear Surrounding Blood Donation Must Be Reduced

One can hardly blame a first-time donor for being somewhat apprehensive regarding the impending process. As much as it is an altruistic act, there are many aspects of the procedure that may be met with considerable bewilderment, with questions ranging from "am I qualified?" through to "how enormous is the needle?" Exhibit 6-2 presents an overview of the different elements covered off regarding the impact of fear and uncertainty.

Areas of Uncertainty and Fear. We all know people who do not like going into a hospital or being associated with anything medical. This type of general *service-class risk* is likely augmented by confusion regarding details surrounding the donation process itself (*service-specific risk*). Where do I go? How long does this take? How does one sign up? What age do I have to be? What are the certifications of the people performing this process? What exactly are they taking from me? How long will it take to recover...can I play golf later in the day? Can I donate if I am taking aspirin for a headache? Much of this could be (and is) handled through FAQs on a Web site or even a short video somewhat similar to what one sees on an airplane prior to takeoff.

Pertaining to *discomfort of adoption*, some first-time donors may be embarrassed they have not donated to this point and/or do not want to look stupid by being the "newbee," displaying ignorance by not having a clue what the procedures are. Others may fear a number of very possible outcomes of the process: rejection, pain, and/or fainting (and the commensurate embarrassment). In line with "unwanted outcomes," I have encountered some people who have informed me they do not want to donate because they do not want to be asked about, or diagnosed with, a given disease. Yet others have indicated they are worried about contracting a disease, even though the reality is all needles are both new and sterile.

During the screening, a number of confidential questions are asked of the potential donor, which may raise concerns regarding the *misuse of information*. While some of these questions are innocuous, such as those pertaining to places travelled in the past five years, others are more probing and broach topics such as illicit drug use and sexual activity. For some, not knowing who has access to this information, what other agencies it will be shared with, or how well safeguarded it is, providing this information may generate some unease. In such cases, assurances of confidentiality will be particularly important.

Given that blood donation does not require an interfacing of technologies, *compatibility with "hard" systems* will not be extensive, granted some physical issues may exist. For example, does the person have easy access to the blood donation clinic? Does the person have the capacity to read and understand the information presented? Does he or she tend to faint easily?

Blood donation is likely very *compatible with "soft" systems*. These would include self-perceptions regarding altruism and generosity, along with moral standards. There is also an extremely positive fit between donation behavior and the values of the community. Granted, there are many other activities, such as working at a bake sale to assist earthquake victims, that may also help to affirm such qualities to oneself and others.

Willingness to Take Risk. As outlined in Exhibit 6-2, there are a number of possible areas where willingness may be particularly low. If people see the process as potentially taking away significantly from their health or dignity (*availability of resources* that are important to them), aversion is going to be particularly strong. This is compounded by the fact that it is not possible to *reverse the decision*—further, this is not the kind of decision that one would normally make on many occasions, with the hope of eventually getting it right. Given that individuals are fully in charge of the decision, *volition* (the ability to make a decision) will be high and, consequently, willingness to take risk will be reduced. Remember, giving people choice may increase perceived risk.

EXHIBIT 6-2
UNCERTAINTY AND FEAR OF BLOOD DONATION

Area of Uncertainty and Fear	Impact	Description
Product/Service Class Risk	★★★	Some may be risk averse to anything medical related.
Product/Service Specific Risk	★★★★★	Given the use of a needle, potential for pain and discomfort as well as the sight of blood, this may be a critical issue.
Transaction Risk	----	Not applicable in this context.
Discomfort During Adoption	★★★★★	May be fearful of being vulnerable and naïve during process. Not being accepted or fainting may lead to much embarrassment.
Misuse of Information	★★★★★	Given the sensitive nature of questions asked during screening (drug use and sexual practices), concerns may be very high.
Risk of Discontinuity	★★★	May be the perception that one will be "out of commission" after donation. Usually the only restrictions are that strenuous activity and alcohol should be avoided for the rest of day.
Start-Up Costs	★★	Perceived start-up costs may be high as individual seeks to understand the process and risks.
Payback Period	★	If donor is volunteer, there is no expected tangible payback.
Compatibility with Physical "Hard" Systems	★★★★★	May be large concern regarding whether donating is compatible with physical system (blood, blood type, drug use/sexual background, fainting).
Compatibility with "Soft" Systems	★★★★★	Donation of blood would be highly encouraged by social forces and personal influences. This would reduce fear.
Rate of Change (Social, Legal, Economic, Political, Technical)	★	Although events such as earthquakes may trigger altruism, the rate of social change is not expected to exert a significant influence.

Willingness to Take Risk	Impact	Description
Availability of Resources	★★★★★	The person may view their blood and physical well being in short supply. This would decrease willingness.
Ability to Reverse Decision	★★★★★	It is impossible to reverse the decision once the donation has been made. This would decrease willingness
Ability to "Play" on Multiple Occasions	★	This is not the kind of activity that one continues to do until one, "gets it right."
Short-Term Thinking	★★★★★	People may concentrate on near-term aspects (pain, fainting, embarrassment) at expense of the long-term benefits (saved lives). Increasing long-term view will increase willingness.
Time Until Final Decision	★★★★★	The level of perceived risk may increase as the time for donation approaches. Could be offset by personal reminders and encouragement as the donation date draws nearer.
Framing (Positive vs. Negative)	★★★★★	Willingness increased by focusing on the benefits of donation (to self and others) rather than just the likelihood of discomfort.
Emotion	★★★★★	Anxiety and fear reduce risk-taking, these must be reduced if willingness is to increase.
Volition and Level of Control	★★★★★	As donation is a voluntary experience, the perceived level of risk will be higher (they are "getting themselves into this"). May be offset by education that gives them control – to reduce the likelihood of being rejected, fainting or having any other adverse reaction.

The willingness to take risk will also decrease as the time of actual donation approaches. Three weeks prior to donation, it may have been an easy decision to book an appointment online. On the day of donation, the apprehension is much stronger. All of this speaks to the need to make sure that the *level of control* is maximized, perhaps through education that informs them thoroughly of the process as well as steps to take to avoid being rejected, fainting, or having any other form of adverse reaction. By doing so, negative *emotions* such as the level of anxiety and fear will hopefully be reduced.

Risk Reduction. Even though most people are familiar with the concept of blood donation, it would seem that understanding could be improved on a number of fronts: (1) the removal of misperceptions regarding negative consequences associated with donation, (2) the elucidation of factors that may disqualify a person from being a donor, and (3) the underscoring of the ongoing need for individuals to donate and the lifesaving value of their sacrifice. Given the innate credibility of the various medical sources providing this information, belief in the truthfulness of the messages provided should not be a major constraint.

If strong apprehensions exist regarding the discomfort that will be experienced, a two-sided information approach will be valuable. This might take the form of, "Yes, you will feel discomfort for a very brief period, but for the second of pain you feel, the benefits to society will last a lifetime." Finally, all communication efforts should be very clear as to what the next step in the process should be. For example, "Go to unitedbloodservices.org, get information regarding how you can donate, find answers to questions you might have, chat live online with a member of the team, and even make an appointment."

Law 4: Independent Influences Impact Blood Donation Behavior

Recall that Independent Influences are factors in the environment that are generally beyond the control of the existing and challenging system.

In the 1990s the North American blood donation system became somewhat infamous due to the contamination of the supply with HIV and hepatitis. Occasionally information also surfaces about wasted blood products due to expiration, and sometimes there are stories linked to a surplus of blood and even people being turned away, as was the case after 9/11. Such accounts may cause one to question the actual benefit provided by the donation. Conversely, there are usually reports pertaining to blood shortages and "good news" stories underscoring the importance of donation. Advertisements promoting donation exist on television and YouTube. Blogs and other supporting Web sites also promote donation. Although I am not aware of a recent movie with a popular actor providing a sacrificial transfusion, it is just a matter of time before one will occur and serve to support the cause as well.

Generation Y, the demographic from whom most first-time donors will be drawn, is very Web savvy—they are easily able to access information provided on various sites. While they tend to be somewhat narcissistic, they also demonstrate a bent toward pro-social behavior. However, a visible increase in the incidence of piercings and tattoos in the Gen Y cohort may result in a decrease to the number of qualified donors in this group. This might be exacerbated by a recent upturn in at-risk sexual activities, especially within some ethnic communities.[4]

While not all people can stomach the idea of giving blood, most respect those who do. Consequently, although the driving force for many people may not be peer approval, such appreciation may provide a supporting influence. Even in cases where the donation is a discreet activity, done without openly seeking public approval, just knowing others admire such activities may have an impact. One would expect the impact of others would be particularly profound in cases where the donation is part of a formal group effort, such as with mobile blood donation events involving an office, school, or church. In these cases, there may be strong expectations of positive social reward and/or the avoidance of rejection and punishment.

Depending on the country, there may or may not be more than one organization responsible for collection of whole blood and blood components such as plasma. For example, in Canada the government has appointed one agency for collection, whereas in the United States there are both non-profit agencies, such as United Blood Services or the American Red Cross, that collect blood from volunteers, as well as for-profit entities that will pay people for providing some blood products. Beyond these organizations that directly compete with each other, indirect competitors may be other charities that allow a person to feel as though he or she is making a societal contribution.

Law 5: There are Biases in Search and Choice Regarding Blood Donation

In the previous sections, reference was made to the benefit of providing information that would clarify the process, reduce uncertainty, and promote the positive aspects of donation behavior. There are a number of encouraging points: (1) much of the information required to provide accurate information regarding the process is available online, (2) most misconceptions would seem to be reasonably straightforward to address, and (3) most individuals in the target demographic are computer literate and have access to the Internet. The key issue that remains pertains to how many people will actively *search* out information to clarify their level of knowledge. Unfortunately, while *ability* to process information is high, for many people the *motivation* to do so will not be.

For those who do commence a search, there may be some difficulty sifting through sites, and the inundation of information may be more confusing than enlightening. For these people, the search process may seem overwhelming and better left to another day. Inspection of material people may come across on the Web reveals there are many types of donations (whole blood, plasma, platelets), and the length of time required for donation may vary as a result (fifteen minutes to two hours). Further, in the United States there are many different agencies supporting or responsible for blood donation. Searches may therefore yield additional and unanticipated questions regarding both the process and the service provider. For the most part, it would seem the sites out there are good at converting technical and medical information into common language if one is patient enough to work through the text.

Recall that decision heuristics are mental shortcuts used to simplify the *choice process*. One common shortcut is to reject an alternative if it does not meet a minimum value on a particular dimension. In line with the analysis presented, it would be interesting to know how many people automatically reject the alternative of blood donation because of one or two particular factors, possibly a fear of needles or fear of contracting a disease. Again, this points to the need to ensure communication efforts are in place to remedy erroneous beliefs regarding the process, countering concerns regarding discomfort and making it clear a very real need exists for donors.

Overall Synopsis Regarding Blood Donation

Neither the value offering of the nondonation option nor the stability of this nonpractice are likely strong contributors to failure to give blood. Rather, resistance to donating blood would appear to come from two main model components: (1) the perceived value offering of the blood donation option, along with (2) the uncertainty regarding the donation experience itself. Communication efforts via the Web to answer factual questions and mitigate fears will be essential, especially for younger demographics who are particularly reliant on electronic resources.

As significant as technology may be, the integral ingredient to successful execution is the presence of professional, knowledgeable, and compassionate personnel at all stages of the process. Of additional importance will be facilities, whether mobile or stationary, that reinforce safety and provide a sufficient level of comfort/minimize discomfort. Further, given the nature of why individuals are participating in this benevolent endeavor, evaluations of higher-order attitudes such as compassion and contribution to society would also seem to be particularly useful.

CHAPTER SEVEN

GOING VEGAN

I have two confessions to make. First, on many occasions I have strongly considered decreasing the amount of meat I consume in my diet to the point where I could become a vegetarian. The apparent benefits to this alternative would seem to have merit—lowered cholesterol levels, reduced calorie intake, increased fiber content—not to mention a reduction in pangs of guilt coming from imagining the last moments of life for one of my alimentary friends. The second confession is that until recently I had failed hopelessly at accomplishing any significant change to the composition of my diet. Hot dogs and hamburgers are still a very real part of my social experience. Nicely fried chicken can be memorable for weeks, and a great steak is pleasantly recalled months later. I frequently talk to people who share a similar perspective—it is not that we are out to take on the animal kingdom one mouthful at a time or that we decry the increased consumption of fruits and vegetables. We have simply found ourselves in a holding pattern.

Let us approach this chapter from the perspective of an adult (age eighteen to fifty-five) who has come from a background where meat has been a regular part of meal experiences. A true vegan does not consume any meat products, eggs, dairy, or anything cooked with animal products, such as piecrusts using lard. There are multiple motivations for engaging in such a diet. The first would pertain to religious or moral absolutes. If this is the basis, the value offering of the vegan diet is self-evident and nonnegotiable. For the sake of discussion, we will assume the underlying rationale for a vegan diet is based on a general desire to increase consumption of healthy foods.

Law 1: There Must Be Superior Value Associated with Being Vegan

Feature-, benefit-, and need-based forms of value communication for a vegan diet are presented in Exhibit 7-1. From a *feature-based* value perspective, one could describe the foods (fruits, vegetables, nuts, grains, etc.) available in terms of their nutritional content and the locations where they may be acquired. A feature-based list would also include individuals who are able to provide advice (nutritionists, retail personnel, vegans online, etc.), as well as ancillary services related to diet (restaurants specializing in vegan cuisine or Web sites filled with recipes and dietary information). However, a vegan diet would seem to serve a number of benefits that are not adequately captured by a mere physical description of the various forms of vegan-friendly food available.

At the core of the *benefits* offered, if one is adequately knowledgeable, a vegetarian regimen is able to provide a highly nutritional diet, rich in flavors and textures. Given that fruits and vegetables do not present the same health risks posed by the storage and cooking of meats, this also increases the ease of use. Beyond this, individuals seeking to leap on the vegan wagon may experience a great deal of enjoyment and pride in their newly adopted life choice—should they choose to do so, boasting of their vegan status is one mechanism to show people around them that they are enlightened and different. Proponents of vegetarian diets are quick to point out that a vegetarian diet is higher in fiber and vitamins and that there is research to demonstrate such food will result in the reduction of some forms of cancer, a decrease in heart disease, and a reduction in strokes and diabetes.[1] Vegetarian diets are also conducive to decreasing obesity.

Some of the basic *needs* met by a vegan diet would include the adequate provision of physical needs required for survival and an optimized level of health and longevity. For many, it is more than just about the physical. Some will delight in the acceptance and inclusion they feel being part of the vegan community; the distinct reputation that their diet provides them among their other social circles; a personal level of achievement; and enhanced skills and knowledge. While for some this foray into veganism may be perceived as providing novelty and adventure, for others there is no doubt a sense of spiritual connectedness. For such individuals, becoming a vegan means relating to the earth and their body in a new way that goes beyond mere nutrients and chemicals consumed.

As with any change context, there are often very different needs depending on the *stage of the process*. Pre-adoption issues may center on presenting the appropriate image, getting health-related information out there, and countering misperceptions like the commonly heard "I am worried I will not get enough protein on a vegan diet." During adoption, the provision of recipes and nutritional information will be critical at facilitating good-tasting, well-balanced meals that meet all dietary requirements. Both during and postadoption, the focus also shifts to the continued ability to find good vegan-friendly products in a wide variety of places.

Law 2: Stability Surrounding the Meat-Based Diet Must Be Reduced

Factors underlying the stability of the existing diet are summarized in Exhibit 7-2. One of these, *complacency*, is undeniably a contributor to the stability of a flesh-based diet. Either a vegan alternative has not been considered (i.e., people are on cruise control with respect to dietary choices) or they have nominal awareness of the practice (e.g., becoming a vegan is something you do if you are of a certain religion). Even for those considering a vegan alternative, the priority assigned to switching diets may not be high. In the short term, it is easier to stay with what is known.

EXHIBIT 7-1
FORMS OF VALUE COMMUNICATION (VEGAN DIET)

"Feature-Specific" Value Communication (3 Cs)

Core (C1)

☐ **Products**

- Wide variety of fruits, nuts, vegetables, grains and spices to choose from. Broad range of aromas, tastes and textures. Extensive array of recipes and "meat alternative" options.
- Vegan diet is able to provide all nutritional requirements.
- Vegan diet is typically higher in vitamins and fiber while being lower in cholesterol, fat, and calories.

☐ **Price**

- Price for a vegan diet is reasonable and typically lower than one that includes meat.

☐ **Services**

- Extensive support services available (provision of food, preparation, information).

☐ **Brand Image**

- Generally promoted as healthy, ethical and eco-friendly.

Conduit (C2)

☐ **Location**

- Vegan compatible foods and products are widely available in most local grocery stores.
- Ability exists to obtain additional products and information through the Web.
- Most restaurant have vegan friendly options.

☐ **Personnel**

- Individuals in health food stores, advice columnists, blogs and so forth bring a great deal of experience to the table.
- Given their belief in the cause, vegan promoters are usually high in terms of empathy and communication.

Communication (C3)

☐ Nutritional information, recipes, FAQs widely available through the Internet, conventional sources (books and magazines) and retail establishments.

▼

"Benefit-Specific" Value Communication

☐ **Product/Service Specific Outcomes**

- Being vegan may provide a highly nutritional diet, rich in flavors and textures.

☐ **Safety and Reduced Negative Output**

- Vegan diet results in a reduced likelihood of heart disease, strokes, diabetes, obesity and some forms of cancer.

☐ **Ease of Use**

- Following initial training, food is reasonably easy to find and prepare.

☐ **Enjoyment/Pride of Use**

- New recipes and food orientation may promote enjoyment and pride.

▼

"Need-Specific" Value Communication

☐ **Physical Needs**
☐ **Optimal Health and Longevity**

☐ **Acceptance and Inclusion (part "Vegan" group)**
☐ **Reputation and Status**
☐ **Achievement**

☐ **Skill/Knowledge Acquisition**
☐ **Novelty and Adventure**
☐ **Spiritual Connectedness**

Depth and breadth of system use would pertain to the extent to which meat is used for many food consumption purposes on many different dining occasions. For many meat-eating individuals, meat, egg, and/or dairy products are a very present and dominant part of every meal. A day may consist of bacon and eggs for breakfast, a hamburger and milkshake for lunch, and chicken for dinner with a bowl of clam chowder on the side. Additionally, meat often serves as a status symbol—consuming a high-priced steak and lobster tail tends to be a greater affirmation of attainment (to oneself and others) than boiled cabbage and alfalfa sprouts. Depth and breadth of use is therefore a strong contributor to the stability of the current diet (you are not removing just one food from one meal).

This depth and breadth is compounded when we consider that meat is an integral part of many cultural rituals. Turkey and ham are often the centerpiece of formal gatherings. Hot dogs and hamburgers are synonymous with picnics and family BBQ events. Popcorn, with real butter, is preferred for movie night. Changing the food would somehow change the event.

The movement over to a vegan lifestyle is facilitated somewhat by the small financial costs of migrating over to a vegan diet. Most, if not all, of an individual's existing food preparation equipment may be used under the new regime. As such, *system removal constraints* are extremely low, and *portability of assets* is extremely high. Further, unless a person has just purchased a large quantity of meat, the *time since last purchase* should not have an incredible impact (especially given that many vegan advocates advise that one should move over to a meatless diet gradually).

The stability of current practices is bound to be impacted by beliefs regarding the sufficiency (*technical adequacy*) associated with the meat-based diet. For many, their existing food choices may be perceived as performing less adequately than desired, but nothing is broken per se. That is, their diet is safe, affordable, provides the basics of nutrition, and is still aesthetically pleasing. Indeed, for forty-some years, it has worked extremely well for me. However, my stability in meat-eating ways has taken a hit in recent times. With aging come additional health concerns. Not panics, but concerns. These can be augmented by visits to the physician, comments regarding blood pressure, and results of lab work pointing to elevated cholesterol counts. All of the sudden the biblical adherence in Isaiah 22:13, "Eat, drink, be merry, for tomorrow we die," goes from being a cavalier attitude to a profound realization that mortality is imminent.

The performance level of some foods changes as new attributes are brought into the equation (e.g., the level of sodium, types of fat, or the number of carbohydrates), and gain in prominence as negative output from previous dietary choices becomes apparent. Now those hamburgers and pieces of fried chicken that seemed to be dear friends are viewed as Trojan horses that look magnificent on the outside, but have killers lurking inside.

The perceived *ability to adapt the existing* diet will also be an issue and will have a dampening impact on the migration over to veganism. For example, if dietary needs shift, there is the ability to control the portion size or the type of meat (e.g., reduced red meat or increased seafood). Similarly, if financial constraints appear, a T-bone steak may be replaced by stewing meat or tuna.

Linking back into the sections above regarding the difficulties of giving up the old systems as well as the discussion of how many foods are inextricably linked with social experiences, it would be naïve to think we do not have some fairly strong *relationships* with the foods we eat. Interviews with contestants on reality television weight-loss shows will often display participants sobbing about their uncontrollable relationship with food. While most of us do not have such breakdown moments, there are very few people who see food as purely nutritional intake. Most would not be satisfied with a tasteless powder dissolved in water taken one time per week. I confess, I enjoy eating food. Hey, it is not just me. Recall from the story regarding the introduction of New Coke in 1985 that a key reason for the failure of this new product was not the taste (it was arguably superior to the old formulation); it was the fact that someone messed with a relationship people identified so highly with. Some of these relationships are bound to be present with meat, egg, and dairy products.

EXHIBIT 7-2
STABILITY OF EXISTING SYSTEM (MEAT DIET)

Stability Factor	Impact	Description
☐ Momentum from Psychological Factors	★★★★★	Complacency with existing diet is extremely high for most people. It is not that they think what they have is excellent, it is just that they do not think about major shifts at all.
☐ Depth and Breadth of System Use	★★★★★	Changing to vegan options will have an impact across all meals and social experiences (where meat is frequently the main part of a meal). Meals are often consumed by multiple members of the same family at the same time. Accordingly, the depth and breadth of food in social settings is extensive.
☐ System Removal Constraints	★★★★	Converting to a vegan based diet does not involve physical costs of removing items, however, mental costs of removing meat may be present if the person has a strong relationship with such food.
☐ Constraints Imposed by Independent Influences	★★★★★	There may be strong pressures from significant individuals and family members that will make becoming vegan more difficult.
☐ Portability of Assets	★★	Almost all assets (e.g., skills and tools) that were useful in preparing meat based meals may be used during the preparation of vegan based meals. Some may feel that they are giving up specialized knowledge regarding meat preparation (e.g., grilling on the BBQ).
☐ Time Since Last Purchase	★	Unless the person has recently purchased a large quantity of meat, this will likely not be a major factor.
☐ Technical Adequacy of Existing System	★★★★★	The perception that the meat based diet is *not* working/healthy will have an incredible impact at destabilizing the current system and will help to migrate people over to a vegan alternative.
☐ Adaptability of Existing Alternative	★★★★★	If it is perceived that nutritional and health benefits of the existing meat based diet may be maintained through different adaptations to the existing meat menu (e.g., different meats, more fish, less fat, etc.), the likelihood of converting to a vegan diet will be greatly diminished.
☐ Affinity Programs and Volume Discounts	---	Not applicable in this context.
☐ Relationships	★★★★★	Relationships with certain types of meat may be deeply ingrained, either because of taste preferences (e.g., steak or fried chicken), comfort (e.g., chicken noodle soup), tradition (e.g., turkey for Thanksgiving), convenience (e.g., meatloaf) or as a signal of success (e.g., lobster).

Law 3: Uncertainty and Fear Surrounding the Vegan Diet Must Be Reduced

Factors influencing uncertainty and fear are summarized in Exhibit 7-3.

Area of Uncertainty and Fear. Some people will be very apprehensive about changing their diet at all (*product-class risk*), let alone the removal of meat in particular (*product-specific risk*). Beyond an issue of nutritional content, concerns may be present that vegan meals may suffer from an aesthetic perspective. Many are used to the meat dish forming the core of a meal experience. Rice, pasta, and vegetables may be present in a supporting role, but they are rarely the star of the culinary show presented daily at breakfast, lunch, and dinner. Some textural elements may also be poorly duplicated by standard vegan meals. Additionally, without changing some aspects of the preparation, a meatless diet consisting of broccoli and rice will be bland to most. Hence, while people many may be mentally convinced that they can take on any nutritional requirements rather quickly, there may be a perceived *risk of discontinuity* —a period where "good" food is absent.

Depending on the extent to which the person feels that he or she must humble himself or herself and solicit help from existing vegans to ask basic questions about his or her food, there may be some *discomfort of adoption.* This will seem especially true if the person feels he or she will be judged for his or her past meat-eating ways. The *start-up costs* will be nominal financially, but larger with respect to emotion and education. Concerns regarding any such costs would be compounded by what is a rather ambiguous *payback period.* If the new diet provides a burst of energy, a rush of new tastes, or immediate feelings of pride, this is wonderful. Anything in the short-term will help to confirm that the vegan decision was a good one. Unfortunately, many health-related issues that may be corrected by a vegan lifestyle will take a longer period of time to determine (e.g., lower cholesterol levels). In fact, some may never be recognized. How does one know what ailments one did not get because of one's vegan choices?

Compatibility with "hard" physical systems will not be an issue. As noted, a vegan diet fits very nicely with existing cooking implements and methods. Done right, it will also fit well with the most important physical system of all—the person's body. As alluded to already, *compatibility with "soft" systems* will be a much bigger issue. Many social gatherings, restaurants, and even family meals are not geared to be vegan friendly. Trying to be a vegan in a sea of carnivores may be difficult. On a daily basis, is the family supposed to prepare two meals—one for the vegan and one for everyone else? Given the centrality of food choices to our everyday being, anger and frustration on the part of both the vegan and family members are sure to follow as divergent dietary objectives are reconciled. It is also possible that the new vegan will no longer be invited to some engagements for fear of offending him or her with different meat dishes present.

Issues may arise at catered business lunches without a vegetarian entrée, and there will be awkward moments asking hosts of parties what ingredients were used in a particular recipe. And even though many restaurants specify vegetarian options, further questions often have to be asked to make sure the restaurant's definition of "vegetarian" is actually vegan. For example, were the zucchini sticks fried in vegetable or animal oil?

When the vegan attends the family get-together, he or she may realize that the family's idea of supporting his or her dietary choice is to not be offended if the vegan brings his or her own food. If children are also switched over to a vegan diet, they may now have to bring their own treats to parties at school because many parents, while sensitive to peanut allergies, are not sensitive to a repulsion to butter. While a vegan lifestyle may not be completely Spartan or equivalent to a martyr's existence, compatibility with common social systems will be an issue.

Now I have started to touch on an area that does concern me personally. I am a fairly conservative person, not known for attacks on foreign whaling ships, arrests during protests against corporate indulgence, or wielding placards insisting pharmaceutical companies be shut down because of animal testing. I am worried that once word gets out that I am a vegan, I will constantly have to say, "Yes, but…not one of those kind." Even there, it is not clear what "those kind" refers to. In reading informational literature from various sources, some types of vegetarians would appear to have as much disdain for other types of vegetarians as they do for flesh eaters. There are fruitarians who do not eat vegetables; some vegetarians do not eat something if it resulted in the death of the plant (e.g., a walnut would be good, a carrot would not); some vegetarians eat dairy products, some eat eggs, some eat fish. This can be somewhat bewildering. I am not sure which one I should gravitate to or why (for what it is worth, I searched for a category of vegetarian that also consumed beef and chicken, but my results were fruitless).

Willingness to Take Risk. There are several factors that should play well to the willingness of a person to take the risk of switching to a vegan diet. First, for most individuals, *availability of resources* is not going to be an issue—they will have access to the food and recipes that they need. Second, the decision is easily reversible (if that food does not work out, they can go down the street to McDonald's). Third, it is the kind of "game" that one can *play on multiple occasions*. If Tuesday does not work out, there is Wednesday, Thursday, Friday, and so on after that.

Willingness to take risk will be diminished by *short-term thinking*, dwelling on near-term consequences of their actions (potentially disappointing food and family frustration), rather than the long-term health benefits of switching. From a *framing* perspective, it is the latter that one needs to be thinking about. From an *emotional* perspective, anger or sadness regarding the state of one's health may prompt an increased level of willingness to try a vegan option. Anxiety and fear will have the opposite effect, and may arise through concerns related to nutritional intake or social reprisal (consequences based on what others might think).

EXHIBIT 7-3
UNCERTAINTY AND FEAR OF VEGAN DIET

Area of Uncertainty and Fear	Impact	Description
☐ Product/Service Class Risk	★★★	Some may be very sensitive to changing their diet in any way.
☐ Product/Service Specific Risk	★★★★★	Many individuals will be very concerned that a vegan diet will not be able to provide all of the required vitamins and protein that a meat based diet does.
☐ Transaction Risk	----	Not applicable in this context.
☐ Discomfort During Adoption	★	Minor embarrassment may be experienced as people seek information from vegans regarding what to eat.
☐ Misuse of Information	----	Not applicable in this context.
☐ Risk of Discontinuity	★★★	There may be a perception that a period of time will exist when food will not be as good/family satisfaction will be lower.
☐ Start-Up Costs	★★★	Although the financial start-up costs are not expected to be a constraint, the mental and emotional costs of switching over to a new diet may be perceived to be particularly high by some.
☐ Payback Period	★★	Even if a vegan based diet has a positive impact, it is not clear how long or what benefits will actually occur. This may cloud the tangibility of the benefit and result in postponement of vegan plans.
☐ Compatibility with Physical Systems	★★★★★	In line with product risk, concern may exist that a vegan diet will actually be able to maintain physical health.
☐ Compatibility with "Soft" Systems	★★★★★	This is perhaps the biggest constraint for many individuals. Any desire to become vegan must take into consideration a broad host of family members and social situations. As such vegan meals may not be compatible with the way people, "do things around here."
☐ Rate of Change (Social, Legal, Economic, Political, Technical)	★	The popularity of vegan diets seem to ebb and flow in the media. However, this is not anticipated to be a major issue.

Willingness to Take Risk	Impact	Description
☐ Availability of Resources	★	Given the low costs of switching, resource scarcity should not be an issue. This will increase the willingness to take risk.
☐ Ability to Reverse Decision	★★★★★	It is straight-forward to switch back to a meat based diet if desired.
☐ Ability to "Play" on Multiple Occasions	★★★★★	It is possible to try different vegan meals on multiple occasions if need be.
☐ Short-Term Thinking	★★★★★	People may concentrate on near-term aspects (potentially disappointing food and family frustration) at expense of the long-term health benefits.
☐ Time Until Final Decision	★★★	Many may "talk big" but opt out at the last minute – waiting for a better time.
☐ Framing (Positive vs. Negative)	★★★	Willingness is increased if the focus is on what is being gained rather than what is being given up.
☐ Emotion	★	Anxiety and fear reduce risk taking. Given the ability to try this on a "part-time" basis, emotion is not likely to play a large rule.
☐ Volition and Level of Control	★★★	Becoming a vegan is voluntary and the perceived level of risk will be higher as a result. This may be offset by education that gives them control (i.e., nutritional information and recipes).

Becoming a vegetarian is an excellent example of how *volition* (what a person actually has control over) can increase the perceived risk. Suppose someone told you and your family, "Sorry, all meat is gone; the truck carrying it had an accident, and another will not be arriving for six years." You might feel sad, disappointed, anxious, and angry, but you would not feel like you were taking a risk by moving to a vegan diet. There were no choices. On the other hand, when you have direct control over whether you adopt a vegan diet or not (for example, you could have bought steak and chicken but decided not to), the perception of risk will be greater. You might find yourself saying something like, "I sure hope I made the right decision and the consequences of my action do not harm me or my relationship with my family members."

Suppose you do make the decision to go vegan. You can still control what fruits, vegetables, grains, and spices you purchase, and, because of the control you are able to exert over this situation, the food is remarkably good and is able to meet or exceed all required nutritional dimensions. This ability to be in control will reduce the perceived level of risk. This does, of course, assume the person has the knowledge, skills, and resources to exert this control.

Risk Reduction. Risk reduction needs to occur on a number of different communication levels. Endorsements from credible individuals and organizations may go some distance to reduce the psychological distance between the individual and a vegan diet. Moreover, though, a huge part of the risk reduction process will be: (1) convincing people of the health benefits of a vegan diet, (2) educating people regarding nutritional concerns they think they may encounter, such as low levels of protein or iron, (3) training people regarding food preparation so that meals can still be exciting and enjoyable, and (4) providing information regarding how different versions of the same basic meal may be made to allow vegans and nonvegans to live together functionally in the same household.

Law 4: Independent Influences Impact the Diet Selected

Multiple trends favor the vegetarian cause. While not all people have signed on as card-carrying members of PETA (People for the Ethical Treatment of Animals), the notion of animal rights has received extensive attention in the popular press and seems to have gained general acceptance in the population. Legal mechanisms have been developed and are routinely applied to deal with those who harm animals. Many formal organizations now exist to promote animal welfare, ranging from the highly respected American Society for the Protection of Cruelty to Animals (ASPCA) through to moderate independent organizations such as the aforementioned PETA, and more radical factions, such as the Animal Liberation Front. Although the definition of animal cruelty may vary depending on the organization you consult, our society has come to a point where animal abuse is tolerated less than ever before. Hence, if a prospective vegan is basing his or her decision in part on the desire to uphold the dignity of animals, more than ever, support for this would be present.

Health trends have also been at the fore of many media stories, and being vegetarian seems to be the rage for many celebrities. In brief, despite my concerns regarding how my friends and family might react, being put into the category of "vegetarian" no longer carries with it the same pejorative connotation it once did. In some circles it might even be considered exotic or chic. While it has been possible to special-order vegetarian meals for flights and conferences for some time, this no longer means a bowl of rice with steamed carrots. As well, a growing number of restaurants also have vegetarian options that go well beyond a chef's salad.

Demographic trends also work in favor of the vegetarian movement. As the cultural diversity of the population increases, with a multiplicity of ethnicities bringing not only vegetarian backgrounds but also an expanding array of food types and preparation methods, finding such foods and "fitting in" has become less problematic. Similarly, the ability to obtain vegetarian foods from mainstream grocery outlets has also increased.

Group influences may also play a role. Hundreds of formal vegetarian-related organizations also exist to provide information assisting those wishing to pursue a vegetarian lifestyle. Such sites provide dietary information, deal with misconceptions, list recipes, give information about vegetarian-friendly restaurants, and, in some cases, provide step-by-step instructions regarding how individuals may slowly reduce the amount of meat they consume, with an eventual goal of removing it from the diet entirely. Some of these organizations often also have frequent formal and informal social gatherings. The ability to connect via many forms of social media also exists. Such virtual community options may be particularly valuable for people who do not have a great deal of support for their vegetarian lifestyle at home.

As brought up extensively when dealing with the compatibility with soft systems, there are *significant individuals* around us who may influence the successful adoption of any new diet.[2] Food is rarely a solo effort. The food I make at home is not just my food. It is inevitable that any change to my diet is going to directly or indirectly influence others.

Law 5: There are Biases in Search and Choice Regarding the Diet Chosen

In the section regarding stability, it was noted many people may not perceive they have any problem with the food they are eating. They do not perceive there is this outstanding need to be filled or that a vegan diet may provide any advantage to what they have right now. If there is no problem or no perceived opportunity for improvement, why would one spend time *searching* for alternatives? Remember, we tend to be in a state of drift more than some constant and willful engagement in change. Further, while some might be interested in searching, many may perceive that they do not possess the skills to process the information once they do come across it (i.e., many people are not chefs or dieticians).

Assuming one can be convinced to commence the search process, there is no shortage of information on the Web regarding the promotion of a vegan lifestyle. While the facts are often mired in musings regarding animal cruelty rather than dietary sense, the information regarding alternatives is out there. Many sources are available to address not only possible concerns pertaining to topics such as protein or vitamin deficiency, but also to provide traditional and adapted recipes, vegetarian lasagna for example. A surprising number of these also take a very moderate stance with respect to "converting" people over, recognizing change often takes time. Although some recipes present new ingredients such as chickpea flour, there is no shortage of menu items consisting of commonly found ingredients.

Once the search has commenced in earnest, one would anticipate bias in the choice process will stem from: (1) persistent fears regarding health benefits/drawbacks, (2) a lack of food options, (3) a shortage of perceived food preparation skill, and/or the (4) perceived reaction of family and peers. Any one of these may be used as a trigger to curtail the adoption of a vegetarian lifestyle. On the positive side, it is anticipated that both the motivation and ability of individuals to process information will be high—while there are emotional issues associated with any choice, a strong intellectual approach will be key.

Recall that a competing alternative is more likely to be placed in the *consideration set* if it is perceived to be similar to other options. In this case, to the extent it is possible to present the vegan diet as something conceptually similar to what has been traditionally practiced, the propensity to switch will increase. However, in their enthusiasm, many vegetable-loving zealots might forget this and get carried away talking about all sorts of different foods, principles regarding holistic diets, and the history of vegan culture in some ancient tribal culture. People considering switching their

diet may find this challenging enough without having to change everything they have ever known about food and social practice.

Overall Synopsis Regarding "Becoming Vegan"

Organizations wanting to promote a vegan lifestyle need to find ways
to reduce the level of perceived risk brought forward in the discussion here.
Although there may be limitations regarding what can be done to reduce
some social risks, solutions that realize a prospective vegan will be in a
blended family would be useful. Such steps might be simple substitutions
for cooking that would not be burdensome and recipes all people in a family would enjoy. More than just dealing with food, it is likely both the
new vegan and the people within his or her family will be concerned with
whether the person will be getting the necessary nutrition. Material underscoring the benefits of a vegan lifestyle, as well as assurances that a properly
composed vegan diet will provide adequate iron, protein, vitamins, etc.,
may help to alleviate such concerns, especially if the data are endorsed by a
neutral and well-known third party, perhaps a federal government agency or
professional organizations representing medical personnel or nutritionists.

Recognizing there may be concerns regarding quality of new foods,
product guarantees, free product trials, and supporting materials such as
recipes will help to reduce the level of perceived product risk. Informational
and social support may also be provided by Web sites promoting veganism. Such sites should consider testimonials from regular (noncelebrity)
individuals with a wide variety of backgrounds. They should also take into
consideration and directly address many of the possible fears a potential
vegan might have.

CHAPTER EIGHT

PERSONAL TASER, ANYONE?

The number of products aimed at consumer markets is overwhelming. Think about the bazillion Web pages you have come across and the thousands of items on grocery store shelves, including a mind-boggling number of shampoos you routinely pass by. Similarly, your life has likely not been devoid of specialty and department stores offering hardware, clothing, perfume, and jewellery. Fast-moving consumer goods (FMCGs) such as toothpaste, soft drinks, laundry detergent, paper towels, shampoo, and coffee are constantly embattled in efforts to encourage switching and maintain market share—the two potential goals of the Comprehensive Change Model. Consumer durables, such as washing machines or cars, face the daunting task of asking individuals to expend a considerable amount of money on a product that will be with them for some time. In this chapter we will be examining an alternative that falls more squarely in the durables camp—a civilian version of a weapon that temporarily incapacitates the recipient through the application of electrical current. This is similar to the "Taser[1]" used by law enforcement officers.

As with all applications, the evaluation of an option must be examined from the perspective of the segment you are targeting. Are you pursuing forty-year-old males in Wyoming who frequent gun shows, or elderly residents of a retirement community? For this example, we will examine the problem from the perspective of a young (18 to 25 years old) female in an urban environment. Let us further assume that she has little in the way of self-defense training. In terms of the ARMS criteria for segmentation, this group would be *aligned* with company objectives and *sustainable* (this group would be reasonably large). It is not immediately clear how easy it is to *reach* (communicate with) this segment. Nor is it clear how easy it will be to get them to *move* and actually purchase such a weapon—much of this will depend on the ability to adequately address each of the five laws.

Factors influencing the value offer, stability, and uncertainty are presented in Exhibits 8-1 through 8-3, respectively. We will simplify this situation by examining only the personal Taser C2 option relative to the status quo (no weapons). A more complex analysis could also jointly consider additional competing options, including basic defensive weapons such as mace, pepper spray, whistles, up to something more extreme like a handgun.

Law 1: There Must Be Superior Value Associated with the Taser C2

Want the defensive capability of a handgun but not blood and death? One answer might be a Taser (an acronym for the Thomas A. Swift Electric Rifle, based on a century-old child's book).[2] On a *feature* level, the Taser C2 (the version intended for civilians) may be described as the size of a handgun (able to be hidden in a purse). It works by shooting high-voltage/low current (the current of the C2 is a small 0.07 joules per pulse, compared to approximately 360 joules per pulse for a cardiac defibrillator) at the combatant. These wires are tipped with stainless steel barbs that stick to clothing or skin. A debilitating charge is then provided, resulting in neuromuscular incapacitation. The general finding has been that when used on healthy individuals, there is typically no lasting effect. Of course, not all recipients are healthy.[3] Nonetheless, 16,200 law enforcement agencies in 107 countries have developed a high regard for the use of the professional version, as they can be used from a reasonable distance and are intended to subdue the bad guy without resorting to lethal force.[4]

The Taser C2 starts at about $400 and among other items includes two cartridges with 15 foot leads, a practice cartridge, a practice target, a user manual and a training DVD. They are available in a wide range of colors, including hot pink. These weapons are available online and through some retail establishments that sell regular handguns. Ancillary services providing training may also be available, either in person or through instructional videos. Financing is also something either the manufacturer or the retail store could potentially facilitate.

Personnel may be a key part of the sales process. The knowledge of the product and the ability to link this detailed understanding with the needs of a given buyer will be important in demonstrating a strong problem-solving orientation. Moreover, for many, empathy will be important. If a person is at the stage of purchasing a weapon, they may have been through one or more personal incidents of a threatening nature.

Communication will also be a core component of any marketing strategy. One would imagine that most within this segment are likely to engage in some degree of Internet search regarding both the types of weapons that will be most appropriate and the retail establishments reasonably close to them. Consequently, an online presence, combined with an ability and encouragement to ask questions (perhaps through online chat or a phone number) will be of benefit, even when the final sale will occur in the store.

Owning a Taser C2 would offer a number of *benefits*. First, these weapons have a demonstrated ability to stop an attacker (the key purpose of ownership) if used properly. Second, the personal units are particularly portable and easy to use. Third, and of particular benefit relative to a handgun, a Taser C2 has less likelihood than a handgun of actually killing someone through accidental discharge.

Needs met by the defensive capability the Taser C2 would include not only physical needs, but also optimal health/longevity, self-sufficiency, and preparedness/versatility. In the event that the individual saw it as a means to protect children or other people close to her, it could also be looked at as a way to increase the strength of the family.

Different factors will be important at each *stage of the adoption process*. Prior to purchase, individuals may be concerned regarding the safety of having a Taser C2 and methods that may be employed to safeguard against accidental discharge. Information regarding the purchasing requirements may allay concerns regarding what may be perceived as a complicated process. Promoting information regarding possible training would also be important to most. Further, given that many women in this demographic may feel they are acquiring something that is a little less than ladylike, assuring the individual this is something wise and rationale may help to quell dissonance between who they are and what they are doing. Following the pre-adoption phase, issues of product use become particularly salient. Product demonstration regarding the basics of holding and firing the weapon would reduce uncertainty in this regard.

Law 2: The Stability Surrounding Nonownership Must be Reduced

One possibility is that the person is in an environment where personal safety is not a concern. Alternatively, it may be the case their life is in peril but either they do not recognize there is an issue or they downgrade its significance—both resulting in some degree of *complacency*. A challenge in this type of scenario is to communicate the dangers without causing undue fear or psychological defense mechanisms, such as denial.

Although it may be physically difficult to simultaneously fire a handgun, discharge a spray bottle of pepper spray, and blow a whistle, the acquisition of an additional protection mechanism does not mean that any existing asset has to be given up. As such, *portability of existing assets is high* and *system removal issues* are not present.

There may be a number of *constraints imposed by independent influences*. Specifically, some jurisdictions may have legal constraints in place that severely restrict ownership of a Taser C2. At present, citizens are not permitted to purchase a Taser C2 in states such as Hawaii, Massachusetts, New York, New Jersey, Rhode Island, Washington, D.C., or Wisconsin.

EXHIBIT 8-1
FORMS OF VALUE COMMUNICATION (TASER C2)

"Feature-Specific" Value Communication (The 3 Cs)

Core

□ **Products**
- Reasonably small, hand-gun sized device in a variety of colors that deploys metallic leads and discharges an incapacitating charge to an assailant.
- Replacement cartridges and holster available.

□ **Price**
- Approximately $400. Depends on extra items ordered.

□ **Services**
- Consultation provided prior to purchase as well as product support after purchase.
- Possible to offer product training, financing and expedited delivery.

□ **Brand Image**
- Promoted as contemporary and powerful.

Conduit

□ **Location**
- Not legal in all places. Where legal, available on-line or through some stores where conventional hand-guns are sold.

□ **Personnel**
- Personnel from Taser and other retail locations (on-line and in-person) may be helpful at answering questions regarding legalities of ownership as well as basic product information.
- Personnel from independent retailers will also be instrumental in selling this product. Their knowledge of (and belief in) the weapon as well as empathy for the individual will be important.

Communication

□ At present, awareness of the Taser used by law enforcement personnel is strong. However, awareness for the Taser C2 (the civilian version) would seem to be much lower.

□ Beyond issues of awareness, communication must focus on issues of effectiveness (will it work as desired), as well as safety. Both of these must be considered relative to perceptions regarding a hand-gun (a likely competing option).

□ An on-line presence will be particularly important given the age and likely Internet savvy of the target audience.

"Benefit-Specific" Value Communication

□ **Product/Service Specific Outcomes**
- Demonstrated ability to stop an attacker.

□ **Safety and Reduced Negative Output**
- Unlikely to kill anyone due to accidental discharge.

□ **Ease of Use**
- Very portable (easy to fit in a purse) and easy to use.

"Need-Specific" Value Communication

□ **Physical Needs**
□ **Optimal Health/Longevity**

□ **Self-Sufficiency**
□ **Preparedness/Versatility**

□ **Strength of Family**

If the individual believes that she may be placed in an inescapable situation where the ability to subdue an attacker is required, she may view her existing skills to be *technically inadequate*. This would effectively decrease stability of the status quo option (continued nonownership). Another possibility would be to examine other forms of self-defense, such as martial arts, thereby *adapting* her existing level of weapon ownership (none) to deal with any potential attack situation.

EXHIBIT 8-2
STABILITY OF EXISTING SYSTEM (NO WEAPON)

Stability Factor	Impact	Description
☐ Momentum from Psychological Factors	★★★★★	Some people may have never thought about getting a weapon such as a Taser C2. This could be due to a lack of awareness regarding options available. Alternatively, this may be because the do not perceive themselves to be in a dangerous environment.
☐ Depth and Breadth of System Use	★★★★★	The existing protection measures may have proven useful in a broad range of conditions, however, attachment to them is likely not strong.
☐ System Removal Constraints	---	Not applicable in this context. No existing systems have to be removed.
☐ Constraints Imposed by Independent Influences	★★★★★	It may not be legally possible to acquire a Taser C2 in some geographical jurisdictions. Even where possible, some background check may be required.
☐ Portability of Assets	★★	Any knowledge/skill they have developed for self-protection will still be of equal value after a Taser is purchased.
☐ Time Since Last Purchase	★★	If they have recently purchased another weapon for self-defense one could argue that the likelihood of purchasing a Taser C2 is lowered.
☐ Technical Adequacy of Existing System	★★★★★	If people perceive that they may be confronted with a situation where they will need to subdue their attacker and they do not believe that they are physically capable of doing this on their own, then they will see their existing system as technically inadequate and the Taser C2 as a possible solution.
☐ Adaptability of Existing Alternative	★★	Individuals may perceive that they can take additional training that does not require a weapon (e.g., many martial arts) and thereby adapt their existing system (no weapons).
☐ Affinity Programs and Volume Discounts	---	Not applicable in this context. There are no affinity programs or volume discounts involved.
☐ Relationships	★★★★★	It is unlikely that many would have a relationship with their "nonweapon" status.

Law 3: Uncertainty and Fear Surrounding the Taser C2 Must be Reduced

Areas of Uncertainty and Fear. If we consider the *product class* to be "weapons ownership," it is foreseeable that this general area will be cloaked in some degree of apprehension. Weapons such as handguns or a Taser C2, by their nature, are bound to be associated with violence. There is also the broader issue of becoming a "weapons owner" and any pejorative connotations the individual may associate with this.

While handguns have been around for a considerable period of time, the Taser C2 has not. Consequently, *product-specific risk* is bound to be present, and the number of questions regarding its use and effectiveness are likely to be high. How does it work? Will it work all the time? How long does the battery stay charged? Can it be reloaded? Will it take long to learn how this works (*start-up costs*)? What if there are multiple assailants? On the other hand, the product-specific risk of a Taser C2 will be reduced relative to a handgun, given the lower likelihood of death, either during an altercation or through accidental discharge. Regardless, all of the questions present, along with the potentially unsettling nature of a weapon purchase, may lead to some *discomfort during adoption*.

The Taser C2 for civilian use was designed to be lightweight and ergonomic.[5] As a result, *compatibility* with the physical characteristics of the individual should be high. Compatibility may also be considered for "softer" systems. For example, because accidental firings are less likely to result in severe physical injury, it is more compatible with individuals with children in the household. Second, it may have a better fit for an individual who wants a weapon with strong debilitating power, but who still has moral concerns regarding the use of handguns. Nonetheless, as noted, compatibility with legal systems will be an issue in many states.

Given the relative newness of the Taser C2 and what many will perceive to be its high-tech nature, concerns may exist regarding the *rate of change* of technology. If it is believed that the technology is not stable or will change in the near future, purchase may be avoided or postponed.

EXHIBIT 8-3
UNCERTAINTY AND FEAR OF TASER C2

Area of Uncertainty and Fear	Impact	Description
☐ Product/Service Class Risk	★★★★	Some degree of apprehension may surround the general category of "weapon ownership."
☐ Product/Service Specific Risk	★★★★★	There may be many questions ranging from its effectiveness and reliability through to where one gets replacement cartridges.
☐ Transaction Risk	---	Not applicable in this context.
☐ Discomfort During Adoption	★★★	People may feel intimidated and naïve asking questions about weapons. This may lead to awkwardness and embarrassment.
☐ Misuse of Information	★	Unlikely to be a major issue. None of the information provided is particularly confidential (assuming no previous criminal record).
☐ Risk of Discontinuity	★★	Unless the person perceives that their life is in imminent danger, this will not be an issue.
☐ Start-Up Costs	★★★	Beyond financial costs, concern may exist regarding the time it will take to learn how to use the weapon effectively.
☐ Payback Period	★★	For most, the payback comes immediately in the form of perceived safety and reduced anxiety. Many would hope that the payback from actual use never occurs.
☐ Compatibility with Physical Systems	★★★★	Given small size, it is compatible with the physical capabilities of most individuals. Would also fit in a pocket or a purse.
☐ Compatibility with "Soft" Systems	★★★★★	Some may have an attitude opposed to weapon ownership. Moreover, in some jurisdictions, ownership is not legal.
☐ Rate of Change (Social, Legal, Economic, Political, Technical)	★★★★★	Concern may be present that the technology is still improving and/or laws are shifting. Either may reduce adoption.

Willingness to Take Risk	Impact	Description
Availability of Resources	★★★★★	Not a particularly expensive purchase, but would still be a reasonably large expenditure for most persons.
Ability to Reverse Decision	★★★★★	Following purchase, many retail outlets may permit refund within a certain period of time (e.g., 30 days).
Ability to "Play" on Multiple Occasions	★★★★★	Given the nature of personal safety, this is *not*, "something you do until you get it right."
Short-Term Thinking	★★★★★	In the short-term it may be easier to rationalize why one is safe rather than make the financial investment required.
Time Until Final Decision	★★	Although people may agree that they want a weapon, as the time to actually invest and take ownership approaches, levels of apprehension may increase.
Framing (Positive vs. Negative)	★★★	Focus must be placed on safety, security and peace of mind.
Emotions	★★★★	The purchase of a weapon is bound to evoke some emotions including fear and anxiety.
Volition and Level of Control	★★★★	The decision to own a weapon (unless under imminent attack) is going to be perceived as one the person will be responsible for. The resulting increased risk may be partially offset by product training (e.g., how to safely use and store it).

Willingness to Take Risk. There are a number of factors that may decrease the willingness of the individual to take on the risk of purchase. This is may be a very substantial *resource* outlay for the person. Second, this is not a purchase that is made on a frequent basis (i.e., it is not as though they can *"play again"* and get it right the next time if the weapon turns out not to be effective). Third, this decision to purchase such a product is not forced on them (i.e., *volition* is high), and if something goes wrong they will have nobody else to blame. Fourth, depending on the return policy of the store, it may or may not be possible to *reverse* the purchase decision.

Risk Reduction. A number of formal mechanisms may be considered to reduce risk. *Guarantees* often help to assure the individual that the company has the confidence to stand behind the product. This is not a daily-use product, though. If you are attacked and your weapon does not fire, a guarantee will be reasonably useless. As well, for many products, a *free trial* may be useful to reduce uncertainty. However, with a Taser C2, training cartridges are limited (typically only one will ship with the unit) and as a result there will be limited ability to practice once it is brought home. Consequently it may be difficult to dispel concerns regarding how to use the product properly in an attack situation or how effective the probes will be in sticking to the assailant.

The fact that virtually all police forces in the Western world now sport a Taser weapon (granted, an upscale model to the C2) should provide some level of *third-party endorsement* for the product. Direct endorsements from self-defense experts and testimonials from people who have successfully used the product to defend themselves would be of merit. Of particular value to the targeted demographic would be testimonials from younger women about the purchase process, the appropriateness of the weapon, and the overall feeling of security they now possess.

Efforts to enhance *product training* prior to purchase may be of benefit. Although a training DVD does come with the product, some may need additional information regarding the product's ease of use before the purchase is made. The belief that support is present following purchase to handle questions, supply replacement cartridges, and so forth will also be important to many.

Key challenges in *communication* will relate to understanding and believability. Specifically, potential customers need to see this product as a safe, legal (where possible), and highly effective defense against a potential assailant. Information regarding where the product may be purchased would also be of merit.

Law 4: Independent Influences Impact the Adoption of the Taser C2

Stories in the news of women being attacked motivate the perceived need for personal protection and other stories about women successfully defending themselves by using a weapon further bolster the cause. Interestingly, just watching the news predicts fear of crime, and this in turn results in a more positive attitude toward handgun ownership.[6] One would imagine that this would apply to Taser C2 ownership as well.

On the positive side, there would seem to be a movement toward a more pacifistic approach to dealing with conflict (stunning an attacker versus killing him). Further, occasional media reports will mention the successful use of a Taser in apprehending individuals. Police who speak on camera also seem to hold the weapon in high regard.

But the impact of the media is not all roses. Think about the number of people you see taken down with guns on popular television programming during a given evening. Now, think about the number of times you have seen a person taken down with a Taser. Alright, perhaps it is not as sexy to see a person incapacitated as electricity courses through the body. In light of the disproportionate imaging of guns versus Tasers, it would not be surprising to learn that people can imagine how the impact of a gun will yield devastating results on the assailant in a broad array of contexts much quicker than they can envision the impact of the Taser.

Although many public demonstrations with volunteers have tried to display how safe Tasers are, not all receiving the shock have fared well.[7] When an agitated Polish traveller died after being Tasered by police in the Vancouver International Airport in 2007, the news media were quick to pick up the story.[8] This was also true of a twenty-year-old man in Maryland[9] and a fifteen-year-old boy in Michigan[10] who also died after being Tasered by police. Many other stories have been reported, and even if the Taser is clear of being the causal factor in the death (the overwhelming majority of cases), perceptions may linger. Incidents like these have served as an impetus for Amnesty International to question how humane these devices are.[11] The net result of all of these stories may be a greatly reduced sense of the nonlethal status of the weapon in the minds of some potential adopters.

The Taser C2 is a defensive weapon. It is therefore anticipated that ownership would generally not be viewed by individuals and groups in the same light as possessing a large handgun might. Not all individuals will have the same reaction. For some, the ownership of a weapon that can inflict pain is going to be viewed as aggressive. A woman packing a Taser C2 may be perceived as less than genteel. However, especially if the ability to conceal the weapon is present, there is not a particular need for people around the individual to know about the ownership at all. That is, just as people might not approve of fluorescent green underwear with spikes, what is private is private.

Stories regarding accidental shootings, especially those involving children, are both reasonably common (each year, approximately eighteen thousand children under fifteen years of age in the United States are harmed) and particularly salient.[12] More generally, approximately one hundred thousand people are killed or injured by handguns each year in the United States.[13] While obviously not all women in their early twenties have children, many either do or are planning to. For some, "gun ownership" and "responsible parenting" are not congruous. Taser C2 ownership may be viewed as a reasonable way to provide defense without the same danger associated with accidental carnage.

Law 5: There are Biases in Search and Choice Regarding the Personal Taser

Many people may not even be aware there is a Taser specially designed for private citizens. If people do not know about the alternative, they will not *search* out information regarding its effectiveness, legality, and so on. For those who are aware of the Taser C2, most of the information is reasonably clear—you press a button and electrodes stream out, incapacitating the recipient. Material regarding the effectiveness of the weapon (e.g., percent of time a person is unsuccessfully incapacitated when a Taser C2 is fired) is not available. Although this weapon is carried in a number of stores, it is not as omnipresent as traditional handguns. As a consequence, the ability to actually conduct an in-person search may be limited for some individuals—leaving them to have to trust the information they can find on the Web.

The Taser C2 presents an interesting alternative to guns, and there may be a tendency to stress how remarkably different they are. One potential problem for some individuals could be that the Taser C2 may be regarded as "too different" and therefore not be included in the consideration set. Hence, while noting the nonlethal nature of a Taser C2 may be valuable, in general, stressing the similarities to guns (something people are familiar with) may help them to consider the Taser C2 as a reasonable option—not just some new technology. Another problem that may cause the automatic rejection of the Taser C2 may be perceptions regarding the efficacy of the unit—will it work as planned? We know guns can kill people, but it would seem we do not hear many stories of civilians successfully thwarting an attack by using a Taser C2.

Overall Synopsis Regarding the Adoption of A Taser C2

For many young women, perceived safety when walking alone at night may be an acute issue. There are a number of defense mechanisms available at a low cost; however, these will typically not deliver the same incapacitating effect that a Taser C2 is able to. As a result, if the fear of attack is sufficiently large, these methods will be perceived to be technically inadequate.

The Taser C2 presents an interesting option. It is a debilitating weapon with a low likelihood of lethal consequences, no bloodshed, and a decreased probability of litigation resulting from severely harming another (deliberately or not). The price tag also tends to be lower than most handguns. With virtually every police force in the Western world having adopted the weapon, indirect support for the unit is present. However, some uncertainty may also exist regarding the efficacy of the unit. Whereas people can go to a firing range and practice with their handgun, the same level of practice is not present for civilians with a Taser C2—for some, the first time it is needed it is the first time one finds out how well it works. The legality of the weapon is also an issue. Ownership by civilians is not permitted in all states or countries. Given the relative infancy of the weapon, it is plausible that regulations will continue to change. If one believes that the standards for Taser C2 ownership will become more restrictive, this may cause a person who is initially attracted to the Taser C2 to more seriously consider the more familiar option of a handgun or purchase nothing at all.

CHAPTER NINE

GEOTHERMAL HEAT PUMPS

In Chapter 5, consideration was given to the growing importance of energy self-sufficiency and the need to find solutions that more efficiently use the energy sources we have available. Some technologies look at ways of more effectively using existing carbon-based energy sources. This may take the form of enhanced extraction (such as the oil-sands of Alberta), better processing (as with clean coal) or improved end usage (through more efficient engines/combustion). In recent years, greater attention has been given to alternative energy production methods, including hydrogen, nuclear, wind, biomass (converting plant material into ethanol and/or electricity), solar, and geothermal.[1] We will focus on some of the issues involved in implementing the latter. Let us consider this from the perspective of a current homeowner using conventional technologies for purposes of heating (gas, oil, or electricity based) and who is considering retrofitting the existing system with a geothermal system. Factors influencing the value offer, stability, and uncertainty are presented in Exhibits 9-1 through 9-3, respectively.

Law 1: There Must Be Superior Value Associated with Geothermal Heat Pumps

On a *feature level*, the general nature of a closed-loop geothermal system is fairly straightforward: put a tube into the earth (or a body of water) and circulate an antifreeze solution (typically ethylene glycol) through the tube, with a heat exchange unit at the surface. This may be used to transfer energy into the earth (cooling in summer) and energy from the earth (heating in winter). Geothermal technology units require minimal maintenance, last for over two decades, and produce very low levels of CO_2 emissions compared to a conventional furnace or air-conditioning system.

Geothermal units are typically not a do-it-yourself project. Adoption of a geothermal system will require the presence of knowledgeable personnel. However, despite the minimalist nature of the technology, not all architects and contractors possess the expertise to design and build geothermal systems suited for a particular application (especially once the specifics of the ground conditions are taken into consideration).

On a *benefit level*, these systems may be used to effectively heat and cool buildings. Following installation, these systems are extremely easy to use, very reliable, and extremely durable. Variable costs are particularly low with a geothermal system, and payback normally occurs within about ten years. In addition to the general "badge of ownership," these systems are generally considered to have a much lower carbon footprint than gas, electric, or oil alternatives.

Geothermal heat pumps may be thought of as contributing on a number of *need levels*. Obviously the heating and cooling meet a number of physical needs. The low levels of maintenance along with the low variable costs of operation also enhance perceptions of preparedness, predictability, and self-sufficiency. Opting into such an eco-friendly alternative may also bolster the sense of acceptance and inclusion into the environmental fold. In addition to any personal sense of achievement, individuals will also likely feel that their small carbon footprint contributes to the earth specifically and society more broadly.

The requirements of the potential adopter will vary greatly with the *stage of the process*. Information and education will be especially important initially. In the pre-purchase phase individuals will be particularly concerned with efficacy (whether it will work), feasibility (whether installation possible given specific physical conditions present), and anticipated return on investment. Due to the up-front costs associated with a geothermal system, financing may assume a prominent role during the purchasing phase. Following installation, information regarding use and maintenance will be of value.

EXHIBIT 9-1
FORMS OF VALUE COMMUNICATION
(GEOTHERMAL HEAT PUMP)

"Feature-Specific" Value Communication (3 Cs)

Core (C1)

☐ **Products**
- Closed loop system of tubes placed in earth or water. Anti-freeze solution circulated through to transfer energy into the earth during summer and energy from earth in winter.
- Considered reliable and durable (lifetime of 2 decades) with minimal likelihood for environmental destruction.
- Very small CO_2 emissions relative to conventional units.

☐ **Price**
- Roughly double that of conventional systems.

☐ **Services**
- May be difficult to find, but services exist for design and installation.

☐ **Brand Image**
- Promoted as cost effective (long-term) and eco-friendly.

Conduit (C2)

☐ **Location**
- Not typically available through general home supply stores. Must be ordered through appropriate contractors or via the Web.

☐ **Personnel**
- Although system is reasonably straightforward conceptually, considerable expertise is required to design the system for the nature of the soil, geographic region and idiosyncrasies of the particular construction site (e.g., location of house and size of lot).
- Expertise will also be critical at providing information regarding the likely payback period of the unit.

Communication (C3)

☐ Currently, communication regarding these systems is present, but not really geared toward helping the average household have a solid understanding about the merits of switching (information tends to be either too basic or too technical).

☐ Much greater Web presence required in order to provide a wide range of information regarding geothermal heat pumps as well as a directory of qualified personnel who can design and install systems.

▼

"Benefit-Specific" Value Communication

☐ **Product/Service Specific Outcomes**
- May help to heat and cool buildings.

☐ **Cost Reduction**
- Variable costs are low. Payback in 10 years.

☐ **Safety and Reduced Negative Output**
- Systems are generally considered to be environmentally safe to install and run. Heating and cooling has small carbon footprint.

☐ **Ease of Use**
- Following installation, very low maintenance.

☐ **Enjoyment/Pride of Use**
- Very high pride of use.

☐ **Stability**
- Extremely reliable.

▼

"Need-Specific" Value Communication

☐ **Physical Needs**

☐ **Structure and Order**

☐ **Acceptance and Inclusion**

☐ **Preparedness/Versatility**

☐ **Predictability**

☐ **Self-Sufficiency**

☐ **Achievement**

☐ **Contribution and Compassion**

Law 2: Stability of Surrounding Existing Heating/Cooling Must Be Reduced

From a demand side, it is possible many people do not give any active consideration to their heating and cooling systems on a daily basis. While such systems have a physical presence, unless something goes wrong, there is not really a need to pay any attention to them. In such cases, *complacency* is bound to be high. Additionally, although many people are familiar with alternative energy sources, many may be underinformed with respect to the cost and environmental benefits of using geothermal energy in a residential application. Even for those who are aware, many have not yet been sufficiently troubled by experiences of energy price volatility or concerns regarding the long-term supply of resources such as natural gas. As such, low priority will be assigned to changing the type of heating/cooling system used.

Although geothermal heat pumps may integrate with existing ducting systems, the general prevalence and acceptance of existing systems (*breadth and depth of use*) among repair personnel, contractors, building product stores, and so forth will reduce the likelihood that the geothermal heat pump is brought forth as an alternative for consideration.

The good news is that traditional heating and cooling systems are reasonably self-contained and the *system removal constraints* are fairly straightforward from a mechanical perspective. However, mentally, removing these physically large units may be seem to be difficult and wasteful, especially if they still have considerable life left to them (for example, if the *time since last purchase* was less than a year ago). Both perceptually and financially, it may make more sense to wait until the existing unit breaks down or starts to cause considerable problems (when *technical adequacy* is particularly low and costs of operation/maintenance are high). Augmenting any perceived mechanical problems, the technical adequacy may also be impacted by rising energy prices (*costs of operation and maintenance*) as well as an increased concern regarding carbon emissions.

For those individuals wanting to do something more ecofriendly, a number of different options that involve the *adaptation* of their existing unit may be more palatable—certainly from a short-term financial perspective. High-efficiency furnaces may replace existing ones. Alternatively, it may be possible to find ways of being more environmentally friendly through buying a programmable thermostat and changing the settings to reduce energy consumption. In brief, there are ways of generating many of the benefits of a geothermal heat pump through less-radical modifications to the existing system.

It is likely that few will have any emotional *relationships* with their existing technology. Nonetheless, it is likely that people will have a great deal of familiarity with them—how they work, the costs of operation, their (general) reliability, and so forth. This "devil you know" relationship may foster the use of more conventional technologies.

Law 3: Uncertainty and Fear with Geothermal Heat Pumps Must Be Reduced

Areas of Uncertainty and Fear. Most would not have a great deal of perceived *product-class risk* associated with "heating and cooling"; however, there are a number of possible areas of *product-specific risk* associated with a heat pump alternative. For most individuals, the pre-existing level of knowledge about the installation and functioning of heat pumps is going to be fairly low and therefore cloaked in some degree of mystery. This is bound to lead to a number of questions. How easy is it to retrofit an existing house? How far down will we have to dig? What is the up-front cost and what will the monthly savings really be? Who do you call to install this type of system, and are they legitimate? Is there a rebate and, if so, when do I get it? Although there are many issues that may need to be covered off, this is likely not a category where people will be embarrassed to ask questions. As a result, any *discomfort during adoption* will be more cerebral than emotional.

EXHIBIT 9-2
STABILITY OF EXISTING SYSTEM (TRADITIONAL HEATING/COOLING)

Stability Factor	Impact	Description
☐ Momentum from Psychological Factors	★★★★★	Complacency with existing heating/cooling systems on the part of contractors and consumers will be extremely high.
☐ Depth and Breadth of System Use	★★★★★	Geothermal heat pump systems may integrate with existing ducting in retrofit situations. Nonetheless, the general prevalence/acceptance of existing systems may constrain growth.
☐ System Removal Constraints	★★★★	For new installations this is not an issue. For retrofit contexts there will be costs to removing existing gas/oil/electrical units. Existing ducting may remain though. Removal costs may be more mental (i.e., feeling bad about removing a system that works).
☐ Constraints Imposed by Independent Influences	★★	Local government regulations may require obtaining a permit prior to installation.
☐ Portability of Assets	★	Following installation, the use of the system is virtually identical to conventional systems.
☐ Time Since Last Purchase	★	The likelihood of retrofitting a system will be inversely related to the age of the conventional system. This is not an issue with new installations.
☐ Technical Adequacy of Existing System	★★★★★	To the extent that the existing system is working well, still has considerable life expectancy and is not costing too much to operate/maintain, it will be harder to convince an individual to retrofit.
☐ Adaptability of Existing Alternative	★★★★★	If the key goal is cost reduction and a reduction in carbon emissions, some individuals may be able to achieve this through the installation of a high efficiency furnace and extra household insulation.
☐ Affinity Programs and Volume Discounts	---	Not applicable in this context.
☐ Relationships	★★★★★	While familiarity with existing technology may have a strong influence, there is not likely to be a strong "relationship" with conventional technology or any particular manufacturer thereof.

Risk of discontinuity may be particularly high. When heating or cooling systems go awry, decisions usually have to be made quickly. Furnaces and air conditioners tend to break down when they are in use (when it is very cold or very hot outside). In northern climates, it would take quite a committed individual, and one with thick clothing, to call a company specializing in geothermal heat pumps when his or her furnace dies in January. Fixing the current system could be accomplished in hours. Putting in a geothermal heating system could take weeks, depending on the expertise and installation capability available. Clearly, the *start-up costs* associated with retrofitting an existing system are going to be greater in the short-term than just living with the existing technology, and although the financial *payback period* is expected to be about ten years, this may be longer than most people are willing to commit to. Even here, this is not a government-backed investment certificate with a fixed rate of return, and there is no guarantee regarding the payback. It may be eight years. It may be fifteen years. It may never occur.

Although the geothermal technologies will work with most existing Heating, Ventilation and Air Conditioning (HVAC) systems, there still may be some physical impediments to implementation due to *compatibility with physical "hard" systems*. Some geographical areas are more suited for geothermal heating and cooling, either by virtue of the climate (a moderate climate is best), the nature of the soil (drilling into bedrock is more difficult than clay), and the amount of space available (systems can be drilled vertically, thereby reducing space requirements, but this will cost more to install).

Energy prices seem to ebb and flow in terms of both their rates, as well as the interest they generate in the media. Nonetheless, most would agree though that the general trend is upward. The same would be true regarding societal support regarding environmentally responsible actions; in general, our respect for such behaviors is increasing. The perceived risk of heat pump adoption would be expected to be lower for individuals who are sensitive to these dynamics.

Willingness to Take Risk. The perceived risk may be exacerbated by a number of factors that may increase the risk aversion of the individual. A geothermal heat pump will require a significant financial outlay—certainly enough to tax the *availability of resources* for most individuals—and if, for some reason, something does not go well with the system, the *ability to reverse the decision* will be low. This process involves digging holes and using materials. Perhaps some elements could be reclaimed; however, the ability to walk back to the provider, hand them your geothermal heat pump equipment, and get all of your money back is not tenable. This is a game that one *"plays" on a very infrequent basis*, and one needs to get it right the first time. This, combined with the typical timing when such decisions have to be made (perhaps in the middle of winter), is bound to lead to *short-term thinking*. Any commitment to a geothermal heat pump, by virtue of the technology, is long-term in nature. To the extent that a longer-term perspective may be maintained and the *frame* is shifted to what is being gained rather than given up, the willingness to take risks will be enhanced.

As with blood donation and a vegan lifestyle, choices regarding the selection of a heating and cooling system are not mandated by law. People will choose what they will choose (they have complete *volition* over the decision). Accordingly, they will also be the ones responsible for anything that goes wrong. Education about the system in general and what they can do to increase its effectiveness will hopefully provide the person with a sense of control and thereby reduce perceived risk.

EXHIBIT 9-3

UNCERTAINTY AND FEAR OF GEOTHERMAL HEAT PUMPS

Area of Uncertainty and Fear	Impact	Description
☐ Product/Service Class Risk	★★★	Product class risk (heating and cooling) will be low to moderate.
☐ Product/Service Specific Risk	★★★★★	There may be an extremely high level of perceived risk surrounding the use of a geothermal heat pump, ranging from issues of installation (individuals installing the system and the process) to effectiveness (i.e., will it work as well as anticipated).
☐ Transaction Risk	★	While people may not be certain about what they are getting, transaction risk will depend on the reputation of the vendor.
☐ Discomfort During Adoption	★	Although people will have questions, they will not feel awkward or embarrassed asking them or getting more information.
☐ Misuse of Information	★	Not likely a concern. No sensitive information is shared.
☐ Risk of Discontinuity	★★	For retrofits, there may be concerns that the heating/cooling will not be available for some time. This concern may depend on the time of the year (for example, in particularly hot or cold periods).
☐ Start-Up Costs	★★★★	Concerns will be present regarding the initial fixed costs, however costs (mental and financial) after that will be minimal.
☐ Payback Period	★★	This will be a critical concern for many. While part may be from being "eco-friendly" many will want financial payback, especially relative to conventional technologies.
☐ Compatibility with Physical Systems	★★★★★	Key issues surround compatibility with existing HVAC system as well as geographic/geological characteristics of area.
☐ Compatibility with "Soft" Systems	★★★★★	Being eco-friendly is extremely compatible with social views, but practice of design/installation may be foreign to some.
☐ Rate of Change (Social, Legal, Economic, Political, Technical)	★	Although concern regarding technology should not be an issue, many will see it as "new" and have concerns about adoption. Rate of change for conventional energy costs may also have an impact.

Willingness to Take Risk	Impact	Description
☐ Availability of Resources	★★★★★	Cost of system and installation will be looked at as a considerable financial investment. Resources will be an issue for many.
☐ Ability to Reverse Decision	★★★★★	While possible, it is not trivial to revert back to conventional.
☐ Ability to "Play" on Multiple Occasions	★★★★★	This is typically a one-shot, "get it right the first time," application.
☐ Short-Term Thinking	★★★★★	In the short-term it will be faster and cheaper to use a conventional system. Benefits of geothermal require a long-term perspective.
☐ Time Until Final Decision	★★	While geothermal systems may be considered initially, perceived risk is likely to increase as time of final choice/installation draws near.
☐ Framing (Positive vs. Negative)	★★★★★	Willingness increases if the focus is on what is being gained rather than what is being given up.
☐ Emotion	★★★★★	This is not likely to be a very emotional decision.
☐ Volition and Level of Control	★★★★★	This decision is voluntary and therefore will be perceived as more risky. Education regarding the technology and optimal installation/use practices will provide some degree of control.

Risk Reduction. In addition to issues regarding communication, a number of formal methods may be employed to reduce risk. Although a full money-back guarantee may not be possible, *guarantees* on the equipment and installation would be. More than this, it might also be possible to provide product support, training, and annual maintenance either for free or at a guaranteed low rate. These steps will help to reduce the uncertainty regarding future financial outlays. Perceived risk may also be mitigated by showing a customer homes and units that are similar to his or hers (something similar to a *free trial*), thereby allowing individuals to actually experience the climate afforded by a heat pump. Documentation regarding energy savings for specific properties, not just vague generalities, will also be of value.

Manufacturers and contractors who are able to provide certification by a recognized third party (e.g., that the contractor is credentialed to install this type of system and is licensed by the state) will also reduce concerns. Testimonials for geothermal heat pumps would also help to reduce the fear that the person is acquiring something that is untested or unstable. Among possibilities, such endorsements may come from government departments, such as the Department of Energy or Environmental Protection Agency, engineering associations, consumer groups, or construction associations.

Law 4: Independent Influences Impact the Choice of Geothermal Heat Pumps

Independent influences are almost unanimously aligned in favor of geothermal heat pumps. Where shall we begin? In the United States, rebates on geothermal installations (30 percent of the cost) were introduced by the Obama administration in 2009. Other nations, such as Canada, have similar programs. This can substantially cut down the burden associated with the initial financial and mental costs and create some degree of impetus to act before any such programs are removed. Some other contributing factors would be:

- The manufacturing and installation of this equipment bolsters the number of "green" jobs. It also serves to foster employment and the economy "at home."[2]

- The overall level of education is increasing in the United States, facilitating a progressive and positive approach to energy consumption and alternative fuels.

- Social trends, including a more socially conscious populous; the entrance of the ecofriendly Generation Y into the housing market; and the more general impact of the environmental movement all work in favor of geothermal energy. This is augmented by a desire to foster domestic energy production.

- Energy prices seem to be in a constant state of flux, but the trend is inevitably upward.

- Regular media coverage regarding all of these issues serves to positively reinforce the geothermal heat pump option.

On the downside, we tend to move homes on a fairly regular basis (popular wisdom suggests every five to seven years), which, for the typical person, may produce a concern he or she will not recoup his or her initial investment.

Law 5: There are Biases in Search and Choice Regarding Geothermal Heat Pumps

Ignorance and apathy may result in some individuals never engaging in the *search process*. For those who do see a need to engage in the search process, a thirst for information will only be partially quenched. There is an ample amount of information regarding geothermal heat pumps, but this information tends to be either too basic or too technical. Finding concrete information regarding the cost of equipment and installation, as well as specific cost savings, can be difficult to pin down—perhaps because of idiosyncrasies associated with each particular installation. For example, the depth and ground material will determine the cost of drilling/excavation; the heat transfer associated with the soil will impact the amount of tubing needed; and, there may be issues dealing with other utilities already buried underground. For most people this is a major investment, and not being able to get a solid grasp of the facts can be disconcerting.

When things do get confusing for the customer, there may be a tendency to fall back on conventional technology such as gas, oil or electricity. It might not be perfect, but there is a high degree of familiarity with it, and it has a record of demonstrated success. Hence, while it will be important to communicate the core benefits in a very lucid manner, it will also be important to stress the benefits of the heat pump in a manner easily related to current knowledge and underscore how it integrates nicely with other existing aspects of the infrastructure, including ducting and thermostats.

There can be an inclination for some to become very excited about a new technology and present it as something particularly unique. Recall that radically different options are often left out of the *consideration set*. Adoption will be greater if it is perceived to be "more of the same" but just much better.

For most who include the geothermal heat pump in the consideration set, the *final decision* will probably involve a great deal of mental effort, with energy cost savings and environmental benefits traded off against the higher up-front cost and the extra burden involved during installation. Even though the price tag is partially offset by government rebates, for some, the initial cost may seem just too high. Consequently, either the lack of sufficient financial resources in hand and/or a perception they will not recoup the investment if they sell in the next couple years may result in this option being rejected very quickly. Financing options and solid information regarding cost savings may ameliorate this issue somewhat.

Overall Synopsis Regarding Geothermal Heat Pumps

Geothermal heat pumps often represent a green and effective mechanism for heating and cooling requirements in both residential and commercial applications. Indeed, this option would seem to be aligned with every independent influence available (e.g., government support, social encouragements, environmental benefits resulting from a reduced carbon footprint, and a decreased long-term cost of energy that reduces the dependence on other nations for energy). Geothermal systems also benefit from being compatible with existing HVAC systems and also tend to have a longer lifetime than conventional units. Although up-front costs are higher (some of this which may be offset by government grants and rebates), geothermal energy is typically cheaper in the long term, with a payoff period of approximately a decade.

Despite all of these positive features, uncertainty regarding this technology may be substantial. Some of the key issues would include technical details regarding how the system works; finding contractors with sufficient expertise; compatibility with specific soil characteristics; and concerns regarding unforeseen costs and the true payback period—there is a certain amount of faith and a number of assumptions involved in the calculation of dollar savings.

Although this technology has had demonstrated success in retrofit contexts, efforts might be more successfully targeted toward new construction. Those with existing systems (e.g., natural gas) may take issue with having to replace what seems to be a perfectly well-functioning system, even if the cost of their current energy input is a little higher than they would like on a monthly basis. The issue here actually becomes more complex. When the existing system does break down, it usually does so at a time of the year when it is in greatest use, and the knee-jerk reaction of most will be to get a quick fix rather than opt for a complete retrofit. Removing an existing system is also bound to bring with it a greater degree of mess and disruption.

CHAPTER TEN

NURSE PRACTITIONER CLINICS

One could argue that the existing health care system is challenged on a number of fronts. Assuming the goal of a nation's health care delivery is to adequately treat its populace, the system in the United States is faltering, with U.S. Census figures in 2006 suggesting forty-seven million people did not have health insurance.[1] This level was greatest for households with lower incomes (24.5 percent for those under $25,000 versus 7.8 percent for those over $75,000).[2] While this number may decline under the healthcare policies initiated by the Obama administration[3], issues of affordability will remain. Specifically, there are a number of areas where the cost and maintenance of the health care system is putting demands on society that are not be tenable going forward. The per capita expenditure on health care has been progressively increasing: $1,100 (1980), $2,818 (1990), $4,789 (2000), $8,086 (2009).[4]

Medicare costs are also projected to increase consistently for the foreseeable future, going from 3.2 percent of the GDP in 2008 to approximately 7.3 percent in 2035.[5] Despite these costs, the quality of health care afforded to all individuals has been criticized, and problems persist with respect to patient safety.[6] The already hefty burden on the system will become even greater as the boomers move into their health-care-intensive phase of life. In brief, it would appear the current system is not sustainable if left alone. While some problems may be particularly acute in the United States, other countries face similar problems.[7]

Many in the United States have pointed to the financial burden imposed by the current health care industry and the importance of universal health care. One mechanism advanced to address this issue is the Nurse Practitioner (NP). Originally created in 1965 in order to combat what people perceived to be a looming shortage of physicians, this role has expanded considerably in recent years to serve in a more active capacity.

The role of the NP has been effectively used in many primary care settings, including initial treatment of common paediatric and geri-atric ailments, as well as dealing with some emergency room cases. They have also been used to provide greater access to health care in rural communities and in some urban areas where the availability of primary care physicians is lower. More recently, freestanding clinics in pharmacies have also been set up to provide a convenient alternative to individuals suffering from reasonably common illnesses that are easy to diagnose and easy to treat, such as a throat or urinary tract infec-tion. Given the potential to reduce wait times for emergency rooms and physicians, some might think such changes would be traveling full steam ahead.

We will be examining this from the perspective of a person who lives in reasonable proximity to one of these pharmacy clinics. Suppose that either this person or another family member has become ill and is considering a number of competing treatment options. These would include the pharmacy clinic (run by an NP), an urgent care facility, or his or her regular family physician. Factors influencing the value offer, stability, and uncertainty are presented in Exhibits 10-1 through 10-3, respectively.

Law 1: There Must be Superior Value Associated with Nurse Practitioners

On a *feature level*, the value offering offered by NPs in pharmacy clinics may be thought of in terms of products offered (vaccines), a lower cost to the health care system for each visit (relative to a primary care physician), services (vaccinations and diagnosis of common ailments), and brand image (promoted as convenient, fast, and competent). Ideally, these clinics are within close physical proximity to an individual, and access to see an NP is often immediate. From my experience, nurse practitioners are knowledgeable, empathetic, and efficient. At present, communication regarding the services offered by NPs within pharmacy settings has been rather passive— an assertive campaign declaring their presence and their value, to the best of my knowledge, has not yet been launched.

On a *benefit level*, the features offered above provide enhanced ease of access (proximity and speed) to a professional who is able to alleviate an ailment. Depending on the individual's health care insurance, this may also be less expensive than a conventional primary care physician or visit to an urgent care facility.

On the *need level*, this enhanced access meets physical needs; enhances the optimal health and longevity of the individual; provides a saving of time; and increases the choices available and thereby the versatility of how a person may deal with such a situation. Depending on whether the individual has children, the provision of this health care option may be perceived as promoting the strength of the family (parents can provide fast care for their children), and this may increase the person's sense of power over health-related situations that may arise.

EXHIBIT 10-1
FORMS OF VALUE COMMUNICATION
(NURSE PRACTIONERS)

"Feature-Specific" Value Communication (The 3 Cs)

Core (C1)

- ☐ **Products (Not Applicable)**
  - Products could include vaccines or sample medications.
- ☐ **Price**
  - Cost of visit may be lower to the health-care system than with a physician.
- ☐ **Services**
  - May provide vaccinations, as well as diagnosis and treatment for variety of common ailments (e.g., sore throat and urinary tract infections).
  - Patients often able to be seen immediately (without appointment or waiting time).
  - Depending on the state, may or may not be able to provide reference to specialist.
- ☐ **Brand Image**
  - Promoted as convenient, fast and competent.

Conduit (C2)

- ☐ **Location**
  - Locations are conveniently placed within local pharmacies.
  - Environment limits privacy to some extent, but examination rooms have similar feel to facilities within a physician's office.
- ☐ **Personnel**
  - Personnel form the critical component of the enterprise. Ideally, these individuals are looked at as knowledgeable, empathetic, quick, honest, and solid communicators.

Communication (C3)

- ☐ At present, communications regarding nurse practitioners in general, and mini-clinics in particular, is somewhat fragmented. In part, this is due to differences among states (legislation and insurance) regarding the role that nurse practitioners are allowed to play in the system.

▼

"Benefit-Specific" Value Communication

- ☐ **Product/Service Specific Outcomes**
  - Ability to receive advice and treatment regarding ailment.
- ☐ **Cost Reduction**
  - Reduced cost to healthcare system.
- ☐ **Ease of Use**
  - The primary benefit of nurse practitioners within pharmacies is the convenience and speed of access.

▼

"Need-Specific" Value Communication

- ☐ **Physical Needs**
- ☐ **Optimal Health and Longevity**
- ☐ **Provision of Time and Efficiency**
- ☐ **Preparedness/Versatility**
- ☐ **Availability of Choice**
- ☐ **Increased Strength of Family**
- ☐ **Power and Efficacy**

Law 2: Stability Surrounding Current Primary Care Options Must be Reduced

Complacency with an existing primary care provider may be present. While most people no doubt recognize that they could switch physicians, many would not have thought of the option of seeing an NP instead. Especially in cases where people have had extensive contact with a physician for multiple purposes (*depth and breadth of use*), the thought of using another provider may be particularly limited. This would be especially true if they felt that any primary care provider needed to have access to their previous medical records, in which case *portability of assets* from the existing system would be an issue. On the positive side, seeing an NP does not preclude one from seeing one's primary care physician as well (the existing system does not need to be terminated, so there are no *system removal constraints*).

It has been noted on a number of occasions that one of the primary benefits of the pharmacy clinic is quick treatment for common ailments. To the extent that the individual's traditional provider is able to open up an appointment quickly, or the insurance provider is willing to cover access to an urgent care/emergency physician who can see the person promptly (there is high *adaptability of the existing system*), the perceived benefit of the pharmacy clinic may be diminished. Of course, one of the chief determinants for many people will be the *relationship* (if any) in place between the individual and his or her physician. Is this someone the individual greatly respects and trusts, or is the NP perceived as being equal or above on these values?

EXHIBIT 10-2
STABILITY OF EXISTING SYSTEM
(PRIMARY CARE PHYSICIAN)

Stability Factor	Impact	Description
☐ Momentum from Psychological Factors	★★★★★	Complacency with existing primary care provider will likely be present.
☐ Depth and Breadth of System Use	★★★	For those with multiple family members, there may be many individuals all seeing the same primary care provider.
☐ System Removal Constraints	----	Not applicable in this context. Seeing a nurse practitioner in a pharmacy setting does not preclude seeing one's regular physician.
☐ Constraints Imposed by Independent Influences	★★★★	There may be some perceived constraints placed on the individual regarding whether health insurance will cover the visit.
☐ Portability of Assets	★★★	People may be hesitant to visit the pharmacy clinic because the NP does not have access to previous health records.
☐ Time Since Last Purchase	---	Not applicable in this context. With the exception of annual check-ups (not covered by nurses in pharmacy clinics), people see a provider on an "as needed" basis.
☐ Technical Adequacy of Existing System	★★★★★	If an individual's existing provider is perceived to be accessible, competent, and covered by their health care system, there will be little perceived need to try something different.
☐ Adaptability of Existing Alternative	★★★★★	To the extent that the current primary care provider can open up an appointment or current health insurance provides access to an urgent care location, the advantage of the pharmacy clinic may be reduced.
☐ Affinity Programs and Volume Discounts	---	Not applicable in this context.
☐ Relationships	★★★★★	Some individuals have a strong relationship with their health care insurer and want to receive coverage. If the pharmacy clinic is not covered by the insurer then the person will likely not use its services unless the situation is very urgent. Moreover though, many people have a strong relationship with their primary care physician. While most of this would stem from trust and competence, many may also have a feeling that the physician truly cares about them.

Law 3: Uncertainty and Fear Surrounding Nurse Practitioners Must be Reduced

Areas of Uncertainty and Fear. Anything medical related is bound to carry some degree of *service-class risk*. A host of *service-specific* questions may also open up as they pertain to NPs in pharmacy clinics. Where are they located? Exactly what are they able to diagnose and treat? Can they write prescriptions? What happens if they do not know what I have—do they refer me somewhere or am I back at square one? Exactly what level of training do they have? What if I have something severe and they misdiagnose me? Will my insurance cover this visit? What do they offer me that my physician does not?

Although one would anticipate low *transaction risk* (will they take my money and not see me?) and low *discomfort during adoption* (awkwardness or feelings of embarrassment), there may be concerns regarding *misuse of information*. After all, this is medical information. To the extent that people feel as though they will need to make additional phone calls to their insurance provider or give a lot of background information to the NP just to get the process going, *start-up costs* will be perceived to be higher.

Unfortunately, if the goal is to make NPs a vital part of primary care provision, in addition to possible noncoverage by insurance policies, there are a number of other issues that exist with respect to *compatibility with existing systems*. Although these vary considerably depending on the state in question, some of the more common issues faced include "soft" (nonphysical) systems, such as regulations preventing/limiting prescribing; decreased autonomy in areas where a supervising physician is still required; difficulties being credentialed by insurers as primary care providers;[8] a lack of clarity among physicians, other health care professionals such as pharmacists or physiotherapists, insurers, and even nurses as to what role the NP is supposed to play;[9] and a constrained ability to refer patients to a secondary care provider like a dermatologist or other specialist. In effect, where these factors are present, the ability of the NP to effectively and efficiently impact the system is reduced. Beyond system regulations, a more general compatibility issue may also be present, with many people wanting to see a "doctor." As such, if an NP is not a physician, some people may not perceive him or her as being aligned with the "way they do things."

EXHIBIT 10-3
UNCERTAINTY AND FEAR OF NURSE PRACTITIONERS

Area of Uncertainty and Fear	Impact	Description
☐ Product/Service Class Risk	★★★	For many, health care issues, in general, may carry some risk.
☐ Product/Service Specific Risk	★★★★★	There may be many areas where there will be high perceived risk regarding the nurse practitioner in a pharmacy clinic. Questions may range from competence and qualifications through to whether this is covered by insurance.
☐ Transaction Risk	---	Not likely a concern. People will be treated once they have paid.
☐ Discomfort During Adoption	★	Very low embarrassment or awkwardness in using NP.
☐ Misuse of Information	★★	Health information is, by nature, often a very sensitive issue. Concern may be present regarding access/security of information.
☐ Risk of Discontinuity	---	Not applicable in this context. Seeing a nurse practitioner will not result in any discontinuity of coverage elsewhere.
☐ Start-Up Costs	★★	Concern may be present regarding the time it may take to start up a new file, provide background information and be sufficiently comfortable with how this system works.
☐ Payback Period	★★	The key payback is health. People will expect the treatment to payback very shortly after the visit.
☐ Compatibility with Physical Systems	★★★★★	Questions will emerge as to whether this is compatible with existing insurance and if it is a convenient distance from home.
☐ Compatibility with "Soft" Systems	★★★★★	For many, this may not be compatible with "how they do things" – many people will want to see a "real doctor."
☐ Rate of Change (Social, Legal, Economic, Political, Technical)	---	Not applicable in this context. The decision to see an NP is likely independent of the rate of change of these factors.

Willingness to Take Risk	Impact	Description
☐ Availability of Resources	★★★★★	Availability of resources may be an issue for many, depending on coverage of service by current insurer.
☐ Inability to Reverse Decision	★	If diagnosis is not perceived to be adequate/proper, it is not necessary to follow through with recommendations.
☐ Inability to "Play" on Multiple Occasions	★	If one is not pleased with this provider it is possible to see either another clinic or a primary care physician.
☐ Short-Term Thinking	★★★★	Short-term thinking may benefit the pharmacy clinic. People typically want treatment as soon as possible and if it is not available immediately through conventional sources they may opt for the nurse practitioner.
☐ Time Until Final Decision	★★	Initial decisions to visit a clinic (given rapid onset of some illnesses) are likely not made well in advance of the appointment.
☐ Framing (Positive vs. Negative)	★★★	Willingness will be increased if the focus is on speed and quality of health care provided, rather than limited services offered.
☐ Emotion	★	This is not likely to be a very emotional decision.
☐ Volition and Level of Control	★★★★★	The decision is completely the individual's. Hence they will be responsible for the quality of treatment. This will decrease willingness to take risk if there are perceived issues about quality.

Willingness to Take Risk. For many people with monthly budget concerns, *availability of resources* will be an issue, especially if they believe that it would be less expensive to go elsewhere (for example, a physician covered by their health insurance). However, there are a number of factors working in the favor of pharmacy clinics as they pertain to the willingness of individuals to take risk. First, going to an NP does not mean that you have to take their advice (there is the *ability to reverse the decision*) or that you cannot also go and see your regular provider (you are still able to *"play" on multiple occasions* until you are happy with the advice provided). *Short-term thinking* may actually work to the benefit of the pharmacy clinic, as people typically want treatment as soon as possible, and if people are not able to see their regular provider, they may opt for the highly accessible NP option. In fact, depending on the ailment and the urgency, people may feel that they have no choice but to see someone who can help them or a family member immediately (they have no perceived *volition* in this situation).

Risk Reduction. From a *communication* perspective, awareness (we are here), understanding (this is what we do), and believing (we do it well) would be important. The believing portion would be supported nicely via *third-party endorsement* from credible sources. These might include state agencies, organizations within the medical community, or individuals (for example, testimonials from people regarding the quality of care). Assurances regarding *certification*, such as their licence to practice, would also enhance credibility.

Law 4: Independent Influences Impact the Choice of Nurse Practitioners

A number of independent influences may impact the acceptance of NPs. Government policies and legislation formalizing and expanding the role of the NP will be critical to a more pervasive acceptance within the medical community. Similarly, collaboration with other stakeholders, such as federal and state regulatory bodies, pharmacists, and the American Medical Association will also be imperative in solidifying their role, clarifying misconceptions regarding what duties they are/are not appropriate for, and providing input regarding the required training NPs must undergo in order to mesh well with the expectations of others.

Public acceptance of NPs is likely fostered by what seem to be daily doom and gloom reports regarding the cost of health care and the need for new alternatives. Further, stories in the popular press regarding the role of NPs and the presence of convenient care clinics serve not only to expand awareness, but also to provide legitimacy, as the journalist indirectly provides a level of endorsement. Over time, groups and significant individuals will also have a significant impact from an informational perspective—positive word of mouth will be important.

Law 5: There are Biases in Search and Choice Regarding Nurse Practitioners

For many potential patients, the existing system is not broken—they get sick, they phone their doctor, they get a prescription, they take their medication, and life is eventually made right. Their level of motivation to search for information regarding NPs is going to be very low. Given that this constraint exists, at least from the patient's perspective, the NP profession cannot afford to be confusing in the information imparted to the community. Material regarding NPs is available online; however, it tends to be fragmented, with different information and resources provided depending on the country and state of practice. Further, when one searches on the Web for "nurse practitioner" and a specific state, the information that tends to come up pertains to jobs and training for NPs—not why the public should seek them out.

If one expands the search to the national level, one finds the American Academy of Nurse Practitioners and the American College of Nurse

Practitioners. These Web sites do contain some material regarding what NPs do and information that would be important to a potential patient, but if the goal is to familiarize the public with the role of the NP, it is important not to bury this material among a plethora of information geared to current and potential NPs (certification, conferences, events and so on). If this material is not clear, the net effect of a search by the potential patient may be confusion rather than elucidation. For patients with decent insurance, in cases where a choice exists between seeing a physician or a nurse practitioner such as those in the convenient care clinics, the benefit of quick access will likely be overwhelmed by the uncertainty associated with the service.

Overall Synopsis Regarding the Use of Nurse Practitioners

In summary, the NP profession does not exist as an island. It is part of a larger integrated, complex, formal, and bureaucratic system that has been established over a long period of time. Changing this system will hinge on ensuring government support and getting other powerful interests onside (e.g., insurance providers and physicians). The development of strong educational programs offered via recognized postsecondary institutions is also key to providing a requisite supply of qualified practitioners and enhancing the profession's reputation. All of these efforts need to be coupled with a coherent and consistent message to the public to help them understand the beneficial and unique role NPs may play, especially in primary care situations such as a pharmacy clinic. If people are either not aware of what role NPs play or practitioners are perceived to be an inferior form of physician, progress will be limited. It would seem that there is a great deal of value that NPs can offer (the value proposition is already there); however, issues of both stability and uncertainty are particularly high.

CHAPTER ELEVEN

ADOPTION OF THE METRIC SYSTEM IN THE UNITED STATES

The following editorial appeared in the *New York Times* on May 14, 1882.

Politicians are constantly professing respect for the judgment of the people and a judgment for their wishes. They acknowledge their support on the support of public opinion, and yet they are constantly misinterpreting popular sentiment and engaging in efforts to carry their ends by methods that awaken distrust instead of inspiring confidence. They either underestimate the general intelligence or else they do not have faith in the soundness and stability of the popular judgment, which they profess to have, for, instead of relying on the people and seeking to obey only their behests, they are continually endeavouring to bring the mass of voters to their support by manipulation and management.[1]

The author of this piece was perhaps a little cynical, suggesting that politicians recognize they need the support of the people but, once elected, implement plans of their own and coax individuals into accepting them through manipulation and management. Whether initially well meaning or not, there are a host of government policies and programs that have not curried favor with a large number of people.

Margaret Thatcher came close to creating a rebellion when she introduced the poll tax in England in 1989. This tax was intended to raise funds for public services. In an effort to be fair, it seemed reasonable that the more people a household had, the more services they would use and therefore the more they should pay. Unfortunately, the optics were not good. A small home with nine people crammed into every nook and cranny would pay more than a couple living on a palatial estate with seventeen Rolls Royces. A similar tax had also failed miserably in Britain in the 1700s—Thatcher apparently thought the uproar had sufficiently died down after a couple of centuries. She was wrong.

The Canadian government has made its share of mistakes. In the opening chapter we discussed the gun control registry. Of a much briefer nature, they also, on a Friday, floated the idea of subsidizing professional hockey teams, and by Monday the idea was dismissed as a misinterpretation of what the government was suggesting. Apparently the public did not think their tax dollars should be paying for nineteen-year-olds to make millions for smacking a hard rubber object on a frozen surface with a wooden stick.

The Vietnam War, stem cell research, the location of a new research facility, social programs, involvement in the private sector, and so forth: it is wishful to think a government can actually appease all of the people, even if they legitimately want to represent the interests of their constituents. I am close to certain that if a given administration announced they had solved poverty issues, cured cancer, and cut income taxes to zero, there would be someone who would oppose this on the basis of principle and declare from his talk-show bully pulpit, "I strongly believe government should not meddle in the affairs of poverty and illness."

We conclude this section of applications with an examination of the metric system in the United States. Created by France in 1795, the system was intended to replace a hodgepodge of measurement systems used throughout many nations. In the United States, the need for common units of measurement was recognized in the Constitution, providing Congress with the power to "fix the standards of weights and measures."[2] Although

President George Washington relayed information regarding the metric system to Congress in 1795, it was not adopted.[3] Since this time, the metric system has gone through cycles of support and near compulsory adoption on many occasions.[4]

The Metric Act of 1866 formally made the metric system in the United States lawful, albeit optional. In 1975, Congress passed the Metric Conversion Act, designating "the metric system of measurement as the preferred system of weights and measures for United States trade and commerce."[5] Federal agencies were to have adopted metric in their use of "procurements, grants, and other business-related activities" by 1992 unless it was impractical or inefficient.[6] The Metric Conversion Act of 1975 was amended by the Omnibus Trade and Competitiveness Act of 1988 (to clarify reporting of implementation) and the Savings in Construction Act of 1996 (this further encouraged the supply of materials in metric units, but also made it clear the provision of metric materials should not increase the cost of a project).

Today road signs are still in miles, commercial scales are in pounds, blueprints are in feet, gas and milk are in gallons, and the National Weather Service displays temperatures in Fahrenheit and precipitation in inches. The Food and Drug Administration requires food be labelled according to metric units, but also requires the U.S. Customary System units. The present approach is designed to gradually introduce the system and minimize costs. This is understandable, but it is questionable how long this somewhat passive approach will take until there is a crossover and metric becomes the mainstay, especially in light of the fact that citizens of other countries that have had the metric system forced upon them (e.g., Canada, Ireland, and England) still use "antiquated measures" in common parlance. For example, in Canada, close to four decades after metric was imposed, based on personal observation, men five foot three and over round up their height to six feet (few could tell you how many centimeters they are). Likewise, people still gauge their weight in pounds, and a shot of liquor is still one ounce.

In the first chapter of the book, we made reference to the quote, "If you make a better mousetrap, the world will beat a path to your door." In so many ways, the metric system is that better mousetrap. In 1900, an editorial in the *Journal of the American Medical Association* noted that within the medical community many were already using the metric system, and they strongly supported legislation to convert to its use.[7] Most people who contrast the U.S. Customary System and the metric system come to the same conclusion. The metric system, based on units of ten, is easy to learn and apply. A system based on pounds, feet, quarts, pecks, bushels, and so on is not. The noted science-fiction writer Isaac Asimov levelled a number of criticisms against the U.S. Customary System, one of which was that it wasted too much time for American schoolchildren, learning arcane units when they could be acquiring knowledge about something more useful. He further quipped that it gave them one more reason to hate school.[8]

So, let us take this one step further and consider a hypothetical government policy that would seek to require the use of the metric system in all sectors of society and seek to curtail the use of the U.S. Customary System in any government or commercial capacity (suppose only metric would be used within five years of being approved on the federal level). Factors influencing the value offer, stability, and uncertainty are presented in Exhibits 11-1 through 11-3 respectively.

Law 1: There Must be Superior Value Associated with the Metric System

From a *feature* perspective, the metric system may be thought of as a service that provides a simplified measurement system that is compatible with world standards. It would be present in all locations where measurement units are required (gas pumps, manuals, packaged goods, road signs, and so on). The system would ultimately be administered by government personnel at all levels who would be responsible for the promotion, education, and enforcement of standards. Educators (elementary through postsecondary) would also be instrumental to the introduction and maintenance of the system. Communication would need to be extensive. First, considerable effort would be required to convince taxpayers that the metric system is worth the cost—one could see the government that implements this program losing votes for taking such action, thereby making it a very political decision. Second, communication would be critical to explain how the system works and to answer questions present. Problems arising will likely range from basics regarding how to convert certain units, through to legal issues involved in compliance, such as whether one can still advertise an apartment in terms of square feet or whether this must be in metric.

From a *benefit* perspective, the relative value of the metric system comes down to ease of use, cost reductions over the longer term (through manufacturing consistency and compatibility with foreign standards), and increased safety (for example, packaging instructions regarding medicine).

A number of *needs* would be met as well. Provision of time and efficiency would (eventually) be created, as would structure and order (a more consistent system would be in place). The heightened ease of use would also mean an increased ability to make predictions based on mathematical calculations. The adoption of metric would also increase acceptance and inclusion on a global scale by bringing the nation into the fold of the official measurement system of virtually every other nation on earth. Not having a unified system of measurement across all people in all industries may lead to disastrous results. Consider the problem faced by NASA's $125 million Mars Climate Orbiter on September 23, 1999. After 286 days in space (416 million miles), it was finally reaching its destination and was ready to circle the Red Planet. NASA used metric (Newtons). Regrettably, their partner, Lockheed Martin, used the U.S. Customary System. As a result, the craft shot through the atmosphere of Mars and is now believed to be orbiting the Sun.[9] Compatibility is important.

EXHIBIT 11-1
FORMS OF VALUE COMMUNICATION (METRIC SYSTEM)

"Feature-Specific" Value Communication (The 3 Cs)

Core (C1)

☐ Products (Not Applicable)

☐ Price
- Extremely high financial cost to convert road signs, manuals, laws and so forth. Long term would result in cost reductions.

☐ Services
- Provision of simplified measurement system.

☐ Brand Image
- Promoted as easier to understand and compatible with the rest of the world's measurement standards.

Conduit (C2)

☐ Location
- Would be present anywhere that measurement units are required (e.g., manuals, textbooks, packaged goods, road signs).

☐ Personnel
- Government personnel would be required to promote, educate and enforce standards.
- Teachers (elementary through post-secondary) would also be instrumental to long-term success.

Communication (C3)

☐ Extensive communication would be required to convince individuals that the metric system should be adopted in full, to educate individuals regarding the metric system and handle questions that would arise regarding the conversion (e.g., how it works through to legal issues).

▼

"Benefit-Specific" Value Communication

☐ **Product/Service Specific Outcomes**
- Would result in reliable and world-standard measurement system.

☐ **Cost Reduction**
- Long-term cost reductions would be present.

☐ **Safety and Reduced Negative Output**
- Conversion to one system would result in less probability of error in applied situations (e.g., medicine and manufacturing)

☐ **Ease of Use**
- Because the system uses multiples of 10 for all forms of measurement (temperature, volume, etc.), it is much easier to teach and employ.
- Calculations are easier and less subject to error.

▼

"Need-Specific" Value Communication

☐ **Provision of Time and Efficiency Achievement**

☐ **Acceptance and Inclusion**
- United States would now be part of same system used throughout the world.

☐ **Structure and Order**
- There would be an enhanced ability of people to understand and use measurement systems for weight, distance, temperature, etc.

☐ **Predictability**
- Increased ease of calculation results in increased ease to predict outcomes.

Law 2: The Stability Surrounding the U.S. Customary System Must Be Reduced

The *breadth and depth* of use of a country's measurement system is phenomenal. Think about how many different places you are affected by your measurement system each day. If you are a native of the United States and the weatherman says it could dip down to 38 degrees, you grab your coat on the way out the door. You tell the person cutting your hair you want an inch off in the back. You order half a pound of meat from the deli, and while you are at it, you pick up a gallon of milk. On the way home you get a speeding ticket for going seven miles per hour over the speed limit. The system is pervasive throughout our social, commercial, and legal environments, and to make changes is more than just a mental effort, it requires a rewriting of manuals, legislation, world records (for example, the fastest recorded pitch in Major League Baseball was thrown by Aroldis Chapman in 2010 at 105 mph; no, strike that, it was actually 169 km/h). This example also underscores how all of our systems are tied together with a common measuring language, just as they are with a common verbal language.

The cost of completely *removing* the U.S. Customary System would be enormous. Among some of the more notable jobs, road signs and manuals would have to be changed, mechanical and construction materials would have to be switched over, education and training would be required, and older people would struggle as they tried to cope with this "newfangled" system. It is understandable why the typical reaction is something like, "Yeah, sounds great...could you get back to me in a decade...maybe then." As noted by Robert Schiesseler, one of the difficulties in advancing the metric system is that although the short-term costs can be clearly identified, the long-term benefits remain vague in nature.[10] Therein lies the problem.

A number of constraints may be present with respect to *independent influences*. Specifically, political and social forces may provide a great deal of pushback. While some groups, such as those involved in the sciences, may embrace change to the metric system, there will also be many who resist. No doubt some will even call it "un-American."

Resistance due to *portability of assets* is a mixed can of worms. On the one hand, the general process of measuring remains unchanged. If you know how to measure ingredients for a cake, you will still be measuring, albeit in different units. However, knowledge regarding the existing system would be made irrelevant and would be as useful as knowing how to speak Lithuanian in Texas. On a tangible level, there are many tools, such as wrenches and drill bits, that would no longer be useful. Granted, many people in industries that require such implements have already purchased metric equivalents.

Although one can easily make the case that the U.S. Customary System is less than perfect when it comes to *technical adequacy*, for the people who use it now, it seems just fine, thank you. Difficulties learning the system and making conversions make it awkward and cumbersome. However, just as people who grow up speaking Chinese do not consider it to be a difficult language to learn, current users of the U.S. Customary System who have an ingrained understanding of its nuances may not view it as technically inadequate. Imagine someone told you English was deemed to be too difficult, so the world was converting to Spanish in five years.

For many, as alluded to already, there is a deep-seated emotional connection with the measurement system. Many remember what it felt like on days when the temperature climbed above the benchmark of 100°F, the nippy days when it went below 32°F, and the fatigue from running a mile flat out. Memories are built around quarter-pound hamburgers, pints and miles. There is a *relationship* with the measurement system itself.

EXHIBIT 11-2
STABILITY OF EXISTING SYSTEM
(US STANDARD SYSTEM)

Stability Factor	Impact	Description
☐ Momentum from Psychological Factors	★★★★★	Most educated individuals are familiar with the existence of the metric system. Nonetheless, most are also likely complacent regarding the need to convert all measurement systems over.
☐ Depth and Breadth of System Use	★★★★★	The existing measurement system is exceptionally pervasive. Although some packages also have metric, the norm in most areas is to present information in US Standard terms (how many miles, feet, inches, ounces, pounds, gallons, etc.).
☐ System Removal Constraints	★★★★	These are enormous. Examples might include removing the current road signs (distance and speed limits), changing quantities in recipes or changing information on drivers' licenses.
☐ Constraints Imposed by Independent Influences	★★	Constraints to change may be present among some formal groups (e.g., political parties) who recognize the cost (financial and political) of switching over. In a broader vein, the electorate may also exert a great deal of unhappiness.
☐ Portability of Assets	★	Portability will be reasonably high. There are usually fairly straightforward conversion systems in place to allow a person with knowledge under the old system to speak coherently in metric. General principles of measurement (e.g., how one measures height or weight) apply to both systems.
☐ Time Since Last Purchase	---	Not applicable in this context. A measuring system does not necessitate change on a frequent basis.
☐ Technical Adequacy of Existing System	★★★★★	The technical adequacy of the existing system is poor by comparison to the metric system. Nonetheless, for everyday purposes the current system does its job and there is a shared understanding among users regarding what the terms mean and it functions well in this regard. From this perspective, the technical adequacy of the existing system is extremely high.
☐ Adaptability of Existing Alternative	★★★★★	The strength of the metric system is that it is based on units of 10. Shy of complete conversion to the metric system, or constantly using converters, it is not feasible to simply adapt the existing system.
☐ Affinity Programs and Volume Discounts	---	Not applicable in this context.
☐ Relationships	★★★★★	Existing relationships with the current system will be strong for both pragmatic purposes (I know how far a mile is and how much is in a Tablespoon), as well as nostalgic/emotional ones (an ounce of liquor, a man who is 6 feet tall, a 4 minute mile). The existing system even infects common forms of speech —"give him an inch and he'll take a mile," or "an ounce of prevention is worth a pound of cure."

Law 3: Uncertainty and Fear Surrounding the Metric System Must Be Reduced

Areas of Uncertainty and Fear. Conversion will be filled with uncertainty, questions, and concerns. How much meat do I order in kilograms without getting a whole cow? OK, so the temperature is going to be twenty…is this good? I guess I would like a liter, or more…or less. My weight…I think I am…could be…sorry, can you speak U.S. Customary? How do I get my stove to convert over? Questions such as this, pervasive through every area of everyday functioning, may lead some to feel rather awkward and embarrassed in social situations (*discomfort during adoption*) if they cannot seem to catch on fast enough. Granted, in most cases this frustration will be manifest as anger rather than embarrassment.

Some of the uncertainty would be mitigated by a period in which both systems are employed, with an emphasis on the metric. This would be similar to a free trial and could help ease many people into the system. Simple tricks such as "double it and add thirty-two to convert from Celsius to Fahrenheit" or "fifty gives you eighty for mph to kph" may help to ease the pain; so too might easy access to converters on the Web. For some, however, the uncertainty will remain profound. A fundamental part of their existence (how they communicate distance, weight, volume, and temperature) will be thrown up in the air, and there will be a perceived *discontinuity* present—a time that they will be "without" an adequate understanding of measurement. This ties into *start-up costs* as well. Yes, there are the rather obvious and incredibly numerous time and financial conversion costs. For many, the real issue will be mental, with the amount of time, effort, and personal frustration being the overarching concern. Hence, on both "hard" (physical) and "soft" (including psychological and cultural) factors, there will be a very real lack of *compatibility*. This may be offset somewhat if there is a general perception regarding the *rate of change* that has existed regarding switching to the metric system throughout the rest of the world and a realization that this change is never going to reverse back.

EXHIBIT 11-3

UNCERTAINTY AND FEAR OF THE METRIC SYSTEM

Area of Uncertainty and Fear	Impact	Description
☐ Product/Service Class Risk	★★★	General risk surrounding "measurement" will be low.
☐ Product/Service Specific Risk	★★★★★	Concern will be present regarding merits of metric system relative to existing system. Will be less on a technical basis (e.g., I do not like a system based on units of 10), more in terms of general understanding (how much gas should I get, how much is in a recipe, and so forth).
☐ Transaction Risk	----	Not applicable in this context. This is a policy decision, there is no transaction per se.
☐ Discomfort During Adoption	★★	Some embarrassment and awkwardness as people learn metric.
☐ Misuse of Information	★	Not applicable in this context. No sensitive information is shared.
☐ Risk of Discontinuity	★★	There will be strong concerns that people will be functionally useless for some period of time (just as if the language switched from English to German). Translators will be possible, but fluency will take a much longer time.
☐ Start-Up Costs	★★★★★	Incredibly large start-up costs for all of the conversions (road signs, manuals, etc.) and getting used to the new system.
☐ Payback Period	★★	Payback comes from the use of an easier system, and one that is used by the rest of world. These have mental and financial implications for daily life and commerce, however, a specific time until payback is achieved is difficult to pinpoint.
☐ Compatibility with Physical Systems	★★★★★	It is compatible with all forms of measurement and the existing system can be converted over.
☐ Compatibility with "Soft" Systems	★★★★★	For many, this is not compatible with the "way they do things". The government in place should expect considerable backlash.
☐ Rate of Change (Social, Legal, Economic, Political, Technical)	★	To the extent that the US sees that the rest of the world has converted to metric but is no longer changing, this will enhance the adoption of the metric system.

Willingness to Take Risk	Impact	Description
☐ Availability of Resources	★★★★★	In tight financial times, expenses required to change (e.g., get new measuring devices) may be considered too large.
☐ Ability to Reverse Decision	★★★★★	While technically possible, it is not practical to switch back other than through the use of calculations.
☐ Ability to "Play" on Multiple Occasions	★★★★★	Conversion is something that has been attempted in stages, but in general it is a "one-time, get it right" deal.
☐ Short-Term Thinking	★★★★★	In the short-term it is much easier to stay with the existing system.
☐ Time Until Final Decision	★★★★★	People may initially agree with the rationale behind the metric system, but begin to panic once time to use it draws near.
☐ Framing (Positive vs. Negative)	★★★★★	Focus must be placed on efficiency and "world standards."
☐ Emotion	★★★★★	This is going to be highly emotional, evoking confusion, anger and frustration. There will be few countervailing positive emotions.
☐ Volition and Level of Control	★★★★★	This decision to switch is made by government and no choice is required other than to go along with it. Control can be enhanced through education.

Willingness to Take Risk. There are many factors that will reduce the willingness of the public to want to engage in the metric experience. Such policy decisions are almost *impossible to reverse*, and the adoption of measurement systems is not something that one continues to do until one "gets it right." There is no ability to play on multiple occasions. Even individuals who recognize the inevitability, and perhaps even the benefit, of the metric system will experience some regret. After all, in the *short term*, the easy thing to do would be to stick with the existing measurement system, no matter how outmoded and cumbersome it is. Willingness to take the metric system on will be fostered by focusing on the long term and *framing* the change in terms of the efficiency and compatibility with world standards that the new measurement system provides.

In a situation like this, where a policy is thrust on the populace, there is no real decision to be made. The level of *volition* is zero. This does not mean that all citizens will be happy, but they will not have the additional burden of wondering whether or not they made the correct decision. One of the key factors will be to provide individuals with the tools and resources they need to exert adequate *control* over the situation and feel like true adopters rather than victims.

Risk Reduction. Although many will not fully comprehend what is happening, some may be swayed by the belief that this is for the better of society in the long term. Endorsement by third parties may provide this confidence. Examples might include support from all of the government agencies, major trade councils and unions, state and city governments, and larger corporate entities. Reminders that this is now the law, as enacted by the government, may also cater to nationalistic sentiment (or foster an uprising). Respected personalities and authorities could also be used to suggest to the layperson that the metric system is the best way to embrace the measurement future.

Such a period of change would not occur without some degree of training. Much of this will not be necessary for people with technical skills or higher education. This, however, does not account for a reasonable portion of society. Legislators must keep in mind there will be wide range of latitude in understanding and acceptance. Hence, beyond education regarding the "how," an essential part of the communication process will be effectively communicating the "why." In order to build national support, people must both understand and believe the rationale underlying the initiative.

Law 4: Independent Influences Impact the Acceptance of the Metric System

Obviously, forces imposed by legal statute or regulatory decree from departments, agencies, and boards will impact any in science or commerce who come under the direct shadow of required metric standards. In turn, this will have spinoff effects—these workers will be more inclined to accept and use metric terms in their everyday life as well. Perhaps the next census will ask if we speak metric at home.

Government programs and initiatives to convert technical manuals and equipment will foster industry support (penalties would work, too, but would not be as well received). Funds to develop educational tools to teach metric, provide people with rulers and thermometers, and other efforts will make conversion easier. For example, downloadable computer programs or free calculators would also further the cause.

Over the course of the long term, the good news is that many younger people are being exposed to the metric system in school. There is also a general trend toward higher levels of educational attainment, and consequently an increased likelihood of meaningful exposure to the metric system. Both of these elements should enhance the acceptance of change. In addition to this, the move toward globalization and the recognition that the United States is the only major country out of step with the measurement language of the world should cause many to recast how they think about metric system.

Finally, the message carried in the media and among major reference groups, including unions and political parties, will have an impact on what bandwagon people decide to jump on. Bringing them online, helping them understand the new system, and convincing them metric will result in an overall betterment in society will further assist in implementation efforts.

Law 5: There are Biases in Search and Choice Regarding the Metric System

If a government policy mandating the complete change to the metric system is put in place, *choice* will not be an option—the key variable will be acceptance of change. Throughout this chapter, the need to provide adequate information to enable individuals to understand the importance of conversion, as well as to adopt the system as part of their daily routine, has been underscored. When developing this information, the capabilities of the "common man" must be kept in mind. While the motivation to process the deluge of information will be high for most, the actual ability to do so may be lacking.

Overall Synopsis Regarding the Adoption of the Metric System

There are very few individuals who would stand up and contest that the U.S. Customary System is in some way stronger than the metric system—in the court of common sense, a *nolo contendere* (no contest) would be declared. With the rest of the world having crossed over to this far more simple and intuitive form of measurement, the pressure on the United States to eventually cross over in a permanent way is present. For two hundred years, in fits and starts, there has even been effort to do so. However, the stopgap measures, while fostering some compatibility with the rest of the world, have still fostered a reliance on the existing system.

Switching problems arise on two major fronts. First, the existing system is used with great breadth and depth by a very large number of people. Just from a signage and documentation perspective, the mechanical cost of removing the existing system will be enormous. Second, fear and uncertainty associated with switching will be high, especially for those who have had years of experience with the U.S. Customary System. A cup of flour, 85° Fahrenheit, and fifty miles per hour have an automatic meaning that their metric equivalents, at least for a little while, will not. The financial and political costs of education may be higher than a political leader with long-term intentions to govern is willing to bear.

NOTES

OVERVIEW

1. Stevenson, Robert Louis (1903), *Across the Plains.* New York, NY: Scribners Publishing Company.

2. Although Ralph Waldo Emerson has been attributed with this quote and may possibly have been delivered in one of his lectures, it does not appear formally in any of his works.

3. For a brief review of the history of Levi Strauss, see: Boulmay, Gardner (1997), "Not by Jeans Alone the Story of Levi's." Case 148-C97A, Babson College.

4. This was captured on the 1981 documentary, "Not by Jeans Alone," part of the *Enterprise Series* filmed by WGBH Boston. Producers were Zvi Dor-Neve and Paul Sloman.

5. Sloane, Leonard (1989), "Home Banking by Computer Hasn't Made Paper Obsolete," *New York Times*, January 7. Retrieved March 17, 2011 from: NYTimes.com http://query.nytimes.com/gst/fullpage.html?res=950DE3D 81F3CF934A35752C0A96F948260

6. Quelch, John A. (1984), "Chemical Bank: The Pronto System," Harvard Business School Case 584-089.

7. At the time there were not many brands of home computer. In North America, the three main home computers were the Apple II, the Commodore 64 and the Atari (for a history of Atari computers, see http://www.atarimuseum.com/computers/computers.html).

8. Retrieved March 17, 2011 from: http://www.bicworld.com/en/pages/faq/

9. Rothenberg, Randall (1989), "Bic Begins Campaign For New Perfume Line," *New York Times*, March 20, D9. Retrieved August 22, 2009 from NYTimes.com.

10. Anonymous (1991) "Scents and Sensibility," *Time Magazine.* Volume 137 (20), May 20, 47.

11. Retrieved March 17, 2011 from: http://en.wikipedia.org/wiki/OS/2 .

12. A chronology of different events, retrieved March 17, 2011 from: http://www.cbc.ca/news/canada/story/2009/10/06/f-gun-registry.html; Other archival material of interest includes: Mauser, Gary (2006) "After the Gun Registry," Fraser Forum, May, 18-20. • Janigan, Mary (2004), "Ready, Fire, Then Aim," *MacLean's*, 117(6), 14 (February 9). • Steel, Kevin (2003) "The Gun Registry Still Shoots Blanks," The Report, February 3, 10-11.

13. Anonymous (2005), "2005 Cars. Top Picks 2005: The Best Models in 10 Categories," *Consumer Reports Magazine*, 20 (April), p. 6.

14. Retrieved March 17, 2011 from: http://en.wikipedia.org/wiki/Honda_Accord_Hybrid

15. Kiesling, L. Lynne (2008), *Deregulation, Innovation and Market Liberalization: Electricity Regulation in a Continually Evolving Environment*, New York, NY: Routledge.

16. Conklin, David W. and Trevor Hunter (2001), "Ensuring the Successful Privatization of Ontario Hydro," *Ivey Business Journal*, 65 (6), 59-65. • Anonymous (2001), "The Energy Calamity in California," *New York Times*, New York, NY, January 27, A14. Retrieved August 22, 2009 from NYTimes.com • Palmeri, Christopher, Laura Cohn, Wendy Zellner (2001), "California's Power Failure: Why the Attempt to Make the Energy Market More Efficient has been a Disaster," *Business Week*, January 8, 34-36.

17. Slocum, Tyson (2008), "The Failure of Electricity Deregulation: History, Status and Needed Reforms," *Public Citizen's Energy Program*. Retrieved March 17, 2011 from: http://www.citizen.org/documents/USdereg.pdf

CHAPTER 1 – THE VALUE OFFERING

1. See, for example: Cooper, Robert (2001), *Winning at New Products*, Cambridge, MA: Perseus Publishing.

2. Biyalogorsky, Eyal, William Boulding, and Richard Staelin (2006), "Stuck in the Past: Why Managers Continue with New Product Failures," *Journal of Marketing*, 70 (2), 108-121.

3. There are countless marketing texts that go through the "4 Ps" or other machinations of representing all of the basic components involved in marketing. Beyond the initial 4 (product, place, promotion and price), services personnel have also added 3 more (personnel, process and physical location).

4. Drucker, Peter F. (1994), "The Theory of the Business," *Harvard Business Review*, September-October, 95-104.

5. Maslow, Abraham (1943), "A Theory of Human Motivation," *Psychological Review*, 50(4), 370-396.

6. See, for example Fieg, Barry (2006), *Hot Button Marketing: Push the Emotional Buttons That Get People to Buy*. Avon, MA: Adams Media.

CHAPTER 2 – STABILITY OF EXISTING SYSTEM

1. Initial academic work in this area is attributed to Samuelson, William and Richard Zeckhauser (1988), "Status Quo Bias in Decision Making," *Journal of Risk and Uncertainty*, 1, 7-59. • For a consideration of different factors contributing to the status quo bias also see: Schweitzer, Maurice (1994), "Disentangling Status Quo and Omission Effects: An Experimental Analysis," *Organizational Behavior and Human Decision Processes*, 58, 457-476.

2. Arkes, Hal R. and Catherine Blumer (1985), "The Psychology of Sunk Cost," *OrganizationalBehavior and Human Decision Processes*, 35, 124-140.

3. Bittar, Christine (2001), "Reflect: A Palatable Model?" *Brandweek*, 42 (14), 18-24.

4. Baughn, Michael K. And Peter A. Finzel (2009), "A Clash of Cultures in a Merger of Two Acquisition Project Offices," *Engineering Management Journal*, 21 (2), 11-17.

5. Parasuramen, A., Valarie A. Zeithaml and Leonard L. Berry (1985), "A Conceptual Model of Service Quality and Its Implications for Future Research," *Journal of Marketing*, 49 (Fall), 41-50.

6. For an excellent review, see: Meyer-Waarden, Lars (2008), "The Influence of Loyalty Programme Membership on Customer Purchase Behaviour," *European Journal of Marketing*, 42 (1/2), 87-114.

7. Meyer-Waarden, Lars and Christophe Benavent (2008), "Rewards that Reward," *Wall Street Journal*, September 22, p. R5.

8. Ward, James C. and Amy L. Ostrom (2006), "Complaining to the Masses: The Role of Protest Framing in Customer-Created Complaint Web Sites," *Journal of Consumer Research*, 33 (September), 220-230.

CHAPTER 3 – UNCERTAINTY AND FEAR OF NEW SYSTEM

1. The 2008 Internet Crime Report, produced by the Internet Crime Complaint Center (a joint initiative between the National White Collar Crime Center and the Federal Bureau of Investigation) may be found at http://www.ic3. gov/media/annualreport/2008_IC3Report.pdf

2. A key part of the calculation to examine payback would be the hurdle rate (i.e., the minimum expected rate of return, for example 5% per annum) for funds invested. For purposes of brevity, issues of discounting cash flows are not considered further, but would be very important for many financially based decisions.

3. Choney, Suzanne (2009) House Votes to Delay Digital TV, MSNBC.com, February 4, retrieved March 17, 2011 from http://www.msnbc.msn.com/ id/29003127/ns/technology_and_science-tech_and_gadgets//.

4. See, e.g.: Wood, Wendy (2000), "Attitude Change: Persuasion and Social Influence," *Annual Review of Psychology*, (51) 1, 539-570.

5. Moore, Gordon E. (1965), "Cramming More Components onto Integrated Circuits," *Electronics*, 38 (8), 114-117.

6. The term was originally coined by: Kahneman, Daniel and Amos Tversky (1979), "Prospect Theory: An Analysis of Decision Under Risk," *Econometrica*, 47, 263-291. • For a review of different theories used to explain this, as well as boundary conditions, see: Li, Shu (1993), "What is Wrong with Allais' Certainty Effect?" *Journal of Behavioral Decision Making*, 6, 271-281.

7. See: Sitkin, Sirn B. and Amy L. Pablo (1992), "Reconceptualising the Determinants of Risk Behavior," *Academy of Management Review*, 17 (1), 9 – 38. • Also: Weber, Elke U. and Richard A. Milliman (1997), "Perceived Risk Attitudes: Relating Risk Perception to Risky Choice," *Management Science*, 43(2), 123-144.

8. See Siegrist, Michael, Heinz Gutscher, and Timothy C. Earle (2005), "Perception of Risk: The Influence of General Trust, and General Confidence," *Journal of Risk Research*, 8 (2), 145-156.

9. It has been suggested that the ability to suffer loss will influence the amount of search activity put into the task in order to reduce risk. See: Dowling, Grahame R. and Richard Staelin (1994), "A Model of Perceived Risk and Intended Risk-handling Activity," *Journal of Consumer Research*, 21 (June), 119 - 134.

10. For a general review, see: Samuelson, Paul (1977), "St. Petersburg Paradoxes: Defanged, Dissected, and Historically Described," *Journal of Economic Literature,* 15, 24–55.

11. The expected value is equal to the sum of the outcomes multiplied by their probabilities. Hence, there is a .5 chance of getting heads on the first outcome with an expected payoff of $1 (.5 multiplied by $2^1 = $1), a .25 chance of getting heads on the second outcome with an expected payoff of $1 (.25 multiplied by $2^2 = $1), and so on. The expected value is therefore equal to $1 + $1 + $1....+$1 = $∞.

12. A number of contemporary approaches to answering the St. Petersburg Paradox have been presented. For example: Blavatskyy, Pavlo R. (2005), "Back to the St. Petersburg Paradox?" *Management Science*, 51(4), 677-678. • Rieger, Marc, and Mei Wang (2006), "Cumulative Prospect Theory and the St. Petersburg Paradox," *Economic Theory*, 28 (3), 665-679. • Lola J. Lopes (1981), "Decision Making in the Short Run," *Journal of Experimental Psychology: Human Learning and Memory*, 7, 377-385. • Tversky, Amos and Maya J. Bar-Hillel (1982), "Risk: The Long and the Short," *Journal of Experimental Psychology: Learning, Memory, Cognition*, 9, 713-717. • Lopes, Lola (1996), "When Time is of the Essence: Averaging, Aspiration and the Short-Run," *Organizational Behavior and Human Decision Processes*, 65 (3), 179-189. • Further support that single-play decisions are regarded as more risky than multiple-play decisions is provided by: Joag, Shreekant G., John C. Mowen, and James W. Gentry (1990), "Risk Perception in a Simulated Industrial Purchasing Task: The Effects of Single versus Multi-Play Decisions," *Journal of Behavioral Decision Making*, 3, 91-108.

13. Alexander, David L., John G. Lynch and Qing Wang (2008), "As Time Goes By: Do Cold Feet Follow Warm Intentions for Really New Versus Incrementally New Products?" *Journal of Marketing Research*, 45 (3), 307-319.

- Trope, Yaacov and Nira Liberman (2000), "Temporal Construal and Time-Dependent Changes in Preferences," *Journal of Personality and Social Psychology*, 79 (6), 876–889. • Trope, Yaacov and Nira Liberman (2003), "Temporal Construal," *Psychological Review*, 110 (3), 403–421. • Trope, Yaacov, Nira Liberman, and Cheryl Wakslak (2007), "Construal Levels and Psychological Distance: Effects on Representation, Prediction, Evaluation, and Behavior," *Journal of Consumer Psychology*, 17 (2), 83–95.

14. Tversky, Amos, and Daniel Kahneman (1981), "The Framing of Decisions and the Psychology of Choice," *Science*, 211, 453-458.

15. Cox, Anthony D., Dena Cox, and Gregory Zimet (2006), "Understanding Consumer Responses to Product Risk Information," *Journal of Marketing*, 70 (January), 79-91.

16. Herzentein, Michal, Steven S. Posovac, and J. Joško Brakus (2007), "Adoption of New and Really New Products: The Effects of Self-Regulation Systems and Risk Salience," *Journal of Marketing Research*, XLIV (May), 251-260.

17. Research regarding one- versus two-sided persuasion attempts can be traced to Carl Hovland's work during the Second World War, see: Hovland, Carl I. (1954), "Effects of the Mass Media of Communication," in *Handbook of Social Psychology,* Gardner Lindzey, ed. Cambridge, MA: Addison-Wesley Publishing Company. • Although somewhat dated, work has also been conducted in marketing contexts, see: Kamins, Michael A. and Henry Assael (1987), "Two-Sided Versus One-Sided Appeals: A Cognitive Perspective on Argumentation, Source Derogation, and the Effect of Disconfirming Trial on Belief and Change," *Journal of Marketing Research*, 24 (1), 29-39.

18. For an examination of fear versus anger on risk perceptions see: Lerner, Jennifer S. and Dacher Keltner (2001), "Fear, Anger and Risk," *Journal of Personality and Social Psychology*, 81 (1), 146-159. • For an examination of sadness versus anxiety, see: Raghunathan, Rajagopal and Michel Tuan Pham (1999), "All Negative Moods Are Not Equal: Motivational Influences of Anxiety and Sadness on Decision Making," *Organizational Behavior and Human Decision Processes,* 79 (1), 56-77.

19. For a review and examination of volition and control, see: Nordgren, Loran F., Joop van der Pligt, and Frenk Harreveld (2007), "Unpacking Perceived Control in Risk Perception: The Mediating Role of Anticipated Regret," *Journal of Behavioral Decision Making*, 20 (5), 533-544.

20. Purohit, Devavrat and Joydeep Srivastava (2001), "Effect of Manufacturer Reputation, Retailer Reputation, and Product Warranty on Consumer Judgments of Product Quality: A Cue Diagnosticity Framework," *Journal of Consumer Psychology*, 10 (3), 123–134. • See also: Moorthy, Sridar and Kannan Srinivasan (1995), "Signalling Quality with a Money-back Guarantee: The

Role of Transaction Costs," *Marketing Science,* 14 (4), 442–466. • David A. Soberman (2003), "Simultaneous Signaling and Screening with Warranties," *Journal of Marketing Research,* 40 (2), 176-192.

21. Menezes, Melvyn A.J. and Jon D. Serbin (1991), "Xerox Corp.: The Customer Satisfaction Program (Case #591055)," Boston, MA: Harvard Business Press.

22. General levels of confidence and trust have been found to reduce perceptions of risk. See: Siegrist, Michael, Heinz Gutscher, and Timothy C. Earle (2005), "Perception of Risk: The Influence of General Trust, and General Confidence," *Journal of Risk Research,* 8 (2), 145-156.

23. http://www.accountemps.com

24. Durand, Richard M., Duane L. Davis, and William O. Bearden (1977), "Dogmatism as a Mediating Influence on Perception of Consumer Choice Decisions," *Journal of Psychology,* 95 (1), 131-138.

25. Erdogan, B. Zafer (1999), "Celebrity Endorsement: A Literature Review," *Journal of Marketing Management,* 15 (4), 291-314.

26. Although the match does not have to be perfect, extreme mismatches should be avoided. See: Lee, Jung-Gyo and Esther Thorson (2008), "The Impact of Celebrity-Product Incongruence on the Effectiveness of Product Endorsement," *Journal of Advertising Research,* 48 (3), 433-449.

27. In general one would expect that negative behavior on the part of the celebrity could harm the sponsor. See e.g.,: Till, Brian D. and Terrance A. Shimp (1998), "Endorsers in Advertising: The Case of Negative Celebrity Information," *Journal of Advertising,* 27(1), 67–82. • Other research suggests that this may not always occur: Bailey, Ainsworth Anthony (2007), "Public Information and Consumer Skepticism Effects on Celebrity Endorsements: Studies Among Young Consumers," *Journal of Marketing Communications,* 13 (2), 85-107.

28. For a review of corporate and spokesperson credibility, see: Lafferty, Barbara A., Ronald E. Goldsmith, Ronald E., and Stephen J. Newell (2002), "The Dual Credibiltiy Model: The Influence of Corporate and Endorser Credibility on Attitudes and Purchase Intentions," *Journal of Marketing Theory & Practice,* 10 (3), 1-12.

29. The response hierarchy is presented as an intuitive understanding of factors that have to be present for a communication attempt to be effective. It stands to reason that if people never even attend to an ad it will not be processed (superficial arguments about subliminal advertising aside). Similarly if people do not understand it, agree with, remember it or act on it, the impact will arguably be reduced. These elements have prima facie value and appeal to common sense. The specific steps involved in the process and the order in which they occur has received considerable attention. For an excellent

review, see: Barry, Thomas F. and Daniel J. Howard (1990), "A Review and Critique of the Hierarchy of Effects in Advertising," *International Journal of Advertising*, 9 (2), 121-135. • Other work has examined other factors involved in advertising effectiveness: Vakratsas, Demetrios and Tim Ambler (1999), "How Advertising Works: What Do We Really Know?" *Journal of Marketing*, 63 (1), 26-43. • Some have also questioned the importance of an information processing model: Heath, Robert and Paul Feldwick (2008), "Fifty Years of Using the Wrong Model," *International Journal of Market Research*, 50 (1), 29-59. • Nonetheless, while the specific model, mechanism and component of emphasis may vary, it is argued that due consideration to attention, understanding, believing, memory and action will be useful to the vast majority of managers in almost all applied situations.

30. The "Cocktail Party" phenomenon was first coined by: Cherry, Edward C. (1953), "Some Experiments on the Recognition of Speech, With One and With Two Ears," *Journal of Acoustical Society of America*, 25 (5), 975-979.

31. For a review, see: Olsen, G. Douglas (2002), "Salient Stimuli in Advertising: The Effect of Contrast Interval Length and Type on Recall," *Journal of Experimental Psychology: Applied*, 8 (3), 168 – 179.

32. This remarkably influential and widely cited theory is nicely presented in Petty, Richard E, John T. Cacioppo, and David Schumann (1983), "Central and Peripheral Routes to Advertising Effectiveness: The Moderating Role of Involvement," *Journal of Consumer Research*, 10 (2), 135-146.

33. In some cases, the required information is present at time of evaluation or choice. In such cases memory may less of an issue. For a consideration of the role of cognitive and affective elements when memory is and is not required see: Rottenstreich, Yuval, Sanjay Sood and Lyle Brenner (2007), "Feeling and Thinking in Memory-Based versus Stimulus-Based Choices," *Journal of Consumer Research*, 33 (4), 461-469.

34. Childers, Terry L., Susan E. Heckler, and Michael J. Houston (1986), "Memory for the Visual and Verbal Components of Print Advertisements," *Psychology & Marketing*, 3 (3), 137-149. • Schmitt, Bernd H., Nader T. Tavassoli, and Robert T. Millard (1993), "Memory for Print Ads: Understanding Relations Among Brand Name, Copy, and Picture," *Journal of Consumer Psychology*, 2 (1), 55-81.

35. As demonstrated by the Picture Superiority Effect, images also tend to be easier to remember than words. See: Nelson, Douglas L., Valerie S. Reed and John R. Walling (1976), "The Pictorial Superiority Effect," *Journal of Experimental Psychology: Human Learning and Memory*, 2 (5), 523-528.

36. For the impact of perceived scarcity on persuasion, see: Cialdini, Robert B. (2001), *Influence: Science and Practice (4th Edition)*, Needham Heights, MA: Allyn and Bacon.

CHAPTER 4 – INDEPENDENT INFLUENCES

1. See, e.g., http://en.wikipedia.org/wiki/Neighborhood_Electric Vehicle, retrieved March 17, 2011.

2. This line is in reference to John Donne's poem, "For Whom the Bell Tolls," taken from an original work entitled, "Devotions Upon Emgergent Occasions." This may be found in: Donne, John and Charles M. Coffin (1994), *The Complete Poetry and Selected Prose of John Donne*, New York, NY: The Modern Library, Random House Publishing Group.

3. Robinson, Rowan (1996), *The Great Book of Hemp: The Complete Guide to the Environmental, Commercial, and Medicinal Uses of the World's Most Extraordinary Plant*, Rochester, VT: Park Street Press.

4. Retrieved March 17, 2011 from dumblaws.com

5. Retrieved March 17, 2011 from: http://www.fda.gov/opacom/morechoices/ mission.html

6. American College of Physicians (2008), *Supporting Research into the Therapeutic Role of Marijuana*. Philadelphia, PA: American College of Physicians.

7. Montana, Jennifer Paige and Boris Nenide (2008), "The Evolution of Regional Industry Clusters and Their Implications for Sustainable Economic Development: Two Case Illustrations," *Economic Development Quarterly*, 22 (4), 290-302. • Feldman, Maryann P., and Johanna L. Francis, Johanna L. (2004), "Homegrown Solutions: Fostering Cluster Formation," *Economic Development Quarterly*, 18 (2), 127-137.

8. Cumming, Douglas and Sofia Johan (2009), "Pre-Seed Government Venture Capital Funds," *Journal of International Entrepreneurship*, 7 (1), 26-56.

9. For an examination of the value of grant and loan programs, see: Jenkins, J. Craig, Kevin T. Leicht and Arthur Jaynes (2008), "Creating High-Technology Growth: High-Tech Employment Growth in U.S. Metropolitan Areas, 1988-1998," *Social Science Quarterly*, 89 (2), 456-481.

10. See e.g., Hemphill, Thomas A. (2006), "US Innovation Policy: Creating (and Expanding) a National Agenda for Global Competitiveness," *Innovation: Management, Policy & Practice*, 8 (3), 288-295. This paper also points out that development of technology must also be paired with development of managerial and organizational strengths.

11. See, e.g.: Ruffa, Stephen A. (2008), *Going Lean: How the Best Companies Apply Lean Manufacturing Principles to Shatter Uncertainty, Drive Innovation, and Maximize Profits*, New York, NY: AMACOM.

12. See, e.g.: Sparks, Glenn G. (2010), *Media Effects Research: A Basic Overview (3rd Edition)*, Boston, MA: Wadsworth. • For an excellent analysis of how changes to manufacturing processes can impact the success of industry members, see: Sinha, Rajiv K. and Charles H. Noble (2008), "The Adoption

of Radical Manufacturing Technologies and Firm Survival," *Strategic Management Journal*, 29, 943-962.

13. See, e.g.: Barnes, Michael D., Carl L. Hanson, Len M. B. Novilla, Aaron T. Meacham, Emily McIntyre and Brittany C. Erickson (2008), "Analysis of Media Agenda Setting During and After Hurricane Katrina: Implications for Emergency Preparedness, Disaster Response, and Disaster Policy," *American Journal of Public Health*, 98 (4), 604-610.

14. Retrieved March 17, 2011 from: http://www.census.gov/ipc/www/idb/worldpoptotal.php. See http://www.census.gov/ipc/www/idb/rank.php for a breakdown by country and year.

15. www.jitterbug.com

16. Twenge, Jean M. and Stacy M. Campbell (2008), "Generational Differences in Psychological Traits and their Impact in the Workplace." *Journal of Managerial Psychology.* 23 (8), 862-868.

17. Trunk, Penelope (2007), "What Gen Y Really Wants," *Time Magazine (South Pacific)*, Issue 27 (July 5), 57.

18. Russell, Cheryl (2007). *Demographics of the United States (Trends and Projections)*, Ithaca, NY: New Strategist Publications.

19. Retrieved March 17, 2011 from: http://bjs.ojp.usdoj.gov/content/glance/tables/viortrdtab.cfm

20. Saad, Lydia (2006), "Worry About Crime Remains at Last Year's Elevated Levels," *Gallup News Service,* retrieved March 17, 2011 from: http://www.gallup.com/poll/25078/Worry-About-Crime-Remains-Last-Years-Elevated-Levels.aspx#1.

21. Gerbner, George, and Larry Gross (1976), "Living with Television: The Violence Profile," *Journal of Communication, 26,* 173-199.

22. US Department of Health and Human Services, Center for Disease Control and Prevention (2009), *Health, United States, 2008, With Special Feature on Health of Young Adults*, Hyattsville, MD: National Center for Health Statistics.

23. Retrieved March 17, 2011 from: http://www.cdc.gov/mmwr/preview/mmwrhtml/mm5526a5.htm

24. Retrieved March 17, 2011 from: http://www.cdc.gov/nccdphp/dnpa/obesity/trend/maps/index.htm

25. The rate of childhood obesity has roughly tripled since the early 1970s. Retrieved March 17, 2011 from: http://www.cdc.gov/nccdphp/dnpa/obesity/childhood/

26. Retrieved March 17, 2011 from: http://www.nflrush.com/

27. Skinner, Brett, and Mark Rovere (2007), *Paying More, Getting Less 2007: Measuring the Sustainability of Government Health Spending in Canada*, Vancouver, British Columbia: The Fraser Institute.

28. See Appendix A pertaining to features, benefits and needs for a discussion of Maslow's hierarchy.

29. At the same time there has been a growing concern regarding the digital divide (i.e., those with access to the internet/information technology and those without).

30. See e.g., Coaffee, Jon (2008), "Risk, Resilience, and Environmentally Sustainable Cities," *Energy Policy*, 36 (12), 4633-4638.

31. Canton, James (2006), *The Extreme Future*, New York, NY: Dutton.

32. Chorev, Nitsan (2007), *Remaking U.S. Trade Policy: From Protectionist to Globalization,* Ithaca, NY: Cornell University Press.

33. Goldman Sachs Global Economics Group (2007), *Brics and Beyond*, The Goldman Sachs Group, Inc.

34. Erixon, Fredrik (2009), "Containing Creeping Protectionism: A Realist Agenda for the G20," ECIPE Policy Brief No. 01/2009. Brussels: European Centre for International Political Economy.

35. French, John R. P., and Raven, Bertram H. (1959), "The Bases of Social Power," in *Studies of Social Power*, Cartwright, Dorwin (ed.), Ann Arbor, MI: Institute for Social Research.

36. Retrieved March 17, 2011 from: http://www.nybg.org/support_the_garden/membership/terms.php

37. Goldstein, Noah J., Robert B. Cialdini and Vladas Griskevicius (2008), "A Room with a Viewpoint: Using Social Norms to Motivate Environmental Conservation in Hotels," *Journal of Consumer Research*, 35 (October), 472-482.

38. For an interesting examination of how member and aspiration groups may influence connections with the brand (with membership groups having a greater impact if the goal was self-verification and aspiration groups having a greater impact if the goal was self-enhancement), see: Escalas, Jennifer Edson, and James R. Bettman (2003), "You Are What They Eat: The Influence of Reference Groups on Consumers' Connections to Brands," *Journal of Consumer Psychology*, 13 (3), 339-348. • On the individual level, research suggests that products touched by attractive individuals, and factors moderating this effect, may be perceived more favourably. See: Argo, Jennifer J., Darren W. Dahl and Andrea C. Morales (2008), "Positive Consumer Contagion: Responses to Attractive Others in a Retail Context," *Journal of Marketing Research*, 45 (December), 690-701.

39. White, Katherine and Darren W. Dahl (2007), "Are All Out-Groups Created Equal? Consumer Identity and Dissociative Influence," *Journal of Consumer Research*, 34 (4), 525-536. On the individual level, research suggests that products touched by attractive individuals, and factors moderating this effect, may be perceived more favourably. See: Argo, Jennifer J., Darren W. Dahl and Andrea C. Morales (2008), "Positive Consumer Contagion:

Responses to Attractive Others in a Retail Context," *Journal of Marketing Research*, 45 (December), 690-701.

40. Fore an investigation of the impact of brand communities on adoption decisions, see: Thompson, Scott A. and Rajiv K. Sinha (2008), "Brand Communities and New Product Adoption: The Influence of Limits of Oppositional Loyalty," *Journal of Marketing*, 72 (November), 65-80.

CHAPTER 5 – BIAS IN SEARCH AND CHOICE

1. Ariely, Dan (2008), *Predictably Irrational*, New York, NY: HarperCollins.
2. Schmidt, Jeffrey B. and Richard A. Spreng (1996), "A Proposed Model of External Consumer Information Search," *Journal of the Academy of Marketing Science*, 24 (3), 246-256. • Hu, Jing, Bruce A. Huhmann, and Michael R. Hyman (2007), "The Relationship Between Task Complexity and Information Search: The Role of Self-Efficacy," *Psychology & Marketing*, 24 (3), 253-270.
3. Seligman, Martin. E. P. and Steven F. Maier (1967), "Failure to Escape Traumatic Shock," *Journal of Experimental Psychology*, 74, 1-9.
4. See, e.g., Jonas, Eva, Stefan Schulz-Hardt, Dieter Frey and Norman Thelen (2001), "Confirmation Bias in Sequential Information Search After Preliminary Decisions: An Expansion of Dissonance Theoretical Research on Selective Exposure to Information," *Journal of Personality and Social Psychology*, 80 (4), 557-571. As noted by this research, bias even greater when information is sequentially versus simultaneously presented.
5. Johnson, Richard D. and Irwin P. Levin (1985), "More than Meets the Eye: The Effect of Missing Information on Purchase Evaluations," *Journal of Consumer Research*, 12 (2), 169-177. • Kunter, Gunasti and William T. Ross, Jr. (2008), "Choice with Inference is Different From Choice Without Inference," Advances in Consumer Research - North American Conference Proceedings, Volume 35, 814-815. • Huber, Joel and John W. McCann (1982), "The Impact of Inferential Beliefs on Product Evaluations," *Journal of Marketing Research*, 19, 324-333. • Kardes, Frank R., Steven S. Posavac and Maria L. Cronley (2004), "Consumer Inference: A Review of Processes, Bases, and Judgment Contexts," *Journal of Consumer Psychology*, 14 (3), 230-256.; Loken, Barbara (2006), "Consumer Psychology: Categorization, Inferences, Affect, and Persuasion," *Annual Review of Psychology*, 57 (1), 453-485.
6. Jianan Wu and Arvind Rangaswamy, Arvind (2003), "A Fuzzy Set Model of Search and Consideration with an Application to an Online Market," *Marketing Science*, 22 (3), 411-434.; Park, Jong-Won and Manoj Hastak (1994), "Memory-based Product Judgments: Effects of Involvement at Encoding and Retrieval," *Journal of Consumer Research*, 21 (3), 534-547.

- Pham, Michel Tuan and A. V. Muthukrishnan (2002), "Search and Alignment in Judgment Revision: Implications for Brand Positioning," *Journal of Marketing Research*, 39 (1), 18-30. • The impact of being able to recall a brand and therefore put it in a consideration set is also considered by: Nedungadi, Prakesh (1990), "Recall and Consumer Consideration Sets: Influencing Choice without Altering Brand Evaluations," *Journal of Consumer Research*, 17 (December), 263-276.

7. Pieters, Rik, Hans Baumgartner and Richard Bagozzi (1999), "Biased Memory for Prior Decision Making: Evidence from a Longitudinal Field Study," *Organizational Behavior & Human Decision Processes*, 99 (1), 34-48. • Braun, Kathryn A. (1999), "Post-Experience Advertising Effects on Consumer Memory," *Journal of Consumer Research*, 25 (4), 319-334. • Cowley, Elizabeth (2008), "Looking Back at an Experience Through Rose-Colored Glasses," *Journal of Business Research*, 61 (10), 1046-1052.

8. See e.g., Elizabeth F. Loftus (1996), *Eyewitness Testimony*, Cambridge, MA: Harvard University Press. • Weingardt, Kenneth R. and Elizabeth Loftus (1995), "Misinformation Revisited: New Evidence on the Suggestibility of Memory," *Memory & Cognition*, 23 (1), 72-82.

9. Tversky, Amos and Daniel Kahneman, D. (1973), "Availability: A Heuristic for Judging Frequency and Probability," *Cognitive Psychology*, 5, 207-232. • Ofir, Chezy, Priya Raghubir, Gili Brosh, Kent B. Monroe and Amir Heiman (2008), "Memory-Based Store Price Judgments: The Role of Knowledge and Shopping Experience," *Journal of Retailing*, 84 (4), 414-423.

10. Shen, Hao and Robert Wyer Jr. (2008), "Procedural Priming and Consumer Judgments: Effects on the Impact of Positively and Negatively Valenced Information," *Journal of Consumer Research*, 34 (5), 727-737. • Berger, Jonah and Grinne Fitzsimons (2008), "Dogs on the Street, Pumas on Your Feet: How Cues in the Environment Influence Product Evaluation and Choice," *Journal of Marketing Research*, 45 (1), 1-14. • Wheeler, S. Christian, and Jonah Berger (2007), "When the Same Prime Leads to Different Effects," *Journal of Consumer Research*, 34 (3), 357-368. • Chartrand, Tanya L., Joel Huber, Baba Shiv, Robin J. Tanner (2008), "Nonconscious Goals and Consumer Choice," *Journal of Consumer Research*, 35 (2), 189-201.

11. Under some conditions, the net effect of time pressure will be the deferral of choice. See: Dhar, Ravi and Stephen M. Nowlis (1999), "The Effect of Time Pressure on Consumer Choice Deferral," *Journal of Consumer Research*, 25 (4), 369-384.

12. Bettman, James, Eric J. Johnson and John W. Payne (1991), "Consumer Decision Making," in *Handbook of Consumer Behavior*, (Thomas S. Robertson and H. Kassarjian eds.), Englewood Cliffs, NJ: Prentice-Hall. • Bettman, James, Eric J. Johnson and John W. Payne (1990), "A Componential Analysis

of Cognitive Effort in Choice," *Organizational Behavior and Human Decision Processes*, 45 (1), 111–139.

13. See e.g., Gensch, Dennis H. (1987), "A Two Stage Disaggregate Attribute Choice Model," *Marketing Science*, 6 (Summer), 223–31. • Shocker, Allan D., Moshe Ben-Akiva, Bruno Boccara, and Prakash Nedungadi (1991), "Consideration Set Influences on Consumer-Decision-Making and Choice: Issues, Models and Suggestions," *Marketing Letters*, 2 (August), 181-197.

14. Moe, Wendy W. (2006), "An Empirical Two-Stage Choice Model with Varying Decision Rules Applied to Internet Clickstream Data," *Journal of Marketing Research*, 680-692. • Urban, Glen L., John S. Hulland and Bruce. D. Weinberg (1993), "Premarket Forecasting for New Consumer Durable Goods: Modeling Categorization, Elimination, and Consideration Phenomena," *Journal of Marketing*, 57 (2), 47-63.

15. Chakravarti, Amitav and Chris Janiszewski (2003), "The Influence of Macro-Level Motives on Consideration Set Composition in Novel Purchase Situations," *Journal of Consumer Research*, 30 (September), 244-258; Simonson, Itamar, and Amos Tversky (1992), "Choice in Context: Tradeoff Contrast and Extremeness Aversion," *Journal of Marketing Research*, 29 (3), 281-295. • Markman, Arthur B., and Douglas L. Medin (1995), "Similarity and Alignment in Choice," *Organizational Behavior and Human Decision Processes*, 63 (2), 117-130.

16. Chakravarti, Amitav and Chris Janiszewski (2003), "The Influence of Macro-Level Motives on Consideration Set Composition in Novel Purchase Situations," *Journal of Consumer Research*, 30 (September), 244-258.

17. Wirtz, Jochen, and Anna S. Mattila (2003), "The Effects of Consumer Expertise on Evoked Set Size and Service Loyalty," *Journal of Services Marketing*, 17 (6/7), 649-665.

18. Alba, Joseph W.; J. Wesley Hutchinson (1987), "Dimensions of Consumer Expertise," *Journal of Consumer Research*, 13 (March), 411-454.

19. For a model examining optimal shelf layout, see: Van Nierop, Erjen, Dennis Fok and Philip Hans Franses (2008), "Interaction Between Shelf Layout and Marketing Effectiveness and Its Impact on Optimizing Shelf Arrangements," *Marketing Science*, 27 (6), 1065-1082.

20. Bitner, Mary Jo (1992), "Servicescapes: The Impact of Physical Surroundings on Customers and Employees," *Journal of Marketing*, 56, 57-71. • Turley, L. W. and Ronald E. Milliman (2000), "Atmospheric Effects on Shopping Behavior: A Review of the Empirical Evidence," *Journal of Business Research*, 49, 193-211. • Garlin, Francine V. and Katherine Owen (2006), "Setting the Tone with the Tune: A Meta-Analytic Review of the Effects of Background Music in Retail Settings," *Journal of Business Research*, 59 (6), 755-764.

• Chebat, Jean-Charles and Maureen Morrin (2007), "Colors and Cultures: Exploring the Effects of Mall Decor on Consumer Perceptions," *Journal of Business Research*, 60 (3), 189-196. • Mattila, Anna S. and Jochen Wirtz (2001), "Congruency of Scent and Music as a Driver of In-Store Evaluations and Behavior," *Journal of Retailing*, 77 (2), 273-289. • Yalch, Richard F. and Eric R.Spangenberg, (2000), "The Effects of Music in a Retail Setting and Perceived Shopping Time," *Journal of Business Research*, 49 (2), 139-147. • Michon, Richard, Jean-charles Chebat and L. W. Turley (2005), "Mall Atmospherics: The Interaction Effects of the Mall Environment on Shopping Behavior," *Journal of Business Research*, 58 (5), 576-583. • Machleit, Karen A., Sevgin A. Eroglu, Sevgin A. and Susan Powell Mantel (2000), "Perceived Retail Crowding and Shopping Satisfaction: What Modifies This Relationship?" *Journal of Consumer Psychology*, 9 (1), 29-42. • Spangenberg, Eric R., David E. Sprott, David E., Bianca Grohmann and Daniel L. Tracy (2006), "Gender-Congruent Ambient Scent Influences on Approach and Avoidance Behaviors in a Retail Store," *Journal of Business Research*, 59 (12), 1281-1287. • Spangenberg, Eric R., Bianca Grohmann and David E. Sprott (2005), "It's Beginning to Smell (and Sound) a lot like Christmas: The Interactive Effects of Ambient Scent and Music in a Retail Setting," *Journal of Business Research*, 58 (11), 1583-1589.

21. Menon, Satya and Barbara Kahn (2002), "Cross-Category Effects of Induced Arousal and Pleasure on the Internet Shopping Experience," *Journal of Retailing*, 78 (1), 31-40. • Mandel, Naomi and Eric J. Johnson (2002), "When Web Pages Influence Choice: Effects of Visual Primes on Experts and Novices," *Journal of Consumer Research*, 29 (2), 235-245.; Dailey, Lynn (2004), "Navigational Web Atmospherics: Explaining the Influence of Restrictive Navigation Cues," *Journal of Business Research*, 57 (7), 795-803. • Richard, Marie-Odile (2005), "Modeling the Impact of Internet Atmospherics on Surfer Behavior," *Journal of Business Research*, 58 (12), 1632-1642.

22. See, e.g., Milliman, Ronald E. (1982), "Using Background Music to Affect the Behavior of Supermarket Shoppers," *Journal of Marketing*, 46 (3), 86-91.

23. Beverland, Michael, Elison Ai Ching Lim, Michael Morrison and Milé Terziovski (2006), "In-Store Music and Consumer-Brand Relationships: Relational Transformation Following Experiences of (Mis)Fit," *Journal of Business Research*, 59 (9), 982-989.

CHAPTER 6 – BLOOD DONATION

1. Linden, J. V., D. I. Gregorio and R. I. Kalish (1988), "An Estimate of Blood Donor Eligibility in the General Population," *Vox Sanguinis*, 54 (2), 96-100.

2. For an analysis of the impact of temporary deferral see: Halperin, D., J. Baetens and B. Newman (1998), "The Effect of Short-Term, Temporary

Deferral on Future Blood Donation," *Transfusion*, 38 (2) 181-183. • See also Piliavin, J. A., (1987), "Temporary Deferral and Donor Return," *Transfusion*, 27 (2) 199-200.

3. Linden, J. V., D. I. Gregorio, R. I. Kalish (1988), "An Estimate of Blood Donor Eligibility in the General Population," *Vox Sanguinis*, 54 (2), 96-100.

4. There is some indication that at-risk behaviors among individuals in Generation Y is decreasing, with a lower engagement in sexual activity and a higher use of condoms. Regrettably, Hispanic and black students did not display this beneficial trend. As well, the use of syringes also increased among these cohorts. See: Centers for Disease Control and Prevention (2008), "Trends in HIV- and STD-Related Risk Behaviors Among High School Students – United States, 1991 - 2007." *Morbidity and Mortality Weekly Report*, 57 (No. SS-30). Center for Disease Control and Prevention, 817-822. • However, a more recent study indicates that incidences of teen pregnancy, syphilis and AIDs among teens and young adults is increasing. Again, these trends tend to impact Hispanic and black individuals to a greater extent. See: Centers for Disease Control and Prevention. (2009) Sexual and Reproductive Health of Persons Aged 10-24 Years – United States, 2002-2007. Surveillance Summaries, July 17. *Morbidity and Mortality Weekly Report*; 58 (No. SS-6). • There is also evidence provided by the Bradley Hasbro Children's Research Center in Rhode Island to indicate that unprotected anal sex among teens and young adults is increasing. See: http://www.lifespan.org/news/2008/11/19/more-at-risk-teens-and-young-adults-engaging-in-anal-intercourse/ , retrieved March 17, 2011.

CHAPTER 7 – BECOMING VEGAN

1. A rather thorough and well referenced article is available at: http://www. vegetarian-nutrition.info/updates/vegetarian_diets_health_benefits.php retrieved March 17, 2011.

2. Paisley, Judy, Heather Beanlands, Joanne Goldman, Susan Evers, and Janet Chappell (2008), "Dietary Change: What are the Responses and Roles of Significant Others?" *Journal of Nutrition Education and Behavior*, 40 (2), 80-89.

CHAPTER 8 – PERSONAL TASER

1. Taser is a specific brand name, registered to Taser International Inc. of Scottsdale, Arizona. As such it is not a general descriptor for the product class.

2. Appleton, Victor (1911), *Tom Swift and His Electric Rifle*, New York: Grosset and Dunlap.

3. This point is nicely made by: Kedir, Shaun H. (2007), "Stunning Trends in Shocking Crimes: A Comprehensive Analysis of Taser Weapons," Journal

of Law and Health, 20, 357-384.: The potentially lethal impact of Tasers is also noted by: Lee, Byron K., Eric Vittinghoff, Dean Whitman, Minna Park, Linda L. Lau, and Zian H. Tseng (2009), "Relation of Taser (Electrical Stun Gun) Deployment to Increase in In-Custody Sudden Deaths," *American Journal of Cardiology*, 877-880.

4. A number of excellent reviews regarding the backgrounds. Kedir, Shaun H. (2006), "Stunning Trends in Shocking Crimes: A Comprehensive Analysis of Taser Weapons," • Adams, Kenneth, and Victoria Jennison (2007), "What We Do Not Know About Police Use of Tasers," *Policing: An International Journal of Police Strategies & Management*, 30 (3), 447-465. • Ready, Justin, Michael D. White, Christopher Fisher (2008), "Shock Value: A Comparative Analysis of News Reports and Official Police Records on Taser Deployments," *Policing: An International Journal of Police Strategies & Management*, 31 (1), 148-170. • White, Michael D. And Justin Ready (2007), "The Taser as a Less Lethal Force Alternative: Findings on Use and Effectiveness in a Large Metropolitan Police Agency," *Police Quarterly*, 10 (2), 170-191.

5. http://www.taser.com/PRODUCTS/CONSUMERS/Pages/C2.aspx, retrieved March 17, 2011.

6. Ibid.

7. Lee, Byron K., Eric Vittinghoff, Dean Whitman, Minna Park, Linda L. Lau, and Zian H. Tseng (2009), "Relation of Taser (Electrical Stun Gun) Deployment to Increase in In-Custody Sudden Deaths," *American Journal of Cardiology*, 877-880. • See also: Bui, Esther T., Myra Sourkes and Richard Wennberg (2009), "Generalized Tonic-Clonic Seizure After a Taser Shot to the Head," *Canadian Medical Association Journal*, 180 (6), 625- 626.

8. http://www.cbc.ca/canada/british-columbia/story/2007/11/14/bc-taservideo.html

9. http://www.cnn.com/2007/US/11/18/taser.death/index.html

10. http://www.cnn.com/2009/CRIME/05/28/michigan.taser.death/index.html

11. Amnesty International prepared a submission to a Justice Department inquiry regarding deaths of individuals after being subdued by a conductive electricity device (ECD). Retrieved on March 17, 2011 from: http://www.amnesty.org/en/library/info/AMR51/151/2007/en

12. Kirkland, Dixie, (2005) "Firearm Safety," *Journal of Emergency Nursing*, 31 (1), 21-22.

13. Curfman, Gregory D., Stephen Morrissey, and Jeffrey M. Drazen (2008), "Handgun Violence, Public Health, and the Law," *The New England*

CHAPTER 9 – GEOTHERMAL HEAT PUMPS

1. For a review of different types of energy sources and the role that they may play going forward, see: Papatheodorou, Yorgos (2007), "Technology Disrupted," *Power Engineering*, February, 20-30. • Kaygusuz, Kamil (2002), "Renewable Energy Sources: The Key to a Better Future," *Energy Sources*, 24, 787-799. • For a review of the role that geothermal energy will play in heating and electricity generation by 2040, see: Demirbas, A. H. (2008) Global Geothermal Energy Scenario by 2040," Energy Sources, Part A, 30, 1890-1895.

2. Anonymous (2008), "New Reports Note the Potential for Millions of Green Jobs," *Consulting-Specifying Engineer*, November, 10.

CHAPTER 10 – NURSE PRACTIONERS IN PHARMACY CLINICS

1. DeNavas-Walt, Carmen, Bernadette D. Proctor and Jessica Smith (2007), *"Income, Poverty, and Health Insurance Coverage in the United States: 2006."* US Census Bureau, Report No P60-233.

2. Ibid. p. 23 • Asch SA, EA Kerr, J. Kessey, J. Adams, et al. "Who Is at Greatest Risk of Receiving Poor-Quality Health Care?" *New England Journal of Medicine.* 354(11): 1147–1156. • Kohn LT, Corrigan JM, Donaldson MS (eds), Committee on Quality of Health in America. *To err is human: Building a safer health system.* Institute of Medicine Report. Washington, DC: National Academy Press, 2000. • McGlynn EA, SM Asch, J. Adams, et al. "The Quality of Health Care Delivered to Adults in the United States." *New England Journal of Medicine.* 348(26): 2635–2645, 2003. • Richardson WC, DM Berwick, JC Bisgard, et al. (eds), Committee on Quality of Health in America. *Crossing the Quality Chasm: A New Health System for the 21st Century.* Washington, DC: National Academy Press, 2001.

3. The Affordable Care Act, signed into law by President Obama in March 2010.

4. https://www.cms.gov/NationalHealthExpendData/downloads/tables.pdf ,Table 1. Retrieved March 17, 2011.

5. 2009 Annual Report of the Boards of Trustees for the Federal Hospital Insurance and Federal Supplementary Medical Insurance Trust Funds.

6. Advancing Excellence in Health Care ww.ahrqu.gov Agency for Healthcare Research and National Healthcare Quality Report 2008

7. Canada, for example, now spends approximately 10.5% of its GDP (approximately $5,170 per capita) on healthcare. National Health Expenditure Trends, 1975–2008.

8. Hanson-Turton, Tine, Ann Ritter, Nancy Rothman, Brian Valdez (2006), "Insurer Policies Create Barriers to Health Care Access and Consumer Choice," *Nursing Economics*, 24 (4) 204-211.
9. Thrasher, Christine and Rebecca J. Purc-Stephenson (2007), "Integrating Nurse Practitioners into Canadian Emergency Departments: A Qualitative Study of Barriers and Recommendations," *Journal of the Canadian Association of Emergency Physicians*, 9 (4), 275-281. • Gould, Odette N. And Louise Wasylkiw (2007), "Nurse Practitioners in Canada: Beginnings, Benefits and Barriers," *Journal of the Academy of Nurse Practitioners*, 19, 165-171. • Burkett, Gary L., Marguerite Parken-Harris, Joan C. Kuhn, and Gerald H. Escovitz (1978), "A Comparative Study of Physicians' and Nurses' Conceptions of the Role of Nurse Practitioner," *American Journal of Public Health*, 68 (11), 1090 – 1096.

CHAPTER 11 – US CONVERSION TO THE METRIC SYSTEM

1. As retrieved from http://query.nytimes.com/mem/archive-free/pdf?_r=1& res=9903E1D8113EE433A25757C1A9639C94639FD7CF on March 17, 2011.
2. United States Constitution, Article I, Section 8, Clause 4.
3. Anonymous (1971), "Past Metrication Efforts in the U.S.," *Congressional Digest*, 50 (12), 293-295, 314.
4. Ibid.
5. SS 1, Sec. 205 b, Metric Conversion Act of 1975, Pub. L. 94-168, enacted December 23, 1975
6. SS 2, Sec. 205 b, Metric Conversion Act of 1975, Pub. L. 94-168, enacted December 23, 1975
7. Editorial (2000), "The Metric System," *Journal of the American Medical Association*, 35, 1560 – 1561. Reprinted in the Journal of the American Medical Association on December 20, 2000 – Vol. 284 (23), 2977.
8. Asimov, Isaac (1971), "How Many Inches in a Mile," *The Saturday Evening Post*, Winter, 96-98, 128.
9. See: Petit, Charles W. (1999), "NASA's Costly Deviation," *U.S. News & World Report*, 127 (14), 63.
   Also, Metric Mishap Caused Loss of NASA Orbiter, September 30, 1999. Posted at http://www.cnn.com/TECH/space/9909/30/mars.metric.02/, retrieved March 17, 2011.
10. Schiessler, Robert W. (1971), "Should the U.S. Approve Pending Recommendations to Adopt Officially the International Metric System? Pro," *Congressional Digest*, 50 (12), 306-307.

Made in the USA
Charleston, SC
13 June 2014